Rendezvous at the Alamo

Highlights in the Lives of

BOWIE, CROCKETT, and TRAVIS

FALL OF THE ALAMO

Painted by T. Gentilz. The twice-repelled Mexican forces are shown beginning the final assault.

Rendezvous at the Alamo

Highlights in the Lives of

BOWIE, CROCKETT, and TRAVIS

by

Virgil E. Baugh

Foreword by Joseph Milton Nance

University of Nebraska Press
Lincoln and London

First Bison Book printing: 1985
Most recent printing indicated by the first digit below:
    3 4 5 6 7 8 9 10

Library of Congress Cataloging in Publication Data
Baugh, Virgil E.
    Rendezvous at the Alamo.

    Reprint. Originally published: New York: Pageant
Press, 1960.
    "Bison book."
    Bibliography: p.
    Includes index.
    1. Pioneers—Texas—Biography. 2. Bowie, James,
d. 1836. 3. Crockett, Davy, 1786–1836. 4. Travis,
William Barret, 1809–1836. 5. Alamo (San Antonio, Tex.)
—Siege, 1836. I. Title.
F390.B38 1985   976.4'03'0922   85-8570
ISBN 0-8032-1190-2
ISBN 0-8032-6074-1 (pbk.)

Reprinted by arrangement with the author

To

My

Mother

CONTENTS

WILLIAM BARRET TRAVIS

ILLUSTRATIONS

LINE DRAWINGS BY THE AUTHOR

Foreword
By Joseph Milton Nance

No event in the early history of Texas is comparable to the heroic self-sacrifice of those who died at the Alamo on March 6, 1836, in defense of the Mexican Federal Constitution of 1824, whose red, white, and green flag floated over that bastion of defense. It was a sacrifice for constitutional government and liberty. The defenders probably would have been more reconciled to their impending fate had they known that representatives of all Texas assembled at Washington-on-the-Brazos had declared on March 2 the independence of Texas from Mexico, a nation whose constitution had been trampled underfoot by the military dictatorship of General Antonio López de Santa Anna, self-styled Napoleon of the West.

Rendezvous at the Alamo is the story of the meeting at the Alamo of James Bowie, David Crockett, and William Barret Travis, whose lives up to then had been full of disappointments and failures. Only by death in the Alamo did they become preeminent among Texas heroes. Except for Sam Houston and Stephen F. Austin, they have probably had more written about them than any other trio in the colonial and republic periods of Texas history.

It was James Bowie who had been sent by Major General Sam Houston at Goliad on January 17, 1836, to San Antonio with instructions to Colonel James C. Neill to destroy the Alamo fortifications and retire toward Gonzales and Goliad.

Bowie was a rough and tumble character, knife-fighter, duelist, opportunist, gambler, land speculator (much of it in bogus money and certificates), poor businessman,[1] rider of mustangs and alligators, successful slave trader and smuggler, and defier of law, whether it be United States or Mexican law. He believed that every man was his own law and never let the law get in his way when it came to money. He had a gift for making money, or for acquiring it by loans from others, but he let it slip freely through his fingers. He drank excessively. It has been said that he never lost a fight and that he never started one. Above all, Jim Bowie was a man of action, and a man with a personality.

Bowie came to Texas in 1828, a wanderer in search of land, silver, and gold. He never found the old Spanish silver mine that he sought in the San Saba area. Soon after his arrival, he settled in San Antonio and became a Catholic and a Mexican citizen. In 1831 he married Ursula de Veramendi, daughter of Juan Veramendi, vice-governor of the state of Coahuila y Texas. His dowry contract actually consisted of bogus land certificates, fraudulent land titles, and other questionable titles to property. Juan Veramendi paid the couple's honeymoon expenses to New Orleans. In the fall of 1833, Bowie's wife, two children, father-in-law, and mother-in-law were all wiped out by a cholera epidemic at Saltillo, where they had gone for the summer. Despondent and restless, Bowie returned temporarily to Louisiana and began drinking heavily. In his seven years in Texas he gained the friendship, confidence, respect, and support of the Mexican population of San Antonio. He had the savvy of men of the frontier and of Mexicans and as a leader was generally well liked.[2]

In the early fall of 1835, General Martin Perfecto de Cós was sent to Texas to enforce obedience to the government and to arrest several individuals whom the Mexican authorities regarded as troublemakers, including William B. Travis, who had recently led a small number of Texans to Anahuac and had forced the surrender of Captain Antonio Tenorio, the customs collector; Lorenzo de Zavala, a distinguished political refugee and enemy of Santa Anna who had fled to Texas; Frank W. Johnson and Samuel May Williams, prominent land speculators; and Robert M. Williamson, later styled "the Patrick Henry of the Texas Revolution." Although Cós had been forced out of San Antonio in December 1835 by troops led by Colonel Edward Burleson, the situation there in the late winter and early spring of 1836 was a very bleak one for Texas. San Antonio, on the frontier of Texas at considerable distance from the Anglo-American settlements, was predominantly a Mexican town.

Soon after Cós evacuated Texas, Colonel Burleson left San Antonio, turning the command of the fortifications there over to Colonel Frank W. Johnson. Johnson was anxious for further military action against Mexico, which would keep the volunteers who had rushed to Texas preoccupied and cause others to come on. He obtained permission from the Council of the Consultation Government to launch an attack on Matamoros, the principal Mexican stronghold on the lower Rio Grande. Early in January, he turned his command at San Antonio over to Colonel James C. Neill and marched off to the vicinity of Refugio and San Patricio with nearly two hundred of the men and most of the supplies of food, clothing, medicines, and ammunition in the San Antonio area. There, he and Doctor James Grant, a large landholder in northern Mexico, sought to put together an expedition to seize Matamoros.

Left behind at the Alamo were a little over one hundred poorly equipped men under Colonel Neill, who appealed to Governor Henry Smith for men and badly needed supplies, complaining that Johnson and Grant, on leaving with the troops, largely volunteers from the United States, for a campaign against Matamoros had stripped the garrison of supplies and clothing. The Consultation had provided for a Regular Army of 1,120 men to be enrolled for two years and had appointed Sam Houston, one of its own members, to the rank of major general in command of that force but had denied him command of the several volunteer forces that existed. Houston named William B. Travis as chief recruiting officer for the Regular Army and on January 17 sent Colonel James Bowie, who did not hold a commission in the Regular Army but was then at Goliad with him, to San Antonio with twenty-five men with orders to dismantle the fortifications there and to retire eastward with the artillery. Upon arrival at San Antonio on January 19, Bowie and Neill agreed that it would be impossible to remove the numerous cannon without oxen, mules, or horses; so, it was easy for them to ignore the orders to abandon San Antonio. Consequently, the fortifications were not dismantled. Who, presumably, had a better view of the situation than Bowie?

In the meantime, Houston, finding it difficult to raise and coordinate the existing forces to meet the threatened invasion from Mexico, took temporary leave of the army and with John Forbes and John Cameron went to East Texas to negotiate with the Cherokees and their associates to keep the peace during the threatened Mexican invasion of Texas. Disorganization and personal rivalries destroyed all possibility of an efficient organization at both the governmental and military levels to repel the threatened invasion, and General Antonio López de Santa Anna entered Texas with strong forces, which began to arrive in the San Antonio area on February 23.

A few days after Houston sent Bowie to San Antonio, Governor Henry Smith, in response to Colonel Neill's frantic appeals for reinforcements and supplies, sent Lieutenant Colonel William B. Travis, recruiting officer for the Regular Army, from San Felipe to the relief of San Antonio. Travis arrived at San Antonio on February 3 with thirty men, constituting the entire Regular Army that had been recruited up to that time. Within the next few days others arrived, including David Crockett with a few "Tennessee boys," spoiling for excitement and a fight. By the time Santa Anna arrived on February 23, there were some 150 defenders at the Alamo (a mission and not a fort), when to man its extended walls fully a thousand to twelve hundred well-trained and well-equipped men were needed.

In the face of internal discord over the command and discipline of the men and the increasingly precarious situation with constant reports coming in of large armies on the march north under President Santa Anna, "the butcherer of Zacatecas," Colonel Neill took leave to see to the safety of his sick family. For nearly three weeks there was chaos in the command of the military force at San Antonio, but such was the situation on other fronts also. Bowie and Travis argued over who should command. Bowie thought he should; he had commanded troops recently in the Battle of Concepcion and in the "Grass Fight"; he was 41 years old and thought himself more experienced; furthermore, he had been a colonel in the militia and outranked Lieutenant Colonel Travis. Certainly, he had the support of the volunteers who made up three-fourths of the troops at the Alamo. He knew how to command. He was worried by the reports of the advance of a large Mexican army.

Travis had his own code of conduct, and he expected everyone else to live up to it. He was strongly in favor of individual liberty, but concerning others it must be his kind. Proud, ambitious, vainglorious, domineering, and impetuous, he was also generous to a fault and was often regarded as a soft touch for a loan. He liked fine clothes and gambled a great deal. He had served in a state militia force before coming to Texas, and had hot-headedly, and without general public sanction, led an attack upon the customhouse at Anahuac in June 1835 and that fall had commanded a scouting company as the Texan volunteer army under General Stephen F. Austin advanced upon San Antonio to drive out Cós. Nevertheless, it could hardly be said that this 27-year-old South Carolinian had real military experience or maturity of judgment.

A lawyer by profession, Travis had killed a man in Alabama whom he thought was attempting to trifle with his wife and had fled to Texas to avoid prosecution. In Texas he early became identified with the radical element critical of Mexican authority and was ever distrustful of Mexicans and disdainful of Bowie's association with them. In Texas, too, Travis's love for his wife Rosanna had soured; he had met other interesting young ladies there, and when a prearranged rendezvous with his estranged wife had been agreed to, she came to Texas and met him at San Felipe, expecting to effect a reconciliation. She quickly concluded that Travis had no love for her when he arrived with Rebecca Cummins, as if this were the way to greet a wife that one had not seen in four years.

Travis disliked Bowie's thirst for liquor and his loud boisterous laughter and camaraderie. Hasty, fiery, and lacking in practical knowledge, Travis was certainly not a frontiersman like Bowie or Crockett. As one writer has so succinctly said, "Travis was not patient like Stephen F. Austin; his was not a cool brain, like Jim Bowie's; he was not full of cunning, like Sam Houston; certainly not a hero like Davy Crockett."[3] However, for having died in the Alamo, he will always be remembered as "the immortal hero," rather than the "immortal heel" that many of the men thought he was.

Crockett's arrival did not solve the problem of command, although he seemed to side more with Bowie. When he came to Texas in the late winter of 1835–36, David Crockett, the humorist, hunter, and renowned backwoodsman, was still smarting over his defeat in 1834 for reelection to the U.S. House of Representatives as a Whig from Tennessee. He was far from being a nobody, being widely known in the United States. He had made a speaking tour to New York and New England and had been widely acclaimed. After serving two years in the State Legislature of Tennessee, he had been defeated for reelection. He then ran for the U.S. House of Representatives on the Democratic ticket and was elected for two terms before being defeated. Running on the Whig ticket for Congress, he won, only to go down to defeat in 1834. Soon after completing his term, he headed for Texas to look the country over, leaving his wife and children in Tennessee. His interest in going to Texas may have been tied to his desire to make a fortune for himself, or he may have been simply a wanderer looking for a challenge. Upon arrival in East Texas, he got caught up in the excitement over the Mexican threats to the liberties of the colonists and headed for San Antonio, where action was expected to take place. His honesty, foresightedness, charm, shrewd simplicity, and cleverness made a strong appeal to frontiersmen and to the ordinary man.

Crockett had fought Indians, and in the Creek Indian War of 1813–14 he had commanded a battalion of mounted riflemen. His arrival was widely hailed, but there was no thought of making him commander of the garrison, nor did he seek the command. Of the three, Bowie and Crockett were rough and tumble, tried frontiersmen. Both were older and more experienced men. Crockett was the oldest, age 49, and in the prime of health. Bowie and Travis argued, tenaciously at times, over the command for three weeks, in the meantime sharing jointly the command. On February 24, the second day of the siege, Bowie was injured in a fall from a scaffold while aiding in the mounting of a cannon. Confined to his cot by his injury and by typhoid-pneumonia, he could no longer command. Travis now assumed full command on February 24 without hindrance and in the dark days that followed became more generally respected. The men came to admire him for his energy and his determination to hold the Alamo at all cost and to buy time for Texans generally to get their affairs in order to withstand the invader. During this time, Travis became pathetic and desperate. He sent out numerous stirring and ringing appeals for aid by couriers, many of whom never returned, though they were not captured. In losing the couriers, he weakened his position, if one can believe that the dozen men sent out at various times could have made any difference. The only effective response to Travis's appeals was the arrival on March 1 of Captain Albert Martin with thirty-two of the several hundred men in camp at Gonzales, bringing the total defenders to 187 or less. By that time the small garrison was outnumbered more than twenty to one and was short of ammunition and munitions of all sorts. Much of the powder on hand was low grade stuff captured from General Cós. Any person with a modicum of military knowledge or experience would have known by that time, if those in the Alamo did not, that the Alamo was a death trap.

On March 3, James Butler Bonham, twice sent out as a courier, returned for the second time to report to his boyhood friend, Travis, that neither James W. Fannin nor anyone else was coming. His return, when he knew that the Alamo was a death trap, ranks him at the top of Texas heroes and shows his devotion to duty and to a friend. The siege lines by then had been tightly drawn, and it was only by luck, shrewdness, and daring that Bonham had gotten through. In the words of one writer, "Their's was a decision to die."[4] The decision to remain was not difficult to make; by now escape was almost impossible, and most of those who might have attempted it would surely have perished in the effort. The stories of Travis drawing the line on the floor of the Alamo and of the escape of Moses Rose seem to be figments of the imagination; yet they have become a part of the folklore of Texas. It has been said that those who fought at the Alamo did so by choice. But was it really "by choice?" They had delayed so long in the hope of reinforcements that their position had become one that permitted no choice but to remain and hope.

Virgil Baugh has searched wide and deep to tell the life stories of Bowie, Travis, and Crockett, and to evaluate the role that each played at the Alamo. There was no premeditated or planned meeting of the three at the Alamo. Bowie and Travis were sent to San Antonio under orders from different sources, and Crockett arrived on his own volition. They met by chance of fate, and each stayed until it was too late to leave and met his rendezvous with death. They elected to defend the place to their utmost ability against overwhelming odds. Any rational man would have left when leaving was possible to fight again, when there might have been a better chance to defeat the invader. As it was, they could now only delay his march into the heart of the settled area of Texas. One might ask, did three frustrated men, who had encountered so many failures in life, become desperate men and act irrationally, hoping to salvage something? Did Travis hold out false hopes to the men? Most of those who died in the Alamo were volunteer immigrant soldiers, brave and courageous, who had come to Texas to fight.

In summation, the stand at the Alamo delayed the invader two weeks; inflicted a heavy toll upon his forces, creating a serious morale problem in the Mexican army; and gave the Texans a rallying cry at San Jacinto to "Remember the Alamo."

Baugh writes with ease and readability. He is convincing, writing with considerable assurance, having made a careful examination of available source materials. His research is thorough and reliable. The scholar and general reader will find this account of the heroic defense of the Alamo by a handful of Texans rewarding and enjoyable.

Notes

1. For a spell, Bowie operated a sawmill in Louisiana, and has been credited with establishing the first steam-operated sugar press in that state. In 1830 with his father-in-law he proposed to establish a cotton textile mill at Saltillo, and obtained a charter for it as the Coahuila Manufacturing Company; but there is no record that the mill was ever built.

2. See J. Frank Dobie, "Jim Bowie: Big Dealer," *Southwestern Historical Quarterly,* 60 (1955–56): 337–57.

3. Lon Tinkle, *Thirteen Days to Glory: The Siege of the Alamo* (McGraw-Hill, 1958), p. 99.

4. Ibid., p. 162.

Preface

My interest in the three men whose biographies form the principal part of this book goes back to that fortunate day I first read *Davy Crockett's Own Story as Written by Himself*. Most people who read that book, particularly when they are young and impressionable, never forget it. And they are apt to be enthusiastic about it. The section on Crockett was written a number of years ago in just such a mood, and it is based largely on this "autobiography." If it causes only one reader to go to the original, I shall be well rewarded for having written it.

As the two other best-known men who fell at the Alamo, Bowie and Travis almost automatically claim the attention of anyone interested in Crockett. But neither of them left an autobiography. The threads of their lives are tangled and scattered; consequently, in preparing even a brief biography of either, one has to sift through a large body of material. And there are some so-called controversial aspects of their lives. Except where these disputed matters have considerable interest in themselves—for example, that subject of indestructible appeal, the "invention" of the Bowie knife—they are dealt with only briefly.

Any life of Travis is bound to be in some measure a pioneering effort, even though some good work, published and unpublished, has been done on him. I hope I have brought him at least part way out of the mists of hero worship that have obscured the man.

Where possible, free use has been made of diaries, personal letters, and eyewitness and other reasonably authentic accounts. It is believed the reader will prefer these to "warmed-over" narratives that cannot possibly convey as well either the subjects of biography or the times in which they lived.

I cannot conclude these brief remarks without expressing appreciation to some of the people who have been of help to me in writing this book. First thanks go to Col. Willard Webb, Mr. Gordon Patterson, and Mr. Alvin Moore, of the Stack and Reader Division, Library of Congress, and to their colleagues in the Rare Books, Prints and Photographs, Loan, and Serial Divisions. Especial thanks go to Miss Winnie Allen of the Eugene C. Barker Texas

History Center for most generous aid; also, to Mrs. Virginia H. Taylor, former State Archivist, and Mr. Dorman H. Winfrey, present State Archivist, of Texas.

Personnel of the Alamo Museum have also been generous with their help, as have the Daughters of the Republic of Texas. Although proper acknowledgment is given elsewhere, I want to emphasize my gratefulness to Mrs. Standish Bradford of Hamilton, Massachusetts, for permission to reproduce the John Neagle portrait of David Crockett, which is, in my opinion, by all odds the best. My thanks go also to Mr. George S. Ulibarri for assistance in translating several Spanish passages into English, and to Mr. Frank H. Mortimer, Director, Division of Typography and Design, Government Printing Office, and to others in that division, for supplying me with some badly needed technical information. And finally, my greatest personal debt is to Dr. Carl J. Kulsrud, a friend and colleague of long standing, for encouragement and help in the planning and in many phases of the writing of this book.

Special thanks are extended to the following for permission to quote or reproduce material: The Bancroft Library, University of California; Mrs. Standish Bradford, Hamilton, Mass.; the Daughters of the Republic of Texas and the Alamo Museum, of which they are custodians; A. C. Baldwin & Sons, Austin; the Eugene C. Barker Texas History Center, Austin; Fish and Wildlife Service, Department of the Interior; Harris and Ewing, photographers, Washington, D. C.; the Prints and Photographs Division of the Library of Congress; the Naylor Company, San Antonio; the *Philadelphia Inquirer;* the Rosenberg Library, Galveston; the *St. Louis Globe-Democrat,* St. Louis, Mo.; the Smithsonian Institution, Washington, D. C.; the *Southwestern Historical Quarterly,* Austin; and the Von Boeckmann-Jones Co., Austin.

V. E. B.

James Bowie

Reproduced courtesy of the Library of Congress

JAMES BOWIE

chapter

1

Bowie's Forebears and Childhood

J AMES BOWIE, whose exploits made his name familiar in almost every American home during his lifetime, and who died in a blaze of glory at the Alamo, had remarkable forebears. According to family tradition, three Bowie brothers emigrated from Scotland to America some time before the American Revolution. Two of them settled in Maryland. The third, who moved on to South Carolina, was James Bowie, the Alamo hero's paternal grandfather.[1] One of the early Bowie emigrants is said to have brought with him a seal with the Bowie coat of arms on it, indicating noble birth.[2] Indeed, one descendant traces the Bowies back to the famed Scot, Rob Roy, and his wife, nee Helen McGregor.[3]

The few known facts about this paternal grandfather are that he was married shortly after settling in South Carolina, was the father of four sons and a daughter, and died young. One of a set of twin sons was Rezin Bowie, born about 1762, the father of the James Bowie who is the subject of this biography. Although Rezin Bowie's life may have been more or less typical of the times, it probably rivaled that of his famous son for excitement, adventure, and romance. Walter Worthington Bowie gives us the following sketch of his early life:

[He] served when a mere boy in the Patriot Army as private soldier under General Marion. At the storming of Savannah he was wounded and taken prisoner. In warding off a blow directed at his head by a British officer, his hand was nearly severed by the saber of the Englishman. While confined in Savannah his wounds were dressed by the patriotic women of that city, among whom was Elve Ap-Catesby Jones, daughter of John Jones, a Welch emigrant. Young Bowie lost his heart with his nurse, and married her in 1782, when not twenty years of age.[4]

The traditional description of Rezin Bowie, Sr. — as we shall refer to him to avoid confusion with his son of the same name — was that he was tall, of fine physique, red-haired, and fearless. (Almost the same description was used later for James.) He has been further characterized as a man of high principles and personal integrity. James's mother was of equally strong character, intelligent, well educated for her times, and as courageous as her husband. She is also said to have been a "devotedly pious woman."[5]

Ten children were born to Rezin and Elve Bowie. Differing accounts have it that from three to six of them first drew breath in Georgia.[6] Lavinia and Lavisia, twin girls, were born in 1783, and died in infancy. John was born in 1785, Sarah in 1787, Mary in 1789, and Martha in 1791. If, as John Bowie stated, his father moved to Tennessee "about the year 1787,"[7] then the two last-named girls may have been born there. Rezin Bowie, Jr., was born on September 8, 1793, probably at Elliott Springs, Tennessee, prior to the family's move to Kentucky in 1793 or 1794.[8] James was born in Kentucky in 1796 and was followed in 1797 by Stephen. The only surviving facts about a fifth son, David, are that he was "a remarkably pious youth," that he was "sickly," and that he drowned in the Mississippi some time in his late teens. He may have been the third child and, if so, he was probably born in 1784.[9]

It is easy to see how the sons of Rezin Bowie, Sr., acquired their love of the outdoors and outdoor life and, in addition, an almost feverish restlessness that James alone could never control. During an interview about his family, published in 1852, John said that his father

...was passionately fond of the adventures and excitements of a woodsman's life, and as the country improved and opened, population increased, and the refinements of civilization encroached upon the freedom of his hunting-grounds, he retired to wilder regions, where he could enjoy those sports and stirring adventures peculiar to a frontier life.[10]

For the movements of the Bowie family from 1782 to 1812, we

also have to rely largely upon John's account. His memory may have been faulty as to details, but the approximate dates and places moved to are as follows: 1787, from Burke County, Georgia, to Elliott Springs, Tennessee; about 1793 or 1794, to Logan County, Kentucky; "in the year 1800 . . . to the state, or rather province of Missouri"[11]; "in 1802 . . . settled on the Bushley Bayou, in . . . the district of Rapides, Louisiana, . . . [then] under Spanish rule"[12] — this bayou is shown on early maps as located in Ocatahoola, part of which became Catahoula Parish, lending weight to other accounts that the family moved to that parish at this time[13]; in 1809, to Bayou Teche; and, finally, about 1812, to Opelousas Parish, where, according to John, his father died in 1819.[14]

One incident that has come down to us concerning James Bowie's parents well illustrates the characters of both. At the same time it must have furnished the strongest example of courage to the Bowie children. The story goes as follows:

In those early days Louisiana was filled with turbulent characters, who, attracted by the possibilities of the new region, flocked there in great numbers. There was little semblance of law, and the strong right hand was often called upon to protect both life and property, but Rezin Bowie was equal to such emergencies, and the turbulent class soon learned he was not to be intimidated. . . . He was fond of hunting, and his rifle ball seldom missed its mark. His wife also was a woman of rugged character, and endowed with masculine courage. Raised in the rough school of border life, she was a fit partner for her sturdy spouse. Many stories are told of their struggles with their aggressive neighbors. On one occasion Rezin Bowie was compelled to defend his property against a set of reckless squatters encamped near him. In the conflict which took place he killed one of his adversaries, and a few days later he was arrested by a sheriff and charged with manslaughter; he was confined in an insecure wooden structure used as the "calaboose," or jail, to await trial. Mrs. Bowie knowing the constable to be an enemy of her husband, suspected he would allow his prisoner to be foully dealt with. Mounting her horse, and accompanied by a Negro servant on another fleet animal, she rode to the jail and demanded admittance to her husband's room. She was allowed to enter, and in a few moments re-appeared at the door accompanied by Rezin Bowie, each with loaded pistols in their hands. While the jailer sought a place of safety, they mounted the horses in waiting and rode away. It is not recorded that he was again molested.[15]

One could wish that some of the "other stories" referred to had also been recorded. No doubt they would make equally good reading!

Little is known about the youth of the Bowie boys prior to their arrival in Louisiana. In 1802 John was only seventeen but already of great assistance to his father, for in those days a youth was expected to assume a man's burdens. Rezin, Jr., was nine, James six, and Stephen, five. They were all strong, fine lads, and James's hair, if not deep red like his father's, was at least fire-tinted, and his eyes were gray.[16] Apparently none of the children had any formal education. John stated that they were reared

... mostly in remote and wild regions, and consequently grew up with but little education, or other advantages besides those inherited by natural endowment, or acquired from parental instruction.[17]

The "endowment" — the strong character, intelligence, and physical attributes of the Bowie parents — was certainly of high order. The "instruction" may also have been as good as the average student received in schools of the day. Elve Bowie had a "finishing school" education and was able to pass on to her children the rudiments of common school subjects. Being a religious woman, she also made up in large measure for the lack of churches in some areas by instructing her brood in the Bible and in Christian principles. John credits her with "much of the information we possessed."[18] Of course, she passed on the arts of home-making to her daughters.

From their father the boys also learned much. Depending upon age, their tutelage must have covered everything from the "know-how" necessary to survive on the frontier to the skills of plantation agriculture. Certainly, it included acquiring skill in the use of rifle, pistol, and knife, and instruction in the care of these weapons: in short, all the hunting knowledge their father had gained in a lifetime on the frontier, from stalking and killing to dressing both large and small game. Knowledge of how to handle themselves in any kind of a rough-and-tumble fight they acquired as a matter of course as did any frontier boy who hoped to live beyond his salad days. Playing with the Indian boys, they would learn the use of bow and arrow, a weapon that later figured in their sports, and Jim would excel in its use, just as he came to do with every other weapon.

The Bowie children also picked up Spanish and French, which they heard spoken almost as often as English.

While John and Rezin, Jr., were old enough to be instructed in running a plantation, Jim was still too young to absorb much along that line, being only thirteen when the family moved to the Teche in 1809. They had a few slaves to do the hardest manual labor, but an overseer or owner of a plantation had to learn many branches of agriculture, among them animal husbandry, raising of feed crops for stock, horticulture, and how to plant, cultivate, harvest, and market cotton and sugar cane, the "money" crops.

Cotton culture was pretty well standardized even in those days, and once planted, sugar cane required little care; however, the production of the syrup was another matter. The work was done by mule power, and two or three barrels a day was considered a good yield.[19] What Rezin, Jr., and later Jim learned from their father about lumbering was to stand them in good stead when they set up their own sawmill.

Rezin Bowie, Sr., must often have despaired of interesting Jim either in business or in any other serious endeavor. The boy grew like a weed. He was muscular, clear-eyed, and intelligent, but he seemed to care for little except adventure and sports. By comparison with coon- and deer-hunting, horse-racing, fishing, and a hundred other amusements afforded by the woods and prairies, plantation tasks were bound to seem dull to him. The father could only hope that he and Rezin, Jr., would outgrow this "adventurin'" craze, which he had to admit he had gone through himself in his youth.

But he looked with more disfavor upon the boys' growing interest in the idle pursuits of planters' sons. A plain, hard-working man, Rezin, Sr., did not "hold" with gambling, duelling, tippling, and wenching. One guesses that his and Elve's disapproval of the ways of wealthy planters may have been one of the causes of their leaving the Teche for the peaceful, less populous, and less pretentious Opelousas Parish.

But the adventure and excitement of life on the bayous never abated for young Jim Bowie. No matter how much shaped by the past, how much chided about obligations to the future, youth is occupied chiefly with enjoying the present. And who would have it otherwise, whether remembering or enjoying that golden time?

Bowie family coat of arms

-- court. Phila. Inquirer

chapter

2

"Those Wild Bowie Boys"

THE OLDER trio of Bowie boys had been almost inseparable for a time, but Rezin was closest to Jim in age and interests. He was always ready to join him in any dangerous undertaking or novel adventure. He even thought up a few himself. The boys' reputation for some of these exploits grew and grew. No one could guess what those "wild Bowie boys" would take up next. We can be thankful that people did talk about them; otherwise, even the few facts we have about some of their pastimes would not have come down to us.

Alligators infested the backwaters of the Mississippi by the tens of thousands. An 1811 traveler from Nashville to Bayou Teche left an account of how, in a passage of eight weeks down the rivers and through the bayous and lakes of Louisiana, the passengers amused themselves by shooting at "thousands of alligators all around."[1] On their passages down rivers during the many Bowie family moves, the Bowie boys must at times also have witnessed this "sport" — although it was more than just a sport, for these reptiles were a serious menace to men and animals. In his book, *Mysteries of the Back-Woods*, T. B. Thorpe describes the trouble one man had when, on "opening a plantation" in southern Louisiana, he

... found, after most of the forest had been cleared off, that in the centre of his land was a boggy piece of low soil covering nearly twenty acres. This place was singularly infested with alligators. Among the first victims that fell a prey to their rapacity, were a number of hogs and fine poultry; next followed most of a pack of fine deer hounds.... The leisure time of every day was devoted to their extermination.[2]

Alligator hunts were often organized in an attempt to reduce the number of these fearsome creatures. One such hunt, held in 1839 in the vicinity of Bayou Chere Amie and Glassy Lake and lasting but two and a half days, yielded

657 of the largest kind, not waisting [sic] a bit of powder upon any one unless he measured good ten feet in length.[3]

The trick was to place the bullet just in front of a foreleg, almost the only vulnerable spot except an eye.

The boys must have quickly learned a great deal about alligators. Day or night, anywhere along the bayous, they could hear the reptiles' big jaws clap shut. They had to be constantly on the lookout for them. It was dangerous even to make camp on a piece of high ground, where a female might have deposited and covered up her eggs.[4] They frequently heard the hoarse mating roar of a bull alligator or saw two of them fighting for the favors of some female. The way they churned the water and tore at each other with their fearsome teeth! Finally a victor emerged, and the female, equally indifferent to the battle and which bull won, waited to be claimed. The boys came to hate those bull alligators because they were the embodiment of evil, killers and cannibals that ate even their own offspring. The female alligator at least had the mother instinct and would protect her young. In fact, often the only haven from its father for a newly hatched alligator was on its mother's head!

Jim apparently never wasted time in fearing anything. He only knew he hated the reptiles because they devoured farm animals and pets and because they scared away or ate the fish, and so spoiled fishing. At first he handled only the small ones. But he had to be careful even of them because their teeth were needle-sharp, and they were full of fight as soon as they emerged from the eggs. An Indian boy showed him how you could turn an adult on its back and hypnotize it temporarily by rubbing its stomach. You had to stand clear if you made a grunting noise like a female seeking a mate. This brought a bull alligator out of his "trance" in a hurry!

Just when and how Jim got the idea of riding alligators is not known. It is known that, as he grew older, his sports became increasingly dangerous. Perhaps he was furious because one of the reptiles had devoured a favorite hound. At any rate, one day he jumped astride an old bull in shallow water. Holding his knife in his teeth and wrapping his legs and arms around the powerful creature, he hung on for dear life, as indeed he had to, for a bull alligator is very strong and cunning. This one probably tried all of his tricks to shake off his rider, and, failing in that, dragged him into deep water where it would be easier to drown him. And all the time he strained to reach one of the boy's arms or legs with his murderous teeth.

Somehow Jim hung on until he could reach a vulnerable spot with his knife. Even then he stayed away from the reptile because he knew that, like a snake, it would show muscular reaction long after it was fatally wounded. He was pretty well scratched up, bleeding in several places, and so exhausted he had to sit down for a time. One wonders if he ever tried such a foolhardy stunt again. It was easier and safer to rope one of the animals around the jaws on land, then ride him like a horse. In any event, he probably had few imitators in either version of the sport.

Jim probably had his first lesson in arrow-fishing on one of the small lakes skirting Bayou Teche, when he was in his early teens. Let us picture him as he walked along the shore of the lake on a day in early spring. . . .

*   *   *

He carried a fishing pole and a can of bait. It was a fine day, and the swamp had been flooded, as it was every spring, by the rising rivers. The water was higher than usual, and it was strange to see grass, flowers, and small bushes submerged, the foliage yet green and alive, the flowers still bright-colored, as if now adapted to this unnatural element. The ground was soft and spongy, so he had to dismount and leave his horse some distance back on higher ground. He spied the end of a large cypress log projecting past some bushes into the water. He might have some good luck dropping a line off the end of it.

An Indian boy of about his own age was standing on the log, hidden from sight by the bushes. Jim did not see him until he reached the shore end of the log. The morning sun seemed to enhance the copper tone of the Indian lad's nearly naked body. He was wearing only a breech clout, moccasins, and a head band. But it was what he was doing that interested Jim. He held a bow and arrow poised ready to shoot into the water. Jim at once guessed its purpose because he had heard of arrow-fishing and had wanted to try his hand at it.

The Indian boy did not notice his approach because he was still looking intently into the water. Jim inadvertently stepped on the end of the log and moved it just as the fisherman released the arrow. The shaft bobbed up at once, and Jim saw with surprise that the arrowhead was not lost, as he had first supposed, because the fisherman pulled it up by a string tied around his wrist. Obviously, he had missed his quarry, but his impassive face showed no sign of disappointment or annoyance as he replaced the arrowhead on the shaft and carefully rewound the string on the middle finger of his left hand, preparatory to making another shot.

Jim guessed that he belonged to the Tackapaw Indians. A few families of this tribe lived in the cypress swamps nearby. He had seen two Tackapaw bucks and their squaws a few days earlier in St. Martinsville.

"I didn't mean to spoil your aim," he apologized.

The Indian turned toward him, his manner not unfriendly. Jim smiled. The other looked him up and down curiously, his eyes resting for only an instant on the hunting knife in the belt around his waist. Jim guessed the knife might be the means of making a new friend, for he well knew the value of such a weapon to an Indian.

"I . . . I'm Jim Bowie," he said.

The Indian boy began to move past him along the log. Then he faced around, his eyes still on the knife. Jim slowly took the weapon from its sheath and held it out, handle first. The Indian searched his face, saw no hostile intent, and slowly took the weapon, which he scrutinized with obvious pleasure, feeling its edge cautiously with his thumb. Then his visage clouded. He was plainly reluctant to hand it back. Jim unbuckled the belt and handed that to him also. The boy looked puzzled but took it.

"They're yours," said Jim, "if you show me how you fish with that bow and arrow."

The Indian nodded an eager affirmative.

"We use boat," he said, and it was obvious he knew only a few words of English. He pointed to a shallow dugout tied to a bush near the shore.

Jim knew the tricky balance of the craft. The other seemed pleased at the gingerly way he got into it, caution that betokened experience. He pointed to the paddle, which Jim picked up. The bowman as carefully took up his position in the bow. Jim noticed that he had already fastened the belt and its precious knife around his waist. It looked odd on his nearly naked body. The slack of the cord leading from the arrow to his wrist was still carefully wound around a finger of his left hand, so it could be taken up freely by the flying arrow.

"Me Tonkwa," said the Indian boy. "Me show you all about it. You learn *pronto!*"

*   *   *

And Jim did learn *pronto*. He found that you fish mainly for carp and buffalo fish for food. Several other species provided only sport. Most exciting was arrow-fishing for gar, one of the largest and fiercest of all fresh-water fish and too dangerous for a couple of boys to tackle. Some gar grow to a length of twelve to fifteen feet. They resemble the common pike, but their jaws are shaped like the bill of a goose and armed with triple rows of sharp teeth much like those of the barracuda. The alligator gar is the terror of the genus, a sort of fresh-water shark, so named because its head resembles that of an alligator.[5]

The bow in use at the time was powerful, of a length suited to the size and reach of the user, and usually made of locust or cedar. The arrows were of ash, about three feet long, and tipped with an iron head of about eight inches. The shaft was fitted loosely into this head, which also had a barb that spread as soon as the fish exerted pressure against it and prevented him from drawing it out. The cord was attached to this head and was fifteen to twenty feet in length. The arrow shaft could thus float free as soon as the arrowhead either found its mark or lost its momentum in the water.

The dugout was the craft preferred by arrow fishermen because of its shallow draft, maneuverability, and resemblance to a floating log. Also, it did not disturb the surface of the water like a canoe or rowboat, but it was so tricky to handle that its occupants hardly dared to breathe for fear of upsetting it. It was definitely not the boat for a "greenhorn."

But with all this equipment, the art of the fisherman was still needed. The fish were so wary that the bowman could communicate with the paddler only by gestures with his bow. Further, he soon learned that he had to allow for the refraction of the water and aim deeper than the fish seemed to be.

T. B. Thorpe has provided a fascinating picture of this kind of fishing. Perhaps we can again imagine that our bowman is properly instructed Jim Bowie and the paddler the Indian boy, Tonkwa:

Yonder is our canoe; the paddle has stopped it short, just where you see those faint bubbles.... The bowman looks into the water — the fish are out of sight.... They are eating busily, judging from the ascending bubbles. The bowman lets fall the "heel" of his arrow on the bottom of the canoe, and the bubbles instantly cease. The slight tap has made a great deal of noise in the water, though scarcely heard out of it. There can be seen rising to the surface a tremendous carp. ...Another moment, and the cold iron is in its body. Paralyzed for an instant, the fish rises to the surface as if dead, then, recovering itself, it rushes downwards, until the cord ... tightens, and makes the canoe tremble; the effort has destroyed it, and without another struggle it is secured.[6]

Imagine the thrill of hitting a fifteen-foot gar! He drags the dugout or canoe along at a great rate, and, in that treacherous craft, his dives and rapid changes of direction can easily upset the occupant into the water. But he finally dies, and can be dragged on shore for his reptile counterparts, the alligators, to eat. He is unfit for human consumption.

* * *

But there is another kind of quarry even more challenging — the wild turkey. Any old-time turkey-hunter will tell you that a turkey gobbler, especially one that has been hunted, is the wariest of game birds. We have no accounts of individual turkey hunts of Jim Bowie, but if he gained a reputation at the sport, as he apparently did, he qualified to enter the select circle of the most accomplished hunters. The difficulty of luring one of these birds within gunshot in the dead silence of the woods can hardly be exaggerated. The slightest noise and he is gone. The call imitative of the hen must be sounded just enough to tantalize. More than that will make him suspicious.

The Bowie boys, notably Jim, are also said to have killed wild cattle with knives. The cattle raised on the lush savannas of Attacapas and Opelousas were domestic species.[7] But there were also wild cattle, said by some to have been the ancestors of the Texas longhorns. They were large, agile, and equipped with rapier-like horns that made them as dangerous as buffaloes. Just how Jim managed to get into a position to kill them with a knife is puzzling. He may have shot them first, then finished them off with his knife. That would have been dangerous enough. We will never know the details, but there seems to be fair evidence that he did perform this feat. (One of many stories of the origin of the Bowie knife connects it with a bad knife cut he received while engaged in this "sport.")

Young Bowie was probably too practical to run down and rope mustangs for anything but the sport of riding them. That was a technique that, at best, would have enabled him to catch only the slower animals. A popular misconception, built up by scores of western motion pictures, is that it is not only possible but easy for a rider on a domesticated horse to single out and run down the fleetest wild horse that ever roamed the prairies. Probably the most successful way to catch mustangs on a commercial scale still is to find some creek crossing or other place frequented by them, construct a pen with a cleverly camouflaged entrance, and drive the horses into it. In this way the best horses can be corralled with the rest, cut out, and roped at leisure.[8]

Although this is by no means a complete catalogue of Bowie's youthful pursuits and sports, it might well end with John's account of a bear trap that he invented and successfully used:

He [Jim] had a way of catching bears which was entirely original. In the summer season, when the bears were constantly ravaging the little patches of green corn of the early settlers, he adopted the following novel plan to entrap them. After finding the place where they usually entered the field, he procured a hollow *cypress knee* of suitable size, which was properly cleaned out, and then sharp iron spikes were driven through it with the points inward and inclined downward, similar to the fingers of a fish-trap. Being thus prepared, some honey (of which the bear is passionately fond) was put in the bottom of the inverted knee, and this put at the place where the bear crossed the fence. In his eagerness to get the honey, Bruin would thrust his muzzle and head down amongst the spikes; and when he would attempt to draw out his head, the spikes would pierce the skin and flesh in such a manner as to prevent him from throwing off the *mask,* and in this blindfolded condition he became an easy prey to his gleeful captors.[9]

Nothing has been written here about Jim as a fighter and wrestler. Perhaps he excelled even more in these sports than in others. He was said to be easy-going, slow to anger, but a demon in any kind of fight with any kind of weapon, once his fury was aroused. But most of his known exploits along that line belong to the period after he had left home.

In his late teens he grew increasingly restless. His father noted with satisfaction that he was casting about for ways to make money. But this ambition may not have been motivated as his parents could have wished. His father cared little for the plantation aristocracy and the kind of life it represented. A plain, freedom-loving man who had fought in the Revolution would not relish being patronized by such people; nor would he and Elve want their children to become like them. But it is doubtful that young Jim shared this view. He may well have wanted to emulate the business success of his older brothers, but he may have yearned even more to live and dress like the young men he saw in Natchez and New Orleans and along the Teche, to frequent the society they represented, and to court the beautiful girls he saw with them. He must have become increasingly conscious that these scions of rich planters had advantages denied to him. Many were cultured and educated to the professions. Since he lacked these qualifications, he would have to depend mainly upon money if he intended to share their kind of life. John gives us a graphic picture of him at the age of eighteen, when he was ready to launch out into the world, a picture that tends to confirm these conclusions:

He was young, proud, poor, and ambitious, without any rich family connections, or influential friends to aid him in the battle of life. After reaching the age of maturity he was a stout, rather raw-boned man, of six feet height, weighed 180 pounds, and about as well made as any man I ever saw. His hair was light-colored, not quite red — his eyes were gray, rather deep set in his head, very keen and penetrating in their glance; his complexion fair, and his cheek-bones rather high. Taken altogether, he was a manly, fine-looking person, and by many of the fair ones he was called handsome.[10]

chapter

3

Fortunes for the Taking

I N 1814, when he was eighteen, James
Bowie left home and settled on Bayou Boeuf, Rapides Parish,
Louisiana, where he cleared a small piece of land and stayed for
several years. He supported himself mainly by sawing plank and
lumber with a whipsaw and boating it down the bayou for sale.
He managed barely to live on his earnings, which were small,
but he used an opportunity to mix with the local society, consisting mainly of wealthy planters. He has been characterized by
his brothers, and by others who knew him, as having a winning
way with people and considerable social grace and talent, in addition to his obvious physical assets. But his interests were not
exclusively social: he knew the value of such connections in business, and he was keeping a weather eye out for ways of making
some money quickly. He had not long to wait.

Settlers were pouring into Louisiana, and land values rose rapidly. He saw the possibility of making large profits in land speculation, but he lacked the necessary capital. He was still, to all intents
and purposes, a poor farmer, and he wanted to better his lot as
soon as possible. The slave trade offered that opportunity.[1] So he
sold his land on the bayou, he and Rezin, Jr., disposed of their
sawmill, and John, who was also interested, joined them in the
new enterprise.

The Bowies had plenty of company in this kind of smuggling.
There were many men ready to employ any means of introducing
slaves into Mexico and the United States, and illegal importation
into both countries had been going on for some time before the
Bowies became interested in it.[2] Slave-running in Texas really
began on Galveston Island before the advent of the Lafittes,

whose name later became practically synonymous with the illegal trade.

The island had remained unsettled from 1686, when La Salle discovered it, until 1816, except for the Carancahua Indians, who used it as a base for fishing operations, and a few privateers who occasionally stopped there. During 1816, however, it was occupied by Don Jose Herrera, whom Yoakum described as "the minister of the Mexican patriots to the United States." With him was Don Luis Aury, whom he appointed as Governor of Texas and Galveston Island. Aury was commodore of a fleet of twelve to fifteen small privateering vessels, commissioned by Mexico and certain Central and South American countries to prey upon Spanish shipping. Also on the island were a Colonel Perry, stationed at Bolivar Point with about one hundred men, and Xavier Mina, another fugitive adventurer and enemy of Spain, with about two hundred men.

This island seemed ideal as a base for their operations. Aury apparently waged a highly successful campaign against Spanish sea commerce in the Gulf of Mexico. He also conducted an admiralty court, deciding on the disposition of the prize vessels and their rich cargoes. The Spanish slavers posed a vexing problem for him because there was little money in Texas to purchase slaves, hence few buyers. The United States seemed a profitable enough outlet, however, to justify almost any risk. This was black gold, wholesaling for a dollar a pound and retailing for any price you could get!

Two ways were found to get slaves into the country: one by water through Bayou La Fourche, the other by land to Bolivar Point, thence to Bayou Boeuf and Alexandria. The purchasers could choose the slaves either at Galveston or at certain intermediate points. The operations of Aury and his colleagues had ceased before the Bowies came to the island to call on Jean Lafitte, but the Lafittes were faced with the same problem of disposing of their slaves, and they were more than happy to solve it in the same way.[3]

Warren D. C. Hall first introduced the Bowies to Jean Lafitte, the privateer. Hall admired Lafitte enough to try to emulate him, but his attempt to set up a buccaneer establishment like the one at Campeachy had failed. Nevertheless they were friends and business associates of long standing. When Hall was introduced to James Bowie at Rapides, Louisiana, he suggested it might be to his advantage to visit the smuggler's stronghold.[4] James agreed, and persuaded his brother Rezin to accompany him.

Early in 1818, when the two Bowies arrived, Jean Lafitte welcomed them personally, and he accorded them one of the lavish receptions for which he was famous, with plenty of Spanish wine to enliven the conversation and keep things going. He liked these Bowies, and they, especially James, liked him. Jean was a man after his own heart: fearless, imaginative, adventurous, and, above all, given to doing things on a grand scale. Rezin declared they even looked alike. Lafitte was an inch taller, had hazel eyes, black hair, and a large black mustache, but they had the same build.[5]

Jean Lafitte dressed in colorful costumes and in his lighter moments was gay and convivial, but he was also realistic in a way that appealed to the Bowies. He knew exactly what he wanted and how to get it. He had built a big house, which he named the Maison Rouge. There he lived like a king, with all of the luxuries obtainable to gladden the heart of a privateer. He was not slow in making a business arrangement with the Bowies that would materially reduce the slave population inside his stockade.

John Bowie has left us our only account of the actual operations of the Bowie boys in running slaves:

James, Rezin and myself fitted out some small boats at the mouth of the Calcasieu, and went into the trade on shares. Our plan of operations was as follows: — We first purchased forty negroes from Lafitte at the rate of one dollar per pound, or an average of $140 for each negro; we brought them into the limits of the United States, delivered them to a custom-house officer, and became the informers [on] ourselves; the law gave the informer half of the value of the negroes, which were put up and sold by the United States marshal, and we became the purchasers of the negroes, took the half as our reward for informing, and obtained the marshal's sale for the forty negroes, which entitled us to sell them within the United States. We continued to follow this business until we made $65,000, when we quit and soon spent all our earnings.[6]

Apparently it was James, always accompanied by his big Negro slave Sam, who made most of the trips, how many is not a matter of record. A run made in the summer of 1819 ended disastrously when Sam went to sleep while guarding thirty slaves. When Bowie woke him, the slaves had vanished. They were in the territory of the fierce and cannibalistic Carancahuas and he guessed that these Indians were the raiders. He gave hot pursuit but never overtook the Indians or recovered the slaves.[7]

James Bowie actually conducted the slave-running operation alone, his brothers being forced to stay home and take care of other business. There is no reason to doubt that they profited to the extent stated by John. A third of $65,000, or $21,666, was a tidy sum for those days, but it was hardly what had been anticipated. But unless they made some other connection they could not have continued their smuggling after 1820, when the Lafittes closed down their establishment.

One can hardly abandon this interesting subject without referring to an account of William H. Sparks of Atlanta, Georgia, a self-styled intimate of the Bowies, concerning a foray into the field of slave-running by Rezin, Jr. Rezin did not actually run the slaves himself but, Bowie-like, acted to save a friend from taking a heavy loss as a result of confiscation of some of his Negroes by the State of Georgia. Not all of the details are clear, and the account may not be completely accurate, but here is Sparks's version of the affair:

About 1817 or 1818 there were imported into Georgia by certain parties a number of African negroes. They were discovered and taken possession of by the State authorities and brought to the seat of government, Milledgeville, and by some process of pretended law were sold into slavery to the number of fifty or sixty. These were carried away and retained by the purchasers when the sale was arrested. The remaining sixty or seventy were retained in custody of the officers of the State. There appeared a claimant by the name of Madraza from Havana, for these slaves. The slave trade then was legitimate in all the Spanish-American possessions. It was proven that John Madraza, of Havana, was the owner of the ship, and the slaves captured in Georgia were all that had been saved from the wreck, which had occurred on the coast of Florida; that they had been taken possession of by parties who had no interest in the ship or slaves, and secretly carried into Georgia. The suit before the court was to recover the money for the slaves sold and those remaining in the hands of the State officers. Madraza appeared with an interpreter, as he could only speak Spanish. At the final trial, proof of the most unquestionable character was produced to establish the identity of Madraza, and that he was a resident merchant of Havana and the owner of the ship and cargo. A recovery was had of the money and the negroes, all of which was paid and delivered to Madraza.

The prime mover and he who had furnished the money to buy and ship these negroes resided in New Orleans. The negroes were purchased in Cuba from a regular trader and shipped to Apalachicola, and sent up to the agency of the Creek Indians, where they were captured. The New Orleans owner knew Rezin P. Bowie, and to him communicated the condition of things and asked his aid. "It is easy enough," said Bowie; "establish a house in Havana, let it claim the negroes, let the ship be lost and the negroes stolen and carried into Georgia, without the consent of the owners." It was all left to Bowie, who was to be amply compensated if successful. He established the house, was himself Madraza, furnished the proof and succeeded, but was never compensated.[8]

If Rezin Bowie could bring off a masquerade of this sort successfully, one must admire his inventiveness and acting ability, whatever one may think of his exploit from the ethical point of view. It is more difficult to believe that he went *unpaid* for his part in it!

There has been a great deal of condemnation of the Bowies for engaging in the slave trade. It is not my purpose to justify such participation, at least according to modern moral standards; but the business ethics and practices of those times were different. Most of the places where the Bowies lived were on the raw frontier, often with little or no established law and order, where a man's fortune depended almost entirely upon his own initiative and his ability either to wrest it from the earth or to take it away from somebody else. Speculation was the quickest way to make large profits, and in a time when almost all men gambled, they saw no wrong in carrying it into business. Most of the men who became the giants of Texas history knew and respected Lafitte and visited him at Barataria. Many respectable merchants in New Orleans regularly handled the goods obtained by his smuggling operations and wholesaled by his brothers Pierre and Henri, while other equally respectable citizens bought them. Men invested in anything their ingenuity could dream up, often without worrying about the right or wrong of it — and slavery was then a widely accepted institution. Condemnation should extend as much to those who bought and kept slaves as to anyone else connected with illegal slave traffic.

At least one writer has maintained that neither Lafitte nor the Bowies killed slaves who fell ill, a common practice among traders.[9] It is also difficult to believe that they were guilty of the brutal excesses of the Spanish slavers. (See Chapter 5, p. 61, for an anecdote about James Bowie freeing a slave being flogged by his master.)

James Bowie did much roving during the period of 1821 to 1828. His business connection with Lafitte must actually have ended some time in 1819; otherwise, he could not have participated in the ill-fated Long expedition of that year. Dr. James Long was chosen at a public meeting held in Natchez in 1819 to lead a company of volunteers in an attempt to invade Texas and wrest it from the Spanish Royalists. The story is too long and complicated to retell here. Suffice it to say that Bowie joined him in this struggle, which failed and ended with Long's assassination in 1822; but few details are known concerning the role Bowie played in this important first attempt to establish and maintain a Texas republic.

James became co-owner with Rezin of plantations in Arkansas and Louisiana and, possibly, with John of certain other properties; but he probably spent little time on any of them. He kept up an interest in Arcadia, the plantation near Alexandria, where he and Rezin set up the first steam mill for grinding sugar cane in Louisiana. John Henry Brown, who traveled with him on the Mississippi in 1829, stated that he "owned a large plantation, called Sedalia, and negroes, near Natchez, on the west side of the Mississippi."[10]

John's assertion that his brother sold most of these properties before moving to Texas is apparently untrue because James's "pre-nuptial contract" of April 22, 1831, states that he owned lands "in the territory of Arcania" (Arcadia?) and "on the banks of the Colorado River and in Wachita of the State of Louisiana," valued at over 100,000 pesos.[11] In any event, these properties could have received only scant attention from him because, for a considerable time prior to his signing of this contract, he was occupied with speculation in Louisiana lands and in litigation over titles to certain other holdings.

John Bowie gives us no details about this activity, stating only that James "went into the land speculation and soon made $15,-

000," but he does add, almost apologetically, that

this business necessarily caused him to spend much of his time in the woods, where natural inclination also gave the employment a charm peculiarly pleasant to him.[12]

Then, suddenly, the Louisiana claims also became entangled in vexing and expensive litigation. About 126 claim cases were brought into the Superior Court at Little Rock for confirmation, all concerning lands located in Spanish grants and sold by the Bowies or other land speculators.[13] No evidence exists that the Bowie claims were spurious. On the contrary, the $15,000 alluded to by John seems to have been James's share of a sizable award of the court.[14] But, with Louisiana land titles in question, it was a good time to get out of trafficking in them, and that is what the Bowies did.

It was natural that James Bowie's attention should turn at this time to Texas. There were both personal and business reasons. His father had died in 1819, and he had settled his mother comfortably at Arcadia. He had not built up the solid business reputation achieved by his brothers; still, he had done some notable things and had made a great deal of money for those times. He had also made some bitter personal enemies among the leading citizens of Alexandria, where he lived for a time. These he had clashed with in the famous Sandbar affair of September 1827. I propose to tell the story of this and other Bowie duels and fights in detail in another chapter. Suffice it to mention here that he was badly wounded in this affray, in spirit perhaps even more than in body. John described him at this time as follows:

After my brother recovered from his wounds, he felt as though he had not been well used, or properly treated by some of his political friends, so he determined to leave the United States and go to Texas. For several years he spent his winters in New Orleans, but during the time was engaged in no business besides what was connected with his land speculations.[15]

It was a form of gambling he liked, and he must have been successful at it because certain of his Louisiana friends commissioned him to buy land in Texas for them. Also, his interest in the cause of Texan freedom had increased until it was always in the back of his mind.

So he left for Texas early in 1828. There he devoted his time chiefly to a hunt for the famous lost San Saba silver mines, about which he had heard much, but he was also scouting around and learning what he could. He did not find the mines, and he had to give up the search temporarily. When he returned to Louisiana some time during this same year, he had already decided that he wanted to spend the rest of his life in Texas.

It was of prime importance that he take immediate steps to become a Mexican citizen. This was difficult to accomplish, even with proper recommendations. If he had been a member of one of the established colonies, it would have been easier. He knew he would have to offer some inducement that the Mexican Government could hardly afford to reject. Marriage to the daughter of some prominent Mexican would also help, and he would have to join the Catholic Church.

The bait Bowie decided to hold out to the Mexican Government was a proposal to set up a cotton spinning and weaving mill at Saltillo, a project to be financed by Rezin and himself. He would need a great deal of money. Apparently his preparations were thorough. When he returned to Bexar in 1830, he had a letter of introduction from Stephen F. Austin and testimonials from other prominent men vouching for his character. He also had ample funds. He at once laid his plan before the officials, who granted him conditional citizenship with the understanding that it was to become final only after he had constructed the mill and put it into operation.

He then bought a house in Bexar. Soon thereafter he began his land-buying activities. According to John, he had only about $1,000 to invest.[16]

There was little speculation in eleven-league land grants in Texas until 1830, but in that year Bowie acquired fifteen or sixteen of them, aggregating over 700,000 acres.[17] His method, which some say he originated, was to induce a settler to apply for a grant, then buy it from him. Sometimes cash was paid, but another method also frequently employed was described by an 1834 traveler as follows:

When an emigrant arrives in the country, he is met by a land speculator, who tells him he knows of a good location, and if he will go and settle on it, he shall have one half of the league for nothing. The land is entered at the land office in the emigrant's name, the speculator pays the fees, and takes a deed of one half, from the emigrant. This is not the worst kind of speculation in the world. . . . The emigrant, at least, seems to have no cause for complaint. He gets twenty-three hundred acres of land, as much as he can ever cultivate, and pays nothing at all for it."[18]

How much land Bowie alienated in this fashion nobody knows. He continued the practice for some years, at one time working with a man named John Mason. Whether he ever actually amassed a fortune of a million dollars, as stated by one writer, is doubtful.[19] At any rate, certain laws were passed in 1834 and 1835 that put a stop to the speculation, so Bowie and most others engaged in the business disposed of their land holdings. He also sold his interest in the Saltillo mill in 1833, after his wife, his children, and his wife's parents were swept away by Asiatic cholera. This tragic loss pretty much took the heart out of him, and he was thereafter preoccupied mostly with matters relating to the Texas Revolution, with a few interludes in which he indulged in dissipation, searched for the San Saba mines, fought Indians, traveled, and engaged in other activities about which little is known.

Perhaps the conclusions to be drawn about James Bowie and his business enterprises and practices are these: He looked at business solely as a way to make money; perhaps it was a bit dirty at times, but unavoidably so. The worst that can be said of him is that he did not always consider moral aspects of his undertakings, the best, that he adhered to the accepted business code of his day, dealt uprightly with all men, kept his promises, fulfilled his commitments, and cheated no one. He did not break the law, but was, on the contrary, ready to put matters to the test of law, as he did with the Louisiana land claims. Samuel G. Bastion, an alleged "Alamo survivor" and one of his chief vilifiers, and some disciples of yellow journalism and phony scholarship, have portrayed Bowie as a man who sold forged land titles, stabbed anyone who disagreed with him, and like drivel.[20] Greatly outnumbering these detractors, however, were other men, many of them Bowie's acquaintances or friends, who testified that he was a man of the highest honor, without a single petty or mean thing about him. Even his bad temper, perhaps his worst trait, he backed up repeatedly by risking his life. But mostly, he fought for principle and justice. Many have fought for less.

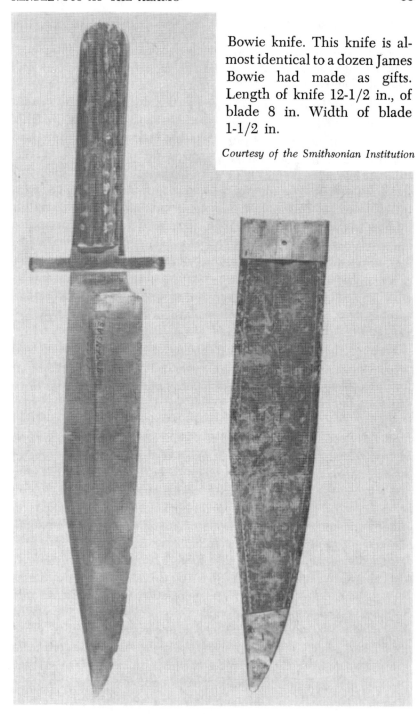

Bowie knife. This knife is almost identical to a dozen James Bowie had made as gifts. Length of knife 12-1/2 in., of blade 8 in. Width of blade 1-1/2 in.

Courtesy of the Smithsonian Institution

chapter

4

The Bowie Knives — a Collective Invention

I HOPE the reader has guessed from the heading of this chapter that it is not a history of the origin of *the* Bowie knife, the one and only "original" or ancestor of all other Bowie knives. Nor is any attempt made here either to name its "inventor" and maker or to fix the time and place of its fabrication. Able investigators have tried to compile such histories, clinging stubbornly to the conviction that every invention must be originated and brought to fruition by one man. They will name their man, describe their knife and the exact circumstances of its creation, even if they have to ignore conflicting evidence to do so. As might be expected, there has been little unanimity in their conclusions.

The reasons for this disagreement among chroniclers of the knife are pretty obvious. The Bowies themselves, their descendants, and their contemporaries, upon whom the historian must depend for most of his facts, are themselves in wide disagreement. This is, without a doubt, one of those historic problems that only seem to recede further and further from solution with each rehashing. Is this not in itself symptomatic? The question "Did Francis Bacon really write the plays attributed to William Shakespeare?" is unanswerable for the same reasons: lack of evidence; too many conflicting stories, the authenticity of which can be neither proved nor disproved; and the impossibility of separating fact from legend. I do not want to add one more erroneous conclusion to those already made, but my research on the subject suggests strongly that there was actually no *one* original Bowie knife. Rather, it was a *collective invention*, going through various refinements and changes at the hands of a number of individuals at different times and in widely separated places, culmi-

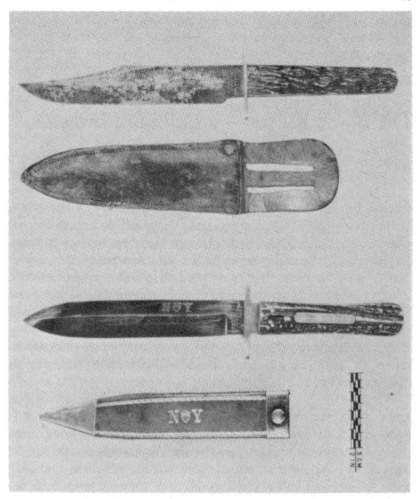

Courtesy of the Smithsonian Institution

Top: Sheffield Bowie-type knife with scabbard. Owned by Henry Vincent Gerrodette while serving in the U.S. Navy during the Mexican War. The blade is stamped "E. K. Tryon Co. Phil Pa. Made in England."

Bottom: Sheffield Bowie-type knife with scabbard. Owned by Frank H. Root, U.S. Navy, during the Civil War. It was made by Alexander of Sheffield.

Bowie knife found on battle-
field of Perryville, Kentucky,
by a Union soldier during the
Civil War.

Courtesy of the Smithsonian Institution

nating in what came to be known as the Bowie knife. Only at the end of that evolution had the main characteristics of the knife become sufficiently well fixed and the weapon widely enough accepted so that it began to have some uniformity of design, regardless of who manufactured it.

The Bowie knife really came into being as a result of a widely felt need. Knives have been part of the accouterment of settlers from our earliest history. Hunters, scouts, soldiers, farmers, trappers, and men in many other walks of life carried and used them for more than a hundred years before the advent of the Bowies. Such men, especially those on the frontier, had, in fact, long had knives made to order by blacksmiths to suit their individual needs. The Bowies were not alone in recognizing the untrustworthy character of firearms of the time. Anyone who used them constantly, as most men did, would have been aware of that. And every man carried a knife for general utility purposes and frequently a dagger as well. He must often have decried the limited usefulness of both pieces of cutlery and longed for some all-purpose knife that would be equal to any situation or purpose. To assert that this need was first felt by the Bowies is absurd. Of course, they were among the first to do something about it, but there is evidence that the earliest-known knife was designed for hunting and general use, not as a personal weapon. (See Rezin Bowie's letter quoted on p. 45.) But whatever else may be controversial in the saga of the Bowie knife, its origin is irretrievably linked with one or more of the Bowie boys and, possibly, with their father. Who of them shared in that origin, and to what extent, remain unanswerable questions. But the stories of that linkage, especially those concerning James, make good reading. Retelling them will not further befog an already befogged issue.

There are more stories connecting James with the origin of the knife than are found for any of the other Bowies. One of these was published in *DeBow's Review* in 1852. Allegedly based upon an interview given by John Bowie to some unidentified writer, it goes as follows:

He [James] had a hunting-knife made, which suited his fancy, by a common blacksmith named Snowden. In after years this knife became famous, owing to some very tragical occurrences which originated as follows: — About the year 1826, James became involved in the political and party squabbles of the day, and his fiery impulsive nature caused him to enlist all his energies in the strife. At this time he resided in Alexandria [Louisiana], on the Red River, and in some of the momentary excitements of the day an altercation took place between him and the sheriff of Rapides Parish, a Mr. Norris Wright, during which Wright shot Bowie in his left breast, while he was unarmed; but had Wright not been rescued by his friends James would have killed him with his fists. This attack so enraged him that he had a neat leather scabbard made for his hunting-knife, and affirmed that he would wear it as long as he lived, which he did. About twelve months after this difficulty, or in September, 1827, the great duel took place at Natchez.[1]

Annie M. Bowie, a granddaughter of John Bowie, son of James, gave another version of this story that appeared in the *Galveston Daily News*.[2] Basing her account upon material obtained from "annals of my branch of the family," she stated that James had the knife made by Lovel H. Snowden, with the intention of using it to defend the rights of a widow who was about to be defrauded of a Spanish grant by certain planters. She implied that they were the same men against whom he employed the knife in the Sandbar affair. (See Chapter 5 for an account of this famous duel.)

There are other stories connecting James with the origin of the knife, but, even as to the main facts, they differ widely. One is that Bowie had the historic knife made by Snowden some time after the Sandbar fight.[3] Another is that the first knife was made for him by a cutler named Pedro in New Orleans. The broken-sword theory, propounded in an article in *Harper's Weekly* in August of 1861, was also given some credence. According to this account, James is supposed to have broken off his sword in a melée with some Mexicans and, having reground the end to a knife point, found it so practical a weapon for close-in fighting that he recommended it to others. This is probably one of the least likely theories of the knife's origin.[4]

If one had to pick his preference among the stories identifying James with the knife's creation, none has more appeal than the one included in an article written by Daniel Webster Jones, Governor of Arkansas from 1897 to 1901.[5] For drama, romance, and all of those convincing details that make for good reading, it can hardly be surpassed. According to Jones, a certain James Black, once a silversmith in Philadelphia, set up as a blacksmith and cutler to gentlemen in Washington, Arkansas, presumably before

1830, for in that year, so the story goes, James Bowie left with him a pattern for a knife and some verbal instructions for its manufacture. Black must have had some enthusiasm for the job because he made not only the knife Bowie ordered but another, modified from the pattern to suit his own ideas. Bowie is said to have expressed pleased preference for the smith's design over his own and bought it instead. *Ergo*, the Bowie knife! Black is supposed to have been the possessor of the "Damascus secret" of making steel, and the ironic sequel is that he was unable to realize his dearest wish to pass it on to Dr. Isaac N. Jones, benefactor of his old age, because of loss of memory at the critical moment.

The Arkansas model of the Bowie knife attained wide currency as "the Arkansas tooth-pick." As a matter of State pride, it could scarcely have been created elsewhere! But this account conflicts with all others placing the knife's creation at an earlier date.

There is also a story that James hammered out his first knife on a visit to Philadelphia. One cannot help but wonder if he was in touch with James Black before the cutler moved to the Southwest.

Another equally interesting tale is that the knife came into being in Gonzales, Texas. Its narrator, A. J. Sowell, relates, on the basis of family tradition, that James Bowie used to come through Gonzales frequently while he was in Texas, usually accompanied by a party of men, and that he and his men were frequently involved in fights with Indians. His story continues as follows:

In one of these fights Bowie made a thrust at an Indian when they were at close quarters, and his hand slipped over the blade of his butcher-knife, cutting him severely. This mishap suggested the idea of a guard between the blade and handle, and he determined to have one made that way. Accordingly, selecting a soft piece of wood, he made a pattern of the kind of knife he wanted, and the next time he went to Gonzales, he went to Mr. Sowell's shop, and showing him the pattern, asked him if he could make one like it. The old man said he thought he could; and selecting a good piece of steel, proceeded to shape one like the pattern, and after it was finished, presented it to Bowie for inspection. He was greatly pleased with it, and paid a handsome price for the work. The old man then asked Bowie if he might name the knife. "Oh yes, Mr. Sowell, certainly," said Bowie, "give it a name." "Well then," said the old man, "I will name it in honor of you; we will call it the 'Bowie Knife.' "[6]

These are perhaps the most important accounts attributing "invention" of the Bowie knife to James, but an equal if not stronger case exists for his brother, Rezin, to whom some modern historians unequivocally assign responsibility for the weapon.[7] They rely mainly on a letter of Rezin to the *Planters' Advocate*, dated August 24, 1838. In it he sought to counteract the "slanderous comment on myself and family" in the newspapers and to attack specifically an alleged "History of the Bowie Knife" that had appeared in the *Baltimore Transcript*. One does not wonder that the author of the "History," who rebutted his accuser in the *Transcript* under date of September 17, 1838, signed himself only "P. Q." The threatening tone of Bowie's letter, coupled with knowledge of the Bowie proficiency with the knife, confirmed the wisdom of his anonymity! Here is what Rezin, Jr., wrote about the genesis of the knife and James's early acquisition of it:

The first Bowie knife was made by myself in the parish of Avoyelles, in this state, as a hunting knife, for which purpose, exclusively, it was used for many years. The length of the knife was nine and a quarter inches, its width one and a half inches, single edge, and blade not curved; so that "the correspondent" is as incorrect in his description as in his account of the origin of the "Bowie knife." The Baltimore correspondent must have been greatly misinformed respecting the manner in which Col. James Bowie first became possessed of this knife, or he must possess a very fertile imagination. The whole of his statement on this point is false. The following are the facts: Col. James Bowie had been shot by an individual with whom he was at variance; and as I presumed that a second attempt would be made by the same person to take his life, I gave him the knife to be used as occasion might require, as a defensive weapon. Sometime afterwards (and the only time the knife was ever used for any other purpose than that for which it was originally destined) it was resorted to by Colonel James Bowie, in a chance medley, or rough fight, between himself and certain other individuals with whom he was then inimical, and the knife was then used only as a defensive weapon, and not till he had been shot down — it was then the means of saving his life. [This is, of course, an obvious reference to the Sandbar affair.] The improvement in its fabrication, and the state of perfection which it has since acquired from experienced cutlers, was not brought about through my agency. I would here assert, also, that neither Col. James Bowie nor myself, at any period in our lives, ever had a duel with any person [whom]soever.[8]

This particular knife, as we shall see, little resembled the Bowie knife in its characteristic form; however, it is obvious that Rezin

Bowie considered it to be the original Bowie knife. He refers to the radical changes in it since this early knife was made. By these changes its value as a duelling weapon was greatly increased, and the knife had come more and more into disrepute, so much so that, before 1840, a number of states had passed laws forbidding its sale, possession, and use as a weapon. Rezin would be stung by this as well as by the many stories going around connecting his brother with some of the more grisly duels and knife fights. Here he is in effect disclaiming any responsibility for the knife's "perfection" and at the same time defending his brother's memory. One can hardly blame him for this, but if only a third of the stories of duels in which James was a principal are true, his last sentence needs a goodly amount of qualification!

An impressive number of Bowie descendants, some of them family historians and all having access either to family papers or to some other sources of information not generally available, went on record as naming Rezin Bowie, Jr., as originator of the knife. They were John S. Moore, a grandnephew of James Bowie; J. M. S. du Fosset; Lucy Leigh Bowie; and Walter Worthington Bowie.[9] All agreed on two main points: that Jesse Cliffe, the Bowie plantation blacksmith, made the knife from an old file and that it was eventually given to James for protection against his enemies, although Moore alone maintained that it was their father, Rezin Bowie, Sr., who presented it to him.

Attribution of the knife to Stephen Bowie is made only once and without convincing evidence being presented to support it.[10]

What did the Bowie knife look like? Again, the answer to that question depends upon what *stage* in its development is referred to. We have to go on descriptions for the early "originals" because none of them has survived, at least none that can be certainly identified. A few presentation knives are in existence, but in some cases it is unsatisfactory to try to deduce anything from them. A clear example of this is afforded by one of Rezin Bowie's knives, obviously commissioned as a gift. (See below, pp. 48-9.) The seeker after the "typical" Bowie knife has to postulate his own. This is at best an arbitrary task. So be it! Let us undertake it anyway.

We can begin by stating what others have postulated on the subject. A British traveler named Charles Hooton drew some pretty sound conclusions from his brief observation of Bowie knives in Texas and elsewhere in the Southwest in the 1840's. He wrote as follows:

> It is made of various sizes; but the best, I may say, is about the length of a carving-knife — cast perfectly straight in the first instance, but greatly rounded at the end on the edge side; the upper edge at the end, for the length of about two inches, is ground into the small segment of a circle and rendered sharp; thus leaving an apparent curve of the knife, although in reality the upturned point is not higher than the line of the back. The back itself gradually increases in weight of metal as it approaches the hilt, on which a small guard is placed.[11]

After a brief analysis of the evolution of the blade as he saw it, Henry C. Mercer settled for three distinguishing points of the Bowie knife: the characteristic, broad main part of the blade, used for cutting, the curved two-edged point for stabbing, and the guard.[12] After stating that the specifications of the weapon are now impossible to determine, J. Frank Dobie, another historian, lists three other characteristics of what he calls the "ideal" knife: the superb quality of the steel used, the unaccustomed weight of the handle, and the over-all balance, adapting the knife well for throwing.[13] There have been other attempts to postulate the knife, but these are probably as close as anyone will come to accomplishing the impossible.

The above postulations or descriptions have purposely been quoted in preference to others because they ignore the actually unsolvable matter of dimensions, while at the same time describing what the typical Bowie knife *became*, and that, in my opinion, is what we mean when we refer to the genus. My own postulated knife, then, is simply a combination of the various characteristics listed by Hooton, Mercer, and Dobie. That is as close as anyone will *ever* come to it; i.e., what is most characteristic of the knife that came to be known as the Bowie knife. The design and details of individual knives, especially of the early ones, change from knife to knife. One might be able to locate a knife that is typical in the sense that it fits a postulated set of specifications, but he could hardly go beyond this. There *is* no "original" or "ancestor" of the Bowie knife simply because it actually was never formulated as such by anybody, even as to what became its main characteristics. It *evolved* in the public mind and through development by cutlers. Rezin Bowie, Jr., complained of this "improvement" — where he was incorrect was in assuming that the knives being manufactured had any real connection with *his* original knife!

The reader will probably be interested in two knives, one of which allegedly belonged to Jim Bowie, the other made by a cutler for Rezin, Jr., who presented it to a friend. These knives, especially the one last mentioned, have unusual value among existing knives because of their apparent authenticity. The word "existing" needs some qualification, as neither knife's present whereabouts may be known.

The only mention I found of the knife once (allegedly) belonging to James is contained in a short article in an issue of the *Honey Grove Special* of unspecified date. The article was reprinted in 1889. The length of the blade — sixteen inches — is certainly not typical, but if the following account is true, the weapon had quite a history:

There is a gentleman living in this city [May's Landing, N. J., the town from which the correspondent wrote] who has in his possession a knife once owned by Jim Bowie, which was given him by Juan Padillo, a man who left the Lafitte band of pirates to follow the fortunes of Bowie, and who is still living. The knife is of tempered steel, the blade sixteen inches long, with a steel guard and buckhorn handle. The handle is dressed smooth where the hand clasps it, and on one side is a silver plate, one and one-half inches long, set into the handle, on which is scratched, in rude characters, "Jim Bowie." On the steel guard of the knife, on the upper side, two notches have been cut with a file, which old Juan Padillo said were cut to mark the number of men Bowie had killed with the knife. On the lower side of the guard are three notches, which are said to represent the number of Indians scalped with the same knife. The knife was given by Bowie to Padillo while Bowie was a resident of San Augustine, Texas, and was presented by Padillo to its present owner in 1862, when the latter succeeded in recovering from the Comanches ten head of horses, which they had stolen from Padillo's ranch, thirty-five miles west of San Antonio. — *Honey Grove* (Tex.) *Special*.

C. H. Carver.[14]

Unfortunately, one of the few authentic presentation knives of Rezin Bowie, Jr., does not completely fit his own description of the knife he claimed to have invented, and it certainly is not typical of our postulated knife. Both edges of the blade are sharpened and curved for its full length, and it lacks the crescent-shaped upper edge at the point. It appears to resemble Rezin's "original" knife in length and width only, because he was specific in his letter in stating that the "blade [was] not curved."[15] Miss Lucy L. Bowie thus appears to be incorrect, at least insofar as this knife is concerned, in stating in a 1917 article that "it may be confidently accepted that the knives given by Col. Rezin Bowie to his friends were exact reproductions of the first one given to his brother."[16] Appearing in the article is a cut of this knife, with a detailed description of it and the name of its owner at that time, a Col. Washington Bowie, Jr.

The type of knife James may have been using in 1835 is much closer to our postulated typical knife. Miss Bowie's article, quoted above, also contains an illustration of a military Bowie knife with which he planned to equip the "Texas troops" — by whom she must have meant the Volunteers he commanded at the Alamo. She states that a knife like the one pictured was presented by James to a Don Augustine Barrera in 1835, and that in 1916 it was in the possession of his grandson, a Dr. Charles A. R. Campbell, of San Antonio.[17] She gives none of the dimensions of this knife.

One question frequently asked is whether James Bowie had a Bowie knife with him in the Alamo. Involving as it does some complex questions of the authenticity of some of the accounts of what went on during and after the siege, it cannot be gone into here; however, a number of accounts have it that his Bowie knife was found beside his corpse. In the account of James's invention of the knife, allegedly based upon an interview with his brother John, James is supposed to have "affirmed that he would wear it as long as he lived, which he did."[18] In the absence of evidence to the contrary, we can hardly assume otherwise. Being long accustomed to wear the knife, why would he have discarded it at a time when its need was most obvious? Also, if he regarded the weapon as important enough to include in the regular equipment of his men, it is unlikely that he would have failed to carry one himself.

The conclusions to which the evidence points are (1) that the Bowie knife was a collective "invention" in which the Bowies shared to an extent now difficult to determine; (2) that it was more an evolution than an invention, extending over a fairly long period of time and to many widely separated places; (3) that there were so many people involved in the creation of the knife that it is vain to look for one originator or exclusive fabricator; and (4) that it is equally futile to try to select a single "original," "best," or "typical" knife. The evidence does not exist upon which one can base a positive determination of any of these matters. But many, including myself, have enjoyed the search for the answers.

But, after all, it is Bowie's employment of the knife that interests us most, whether we approve or disapprove of it. There is little doubt that he mastered the weapon to a degree achieved by no one else before or after him. To what degree it may have mastered *him*, the reader will have to decide for himself.

An "Arkansas Toothpick"

chapter

5

Bowie Knives and Duelling Pistols

WHEN IS a duel not a duel? According to the terminology of Bowie's day, a fight could be a "free-for-all," a "fracas," a "medley," a "transaction," or a "difficulty." Just what the distinctions among them were, nobody now knows; perhaps they were rather nebulous at the time. They probably encompassed all common kinds of unscheduled personal conflict, with or without weapons. But the formal duel, usually fought with pistols, was the order of the day among "gentlemen." The code duello was printed in this country as early as 1836,[1] perhaps earlier, and supersensitivity of honor had been developed to a degree equal to that of the most punctilious European practitioner of the art.

But duelling was by no means universally accepted. There was much caustic editorial comment against it in newspapers of the early 1800's, continuing well past the half-century. The churches, the Masons, and other religious and secular groups opposed it; and laws prohibiting duelling had been passed in several states, including Texas, prior to 1840.[2] There was also considerable early support in Congress for similar Federal legislation.[3]

James Bowie probably had little use for the niceties of formal duelling. But, as we shall see, Rezin, Jr., was not entirely truthful when he insisted that neither he nor James had ever "had a duel with any person [whom]soever."[4] He must also have known that many of James's knife fights were gorier than most duels. Estimates of the number of men James killed in "non-military" encounters vary between fifteen and twenty; however, the seeker after cold-blooded killings is doomed to disappointment. More often than not, he fought to help a friend, to rescue somebody who was being maltreated, or to bring about justice. Oddly enough, it appears to have been his good traits as often as his bad ones that got him into many encounters. And, undoubtedly, some of them can be blamed on the temper of the times.

Let us give the positive side of it first. Frontier conditions actually operated to cause a great many duels, apart from the unbridled passions and lawlessness that were then so common. Timothy Flint, writing in 1826, explained that adventurers and people of scant worth back home found they could carve a place for themselves by displacing men who had already attained public favor in frontier communities. One way of doing this was to kill them in duels or fights. The only qualifications necessary for this dangerous game were steady nerves and more than ordinary skill with weapons. According to Flint, men without education, character, or any of the other attributes of gentlemen except gentlemanly attire, were thus able, at least by tacit consent, "immediately [to] pass for men of honour and truth."[5] It was a case of people being afraid *not* to accept them, however false their pretensions.

It is easy *now* to disparage the "false ideas of honor" the code duello represented, but a man had to live among men, and the brutal truth is that, if he received a challenge and refused to accept it, he was branded a coward and thereafter treated with contempt.

James Bowie was widely known, with something less than complete accuracy, as the "inventor" of the Bowie knife. Few would deny that he was among its most skillful users. There is some evidence that he was sought out by bravos who wanted to test his mettle and, perhaps as much, their own, in somewhat the same way tyro gunmen picked fights with Wild Bill Hickok and other Western gunmen. Sometimes Bowie had to kill or be killed by these youngsters. There were also more expert knife wielders of the type who "had to be showed." A few of them lived on, if Bowie felt merciful at the time, but more of them undoubtedly paid for their bad judgment with their lives.

Bowie's good qualities that got him into trouble were his strong sense of fairness and justice; his generosity; his fidelity to his relatives and friends; his gallantry, both in the heroic sense and toward women; and his fearlessness. He was not, as asserted by some, ready to seize a knife on the least provocation. More often than not, he shook hands and forgave, if a misunderstanding was explained or an apology made.

This brings us to his bad qualities. Once aroused, he had a fierce temper. He was, perhaps, oversensitive in matters involving his honor. He was capable of the bitterest hatred of an enemy, malignity so intense that it could be satisfied with nothing less than his life. In illustrating this last trait, it has been said, with perhaps some basis in fact, that he would attack an enemy anywhere, with any weapon at hand, and under almost any circumstances. He seemed unable to tolerate the presence of anyone inimical to him. Again, let us remember that some of his enemies were equally ruthless and passionate in their hatred of him and worked equally hard at trying to kill him!

Of the fights and duels of James Bowie only three can be dated certainly: his fight with Major Norris Wright in 1826, the noted Sandbar fight of 1827, and his knife fracas with "Bloody" John Sturdivant in 1829. The first two are linked together clearly, while the third is thought by a recent historian to have been an aftermath of the Sandbar affair.

Major Norris Wright was a neighbor of the Bowie boys against whom James had several grievances. The Bowies had once opposed him in a race for sheriff. He belonged to a faction competing with them in speculation in certain Louisiana lands, and he had been instrumental in preventing James from getting a loan from a bank of which he was a director.[6] Each was spoiling for a fight when, one day in 1826, they met accidentally on the street in Alexandria, Louisiana. Wright whipped out his pistol and fired at Bowie. One story has it that the ball struck and was deflected by a silver dollar in Bowie's breast pocket, and his life thus saved. Furious, Bowie drew and tried to fire his own pistol but it misfired — or he was unarmed, as others tell the tale. At any rate, he waded into Wright with his fists and, had friends not intervened, might have beaten him to death. The reader may recall that it was after this encounter that Rezin, Jr., allegedly presented him with the first Bowie knife as insurance against faulty firearms. If he did so, James would have needed little urging to take it, having had such a close call. Perhaps he sensed he might soon need it.

There is no version of the noted fight on the Vidalia Sandbar that is correct in all details, but the one written by Walter Worthington Bowie, family historian, is as authoritative as any and briefer than most. He described the affray as follows:

The "Sandbar duel," as it was called, which took place on a little island in the Mississippi River opposite Natchez, September 19, 1827, has been more written of, perhaps, than any other of his [James's] numerous fights. . . . The following statement of that celebrated fight is based on a letter written two days after the duel by one of the participants, and an article in a Southern paper, published a short time after the occurrence. For many years a feud existed between two parties in the Parish of Rapides, on Red River [i.e., Samuel L. Wells and Dr. Thomas H. Maddox]. On one side was Col. James Bowie, Gen. Momfort Wells [the Bowie family historian undoubtedly meant to write here instead, Thomas Jefferson Wells], Samuel Wells, General [Samuel] Cuney, Dr. Cuney, and [George C.] McWhorter. On the other Dr. T. H. Maddox, of Charles County, Maryland; Maj. Morris [sic] Wright, of Baltimore; Col. Robert A. Crain, of Fauquier County, Virginia; Alfred and Edward Cary Blanchard, of Norfolk, Virginia . . . ; and Dr. Denny composed the leaders of the two parties. Their quarrels finally resulted in arrangements for the fight on the Sandbar, the principals, however, being Dr. Maddox and Samuel L. Wells, the others as witnesses, seconds, and surgeons. After two ineffectual exchanges of shots, Wells and Maddox shook hands, but [General] Cuney stepped forward and said to Colonel Crain, "This is a good time to settle *our* difficulty"; Bowie and Wright also drew, and the firing became general. Crain killed Cuney and shot Bowie through the hip. Bowie drew his knife and rushed upon Colonel Crain. The latter, clubbing his empty pistol, dealt such a terrific blow upon Bowie's head as to bring him to his knees and break the weapon. Before the latter could recover he was seized by Dr. Maddox who held him down for some moments, but, collecting his strength, he hurled Maddox off just as Major Wright approached and fired at the wounded Bowie, who, steadying himself against a log, half buried in the sand, fired at Wright, the ball passing through the latter's body. Wright then drew a sword-cane, and rushing upon Bowie, exclaimed, "Damn you, you have killed me." Bowie met the attack, and, seizing his assailant, plunged his "bowie-knife" into his body, killing him instantly. At the same moment Edward Blanchard shot Bowie in the body, but had his arm shattered by a ball from [Thomas] Jefferson Wells.

This ended the fight, and Bowie was removed, as it was supposed, in a dying condition. Of the twelve men who took part in the affray, Wright and [General] Cuney were killed, Bowie, Crain, and Blanchard badly wounded; the remaining seven men escaping any serious injury. Colonel Crain, himself wounded, brought water for his adversary, Colonel Bowie. The latter politely thanked him, but remarked that he did not think Crain had acted properly in firing upon him when he was exchanging shots with Maddox. In later years Bowie and Crain became reconciled, and, each having great respect for the other, remained friends until death.[7]

But Bowie's reconcilement with Colonel Crain was a long time in the future. His animosity endured, not only against Crain but, after the manner of feuds, against his friends. Among these friends — if indeed he could be called a friend of anybody — was one John (nicknamed "Bloody") Sturdivant, who operated several of the worst gambling and vice dens in Natchez-under-the-Hill, then the disreputable section of Natchez, Mississippi. He was a double murderer, an arsonist, and a counterfeiter.[8] He was, in short, just the kind of man Bowie detested, even if he had not been aligned with the opposition.

One night in 1829, when Bowie was in Natchez-under-the-Hill, he had an opportunity to tangle with Sturdivant, if he was looking for one. The story of that meeting and what he did are so perfectly characteristic of him that it is hard to believe it is not true in every respect.

It seems that a Dr. William Lattimore, a wealthy neighboring planter and a warm friend of Bowie, sent his son to Natchez to dispose of the year's cotton crop, with instructions to bank the money. The boy, who was rather callow and probably a bit set up by being given all this responsibility, may have been looking for adventure. If he was, he found it. One of Sturdivant's "runners" accosted him and lured him into one of that ruffian's dives, where he treated him to several "shots" of strong liquor. After that, it was a pretty easy matter to entice him into a game of faro. The game probably looked simple enough to the boy's drink-befuddled mind, especially since he was allowed to win a few times. In a short time he was losing heavily, but he must have gone doggedly on, becoming more and more desperate in his attempts to recoup his losses, because he lost everything — how many thousands of dollars nobody now knows. Then Sturdivant or one of his bullies tossed him out into the muddy street, with a warning to keep his mouth shut about what had happened to him.

Bitter and ashamed of what he had done, young Lattimore may have indulged in a little unmanly weeping. Red-eyed, hopeless, he had the great good fortune to run into Bowie, whom he at once recognized. He was desperate and Bowie was determined to get at the cause. With very little encouragement, Lattimore must have blurted out the whole story of his folly. Later, he found it necessary to identify himself.

"Lattimore!" exclaimed Bowie in surprise. "Doctor Will Lattimore's boy! You've shot up some since I saw you, and I guess you can't blame me for not knowing you, with all that mud on your face!"

Young Lattimore nodded shyly but returned Bowie's handshake with obvious relief. He felt better already.

Bowie shifted his pistol closer to his right hand and also checked to see that his knife was within easy reach. His face was grim with purpose as he turned toward the door of the dive. Lattimore must have swelled with pride over having acquired such a champion.

"You stick with me, boy, and we'll get your money back. I know any game in Sturdivant's dens is crooked, and I've handled his kind before. Come on!"

Lattimore, knowing Bowie's reputation, would not doubt that he could accomplish anything he set out to do. As the story goes, Bowie got into the faro game, and it did not take him long to spot the crooked dealer. He got up, stuck his knife into the table top, and said that he would use it on the next man who cheated. Although not a gambler, he was adept at cards, and in a few hours he had won back all that Lattimore had lost. He gave the money to him and sent him on his way, with a stern warning to eschew faro and stay out of the dives in Natchez-under-the-Hill, especially those run by "Bloody" Sturdivant.

But this was not the last Bowie saw of Sturdivant. The outlaw had bragged that, if he had been one of the participants in the Sandbar affair, he would have seen to it that Bowie was dead instead of just cut up. Bowie came back into the dive to give "Bloody" John the opportunity to make good his boast.

Sturdivant's desire to cut up Bowie must have been given an even keener edge when he considered the humiliation of being beaten at his own game. He knew Bowie's reputation with sharp cutlery, but he fancied himself as also quite a boy with a knife. So when Bowie returned, he left no doubt as to his bitterness and at once proposed a fight with knives, the left hands of the two men to be tied together across a table. Bowie promptly accepted and, at the first stroke of his knife, disabled Sturdivant's right arm with a fearful cut. He magnanimously spared the outlaw's life, but Sturdivant's rancor toward him only festered and grew like a boil. The outlaw later hired three assassins to ambush and kill him. No details of the gory conclusion to the tale have survived, but Bowie is supposed to have eliminated all three of them "in his first fight using Black's knife."[9]

There are two other stories in which Bowie was the rescuer of victims of Mississippi river boat gamblers. The main events related in each are closely similar; however, one version, written by Major Ben C. Truman, gives the year as 1833, while an anonymous account reprinted from another newspaper in the *Democratic Telegraph and Texas Register* for June 20, 1850, dates the events in 1835 and identifies the crooked gambler Bowie had to fight, a detail omitted from the Truman narrative. In one story the river boat is the *Orleans,* in the other, the *Rob Roy.* As usual with Bowie yarns, you pay your penny and take your choice.

Major Truman stated that his account, which is the more realistic of the two, was based upon a "recent conversation with an old steamboatman [of] a reporter of the St. Louis *Republican.*"[10] In the early 1830's, so he relates, organized bands of gamblers began to infest the river steamers. Members of this gentry made arrangements with barkeepers, hotel clerks, and others, mostly riffraff, to keep them informed of the movements of wealthy travelers. If a prospect boarded a river boat, every effort was made to inveigle him into one of the crooked games, where they could take his "roll" with at least a semblance of honesty. Failing in that, there were, of course, innumerable other ways, some considerably more direct, of separating him from his money.

In the summer of 1833 a young gentleman of Natchez, accompanied by his new bride, made an extended trip to the North and East, in the course of which he collected a large sum of money. He was spotted "by several of the gambling fraternity"[11] on the way back to Natchez, and they made every effort to get him into a game. He resisted them until he and his wife reached Pittsburgh, where they were to board another steamer for Louisville. There he succumbed.

The game was "20-card poker." It was played with only tens to aces of the deck, and four was the maximum number of players. If three of them worked together they could easily force the other one to bid everything he had. Standard procedure was to let the "sucker" win several hands. So they did with the young traveler, who soon came to believe he knew the game as well as his pretended teachers. He was thus ripe for the picking when he boarded the *Orleans* at Louisville.

The game was resumed and, to be brief, he lost his shirt. Enter a "tall, straight, and dignified gentleman,"[12] in this instance Mr. James Bowie. According to the story, the wife tried repeatedly to get her husband away from the game, but he as stubbornly stuck it out until he had gone broke. When she was about to lose a battle to keep him from throwing himself into the river, Bowie intervened and, "with a grip of iron,"[13] pulled him back. He then exacted a promise from the young couple that they would stay in their cabin until he could set matters right.

Bowie used an old ruse to fool the gamblers as to his real purpose by asking for change for a hundred-dollar bill. He deliberately exposed a "well-filled Wallet"[14] in the process, and the gamblers at once took the bait, thinking they were about to fleece another victim. Needless to say, Bowie was setting his own trap. While he carefully watched their actions, he bet heavily and thus forced the trio to do likewise until, at last, there was a pot of about $100,000 on the table. He was noted for carrying a lot of money, and this time he must have been really well-heeled!

The following climax reads like something from a dime novel:

Whilst the betting was going on the stranger [Bowie] had kept his eye on the dealer and had . . . prevented any changing of cards. Toward the last he saw a card slipped by the dealer to the man who had made the blind, when, seizing him by the wrist with one hand, he drew a murderous looking knife with the other and forced the gambler to lay his cards on the table face down. All sprang to their feet and the stranger quietly said that when that hand was raised and it should be found to contain six cards, he would kill the owner; telling the other to show his cards, he threw down his own hand, which consisted of four kings and a ten spot. The baffled gambler, livid with rage and disappointment, swore that the stranger should fight him, demanding, with an oath, to know who he was anyway. Quietly, and as if in the presence of ladies, the stranger answered, "James Bowie." At the sound of that name two of the gamblers quailed, for they knew that the man who bore that name was a terror to even the bravest; but the third, who had never heard of "James Bowie," demanded a duel at once. This was acceded to at once by Bowie, with a smile; pistols — derringers — were the weapons selected, the hurricane-roof the place, and the time at once. Sweeping the whole of the money into his hat, Bowie went to the room where the unhappy wife sat guarding her husband's uneasy slumbers, and, rapping on the door, he handed her, when she had opened it, the hat and its contents, telling her that if he did not come back, two thirds of the money was her husband's and the balance his own. Ascending to the hurricane-roof the principals were placed one upon the top of each wheel-house. This brought them about twelve yards apart, and each was exposed to the other from the knee up. The pistols were handed to them and the gambler's second gave the word, "one, two, three, fire, stop," uttered at intervals of one second each, and they were allowed to fire at any time between the utterance of the words one and stop. As "one" rang out in the clear morning air both raised their weapons, as "three" was heard the gambler's pistol rang out and before the sound had ceased and whilst the word "fire" was being uttered, Bowie's pistol sounded, and simultaneous with this sound the gambler fell, and giving a convulsive struggle rolled off the wheel-house into the river. Bowie coolly blew the smoke out of his pistol, shut down the pan . . . , and going down into the ladies' cabin obtained his hat and divided the money which it contained into three portions. Two of these he gave to the young wife and the other he kept, as it was his own money. Having awakened her husband, the fond wife showed him the money, and told him all she knew about the affair, not having heard of the duel. When the husband became acquainted with all the facts, his gratitude to his benefactor was deep and lasting. Not desiring to be made a hero of, Bowie, when the boat reached Rodney, determined to go ashore. . . . [15]

The reader may think Major Truman erred in stating that this duel was fought with "derringers," a term that now applies only to a small pocket pistol once carried as a reserve weapon. But contemporaneous with this duel there also existed a Deringer U. S. Pistol sometimes used in duels. This may be the type of "derringer" to which Truman referred.

In the anonymous account referred to, the scene of this fracas was the river boat *Rob Roy,* and the time "the evening of the 4th of June, 1835 . . . . " The leader of the gamblers was an overinsistent bully who had tried to persuade almost every man on board to join him at cards. Despite his huge size and fearsome mien, all his overtures failed until at last he ensnared a "wealthy young merchant of Natchez." One pictures this youth as timid, perhaps afraid to refuse the bigger man's invitation. In this version, there were only two in the game, but it ran the same course, weeping, frantic wife and all, up to the point where the handsome stranger appeared, watching events imperturbably but always "with thin firm lips [that] wore a perpetual smile," even when the merchant lost his last $5,000, and he and his wife fainted and were "borne away insensible to the ladies' cabin."

Our anonymous imitator of the dime novelist went even further in his melodramatic account of what followed. The triumphant "hoarse laugh" of the villain had hardly died on his lips before Bowie challenged him to a game.

> "I am James Bowie, of Texas . . . and you are John Laffite [sic!], a natu-ral son of the old pirate!"
> The gambler . . . asked in a firm tone:
> "What game do you wish with me?"
> "*Poker* first, and *pistols* afterwards, if you play foul," replied Bowie.

The amount on the table in this version was a mere $20,000, and Bowie raked it in, even though the gambler had four queens to his four jacks. The author claims only the slightest knowledge of the game of poker, but it would seem this was hardly according to Hoyle! Nor did it set at all well with the "natural son" of Jean Lafitte.

> " 'To the hurricane deck, and let pistols be trumps . . . !' "

Bowie accepted his challenge and, once they had taken their places, even let the gambler fire first! When the smoke cleared away Bowie was minus "one of his golden locks," which had been snipped off by a ball; but he was much the better off of the two, for "the gambler was shot through the heart, and . . . tumbled into the river."[16] As in the Truman version, the young merchant and his wife got their money back and were dutifully grateful to Bowie.

Another of Bowie's fights was with a Spaniard who owned a plantation neighboring his on Bayou Terrebonne. The story is that this "haughty hidalgo" used every opportunity to annoy him with petty insults until Bowie could endure it no longer and so challenged him. As the one challenged, the Castilian could name the weapons. He chose knives, being possessed of a fine hunting knife with a long blade. For Bowie there was, of course, only one knife: "Old Bowie." They were to be naked to the waist and sit astride a "trestle," by which was meant, it is supposed, some kind of a low bench, the legs of which were to be buried part-way in the ground. When the time for the fight came, Bowie's shorter blade evoked considerable scorn from his antagonist, who felt that he had a telling advantage. But he had to draw his longer-bladed weapon back before he could make a pass, and while he was doing so, Bowie made a quick forward thrust with his knife into his antagonist's abdomen, and, "drawing it quickly across, disembowelled the Spaniard in the twinkling of an eye."[17]

In another version of what is obviously the same anecdote, the left hands of the two men were tied together. Bowie killed his opponent with a single stab, "then, coolly cutting the cords that held them, he allowed the corpse of his adversary to sink to the ground."[18]

The following incident is also worth relating. It seems Bowie was riding across a plantation near Bayou Rapides when he saw a man cruelly beating his slave, whom he had tied to a tree. Jim dismounted, went over, calmly cut the cords binding the Negro, and set him free, and, some say, laid the whip over the owner's back. In any event, the other man flew into a rage, drew his pistol, and attempted to shoot Bowie. The pistol misfired and Jim closed with him, slashing his wrist with his knife so as almost to sever his hand. The injured man probably expected to be finished off; instead, Bowie calmly fashioned a tourniquet of his neckerchief to stanch the flow of blood, took him to the nearest doctor, and paid for medical attention. Added details are that Bowie gave himself up to the law, "purchased the slave at double his value, and gave him his freedom."[19] Whether these are just embellishments of an already good story, nobody knows.

Bowie is also supposed to have had numerous other knife fights under all sorts of circumstances, the most incredible being in a darkened cabin, with his and his opponent's buckskin breeches nailed to a log, there to stab it out to the death! He is said to have fought a "duel" with a creole who offered an insult to his friend, John James Audubon, although we have no details of this encounter.[20] He must also have fought at least one formal duel, if the following item from the *Jacksboro* (Texas) *Echo* of May 25, 1877, can be credited:

ONE OF BOWIE'S DUELS
At the appointed hour all parties were on the ground, Bowie, as

usual, very cool, the Spaniard very furious and excited. The Spaniard's second won the choice of position, which gave the second of Bowie the word. They were to stand back to back, rifles perpendicular, upward or downward — to wheel, as before stated. Here arose an instance of genius over routine. In the army the maneuvers are intended for regularity before time; but, in such cases as this, regularity was of no moment, but time was everything. When the Spaniard heard the word to "wheel," he, of course, executed it in true military style, in "three motions," but Bowie, whose whole life had been spent in depending upon himself, not regulating his movements by those of others, who had been compelled, in his warfare against Indians or in procuring game, to take every position, executed every change of body necessary for the occasion to insure success; instead of wheeling, as the Spaniard was doing, simply turned the body from the hips, or on the hips, holding the feet firm, which, of course, brought him around quicker than his antagonist, and enabled Bowie to fire first, and to drive his ball through the brain of his antagonist. This Bowie said any body could do if they only possessed the requisite nerve. — *Wilke's Spirit of the Times.*[21]

There are several anecdotes told about Bowie in which he relied upon his fists rather than upon weapons. His encounter with Major Norris Wright on the streets of Alexandria has already been described. He is said to have also had a fist fight with Edwin Forrest, the actor, over a girl in a gambling house — place, date, and outcome unspecified.[22]

On several other occasions Bowie's presence alone had a pacificating effect. One anecdote concerns his quieting an unruly congregation. A Methodist preacher, one of the first to be sent by his church to preach in Texas, related the incident from his own experience. He had just ridden up the Red River from Louisiana, thence into Texas, when he was overtaken on the trail by Bowie, whose identity he did not then know. He did notice, however, that his chance companion was intelligent and a thorough gentleman.

In a few days they reached a small town which, so it turned out, was a notorious refuge for outlaws. There being no church, the minister announced he would preach at the courthouse. That night the building was crowded with an all-male congregation. The moment the preacher tried to begin his sermon, however, there was braying, hooting, cat-calling, and all sorts of other vocal interference, so that it was impossible for him to continue. At this point Bowie stood up and delivered himself of the following warning:

> "Men, this man has come here to preach to you; you need preaching to, and I'll be d——d if he shan't preach to you! The next one that disturbs him shall fight me — my name is Jim Bowie."

The preacher is quoted as stating that, thereafter, "he never had a more respectful audience, such was the influence this man exercised over the minds of these desperate characters."[23]

Bowie once clashed with a bully on a stage coach. He was the "half-horse, half-alligator" type, and the cigar he was smoking became offensive to the other passengers, especially so to a young bride. Her husband politely requested him to put out the offending cheroot, but the bully refused. Bowie stood it as long as he could; then, holding the point of his knife under the smoker's nose, he made it very clear that if he did not throw the cigar out of the coach at once, he would use the knife to aerate his intestines. Looking at the cold blue of Bowie's blade and his even colder eyes, the bully turned green, ejected the cigar, remained discreetly quiet, and got off quickly at the next regular stop.[24]

There seem to be few stories of duelling in which Rezin Bowie, Jr., figured, and none were found in which he was a principal. He did act as a second to John T. Bowie, one of the Maryland branch of the family who moved to Natchez in the 1830's; but this duel was never fought because Colonel Nicholson, the other principal, got cold feet at the last minute and fled.[25]

I hope the reader finds assurance in the above rather long recital of Bowie's fights that he seldom fought without provocation and then only to help someone in distress or danger; that he was no more given to violence than most men of his day; and that the code he lived by was, if not that of every man, at least that of many of his class. I have also attempted to show the obvious embellishment of some of the stories of his encounters, at the risk of making them ludicrous. In doing so it is not my intention to ridicule James Bowie but rather the literary embroiderers who make the job of writing factual history and biography sometimes only difficult, at other times almost impossible.

chapter

6

Love and Lipan Silver

JAMES BOWIE's love life prior to his one serious courtship is practically unknown. All we have are a few rumors and the names of several women with whom he was allegedly involved. One account is that he had "hectic affairs" with at least three beauties, one of aristocratic birth, the other two of lesser pretensions. Judalon de Bornay is described as a "highborn Creole maid of New Orleans"; Catherine Villers as a quadroon and one-time mistress of Jean Lafitte; and Sibil Cade as a "Cajun" or "swamp girl."[1] In his choice of women Bowie was apparently governed by personal rather than class considerations.

At this late date it is hardly necessary to prove that Bowie was a gentleman. He could be as gallant as the occasion called for and as romantic as a woman expected him to be. But he had traveled far and wide over the frontier, mixed and lived with all classes of people. That is why he was as much at home at an Indian campfire as he was at a fashionable ball in New Orleans.

There is no evidence that he was a "chaser" or libertine, but it is just as unlikely that he was a prig. In his forays into Natchez-under-the-Hill he could hardly have avoided seeing vice in all its forms, including prostitution, but it is pretty unlikely that he was a patron of such low-class dens. It is equally difficult to believe that he would have taken advantage of a slave woman, but he could not have been unaware that plantation overseers and even the planters themselves often "carried on" with them, as testified to by the sizable plantation and city populations of mulattoes. In some Indian camps, such as he must often have visited, male guests were commonly furnished squaws as bed companions. In others it was probably a superfluous courtesy, as the squaws of certain tribes did not rate their virtue very high among tradable commodities!

It would be unfair to generalize about Bowie's affairs on the fleshly level, but we can hardly assume that he did not have any. And he undoubtedly carried on many a flirtation on the innocent level with pretty daughters of planters, begun one week, forgotten the next. All of these were superficial play at love.

Bowie met only one woman he could not forget, and she undoubtedly had more to do with his deciding to stay in Texas than anything else, although he did not meet her until after he had arrived. Actually, he left Louisiana mainly because he was dissatisfied with the business, political, and social life there, not because of any disappointments in love. He was also embittered over the Sandbar duel, and he had still not fully recovered from his wounds. He felt restless and empty; he was tired of his old haunts; and, worst of all, he had run out of fields to conquer.

Texas, on the other hand, offered the prospect of new business ventures. Land speculation, which had played out in Louisiana, Mississippi, and Arkansas, was just opening up there. This time he felt certain he could make a fortune at it. So, apparently, did some of his friends, who commissioned him to buy Texas land for them.

Texas had several other attractions. His connection with the Long expedition had already interested him in Texas liberation, although it probably was not then the consuming passion that it became later. The easygoing, informal life of the Mexicans may also have appealed to him. Nor could he have been indifferent to the dark-eyed senoritas who scrutinized his handsome face and figure as he rode by. And he already knew that the vast open country offered opportunities to roam far and wide and to live the adventurous life he loved. He may already have become interested in locating the famous "lost" San Saba silver mines. . . .

When Bowie arrived in San Antonio early in 1828, events moved with such rapidity that the prospects for an easygoing life vanished. His name was known even there, and it was only a short time before he had met most of the important men in the town, including Don Juan Martin de Veramendi, soon to become Vice-Governor of Coahuila and Texas. He could hardly have made a more advantageous connection, for no one could better help an alien to gain acceptance in a strange land. As an emigrant, he had to comply with certain laws, and, as related previously in another connection, he had to make certain inducements to the Mexican Government before it would grant him citizenship. With his new-found backing he succeeded in taking out preliminary citizenship papers on October 5, 1830. Don Juan had already acted as his sponsor when he was baptized into the Catholic faith on June 28, 1828.[2]

For a time he devoted himself chiefly to business matters. He took advantage of Mexican colonization laws to purchase fifteen eleven-league land grants, then sold them to his Louisiana clients at a good profit. By this time he had largely recouped his fortunes and was able to make a large loan to Don Juan de Veramendi to finance his co-partnership in the textile mill at Saltillo. But, as with most of his enterprises, as soon as its success was assured, he began to lose interest. Shortly thereafter he turned the operation of the mill over to his future father-in-law.

Then he began to take a serious interest in Don Juan's daughter, Ursula. Just turned eighteen, she was justly celebrated for her beauty. Theresa M. Hunter has given us a romantic but not improbable fictional account of their first meeting. He is portrayed as rescuing her from the path of a runaway coach, thereby earning the gratitude of both daughter and father.[3] From that time until their marriage in 1831 he continued to pay steady court to her; however, there was one brief interruption to his suit.

Some time in 1829 he returned to Louisiana on business. While there he persuaded his mother and Rezin to return with him to Texas for at least a temporary stay, and they accompanied him when he returned early in 1830. He needed his brother's help in his business ventures, but he wanted even more to enlist him in the hunt for the fabled San Saba silver mines. He knew that Rezin would be as unable as he was to resist such an adventure.

But as soon as he saw Ursula again, he knew he must have her. He entered into a so-called prenuptial contract on April 22, 1831. Entitled "Promissory Note to the Dowery," it describes his property holdings and other wealth. Some reference having already been made to its contents in another connection, there is no need to do so again. He and Ursula were married by Father Refugio de la Garza in the San Fernando Parish Church at San Antonio, Texas, on April 25, 1831. Apparently the union had the blessing of both sides of the house, and the ecstatic couple took a leisurely honeymoon trip by schooner to New Orleans. Returning, James built a stone house, said to have been located near the San Jose Mission in San Antonio. There he lived with his bride for a time, and deluded himself temporarily into believing he would be contented for long with the domestic life. John Henry Brown gives a picture of the newlyweds eight months after their marriage:

I first met Colonel Bowie and his wife at a party given them on the Colorado on Christmas Day, 1831. Mrs. Bowie was a beautiful Castilian lady, and won all hearts by her sweet manners. Bowie was supremely happy with her, very devoted and more like a kind and tender lover than the terrible duellist he has since been represented to be.[4]

But perfect as their life was together, Bowie caught himself thinking often about the already postponed expedition to the San Saba.

Among the "lost mines" of the West, none has a longer or more fascinating history than *"Los Almagres"* (meaning red earth). Located in the San Saba country of Texas, it was first operated by the Indians, then seized by the Spaniards and operated with Indian labor, then repossessed by the Indians of the Lipan tribe, who were working it at the time Bowie's search for it began in the middle or late 1820's.

There are in existence some Spanish documents that show that the location of the mine was known at that time, and that Emperor Agustin de Iturbide was intensely interested in operating it.[5] But after his abdication on March 19, 1823, government interest in it fizzled out. Without the protection of troops, operating it was practically impossible because of the presence in the area of hostile Indians, chiefly Comanches, Lipans, Carancahuas, and Apaches, all of whom were determined to keep the mine out of the hands of the white man. The Spaniard had given them a foretaste of what he would do for silver and gold. Even tribes ignorant of the location of the lode wanted him kept out of the San Saba country. They well knew that his rapacity extended to things other than precious metals: to their lands and everything else by which they were able to live.

How many white men ever found the mine is not known. If some succeeded, they must have died before they could tell anybody about it, for nobody now knows where the earth harbors her fabulous secret.

Bowie may have secured some maps once owned by Louis Juchereau de St. Denis, an early French-Canadian explorer who not only found the mine but successfully held the Indians off long enough to extract a fortune from it. Eventually they murdered him. His beautiful wife, who shared his lonely life, living much of the time alone in the large stone house he had built for her, escaped to remarry. Then she retired to Spain, where she lived in opulence the rest of her life, presumably on San Saba silver.

An account by one who chose to remain anonymous under the pen name "Brazos" appeared in a November 1898 issue of the *St. Louis Globe-Democrat.* In this article Brazos relates the story of one of Bowie's early trips into the San Saba country as follows:

> . . . By some means he [Bowie] had got possession of a lot of old maps of Western Texas, and upon many of these were marked places that had been abandoned for a hundred years.

* * *

> Possibly Colonel Bowie secured his old maps through his wife. . . . It is certain that he had not been very long married before he began to talk of recruiting an expedition in search for St. Denis' silver mine, and the old house, which at that period, was in the very heart of the country of the terrible Comanches. At that time the house was only a little more than a hundred years old, and there was not a white man in Texas who had ever seen it. Colonel Bowie knew that there was such a place on his old map, and he had heard many stories of the wonderful wealth that St. Denis had gathered in the mountains near the old house and he did not allow many days to pass before he found himself at the head of some twenty five or thirty adventurers prowling about in the mountains of the Guadalupe, southwest of San Antonio. After searching for more than a week, Bowie himself discovered St. Denis' old log house. . . . there was St. Denis' name and the date, 1714, carved on a rock.[6]

As the story continues, Bowie and his party were forced to take refuge in the old house by the Comanches, who besieged them for two weeks. They lost more than half of their men, and the rest were able to escape only under cover of a storm. But Bowie was the sort of man upon whom danger and difficulty operate only as spurs. He returned again and again. He carved his name on a gatepost of the St. Denis structure in 1832 and was purportedly planning another expedition to the San Saba in 1835 when the invasion of Texas changed his mind. Whether he ever discovered *Los Almagres,* or returned from it periodically with rich cargoes of silver, celebrating each time with "feasting and revelry [that] lasted for several days"; whether he ever had his "favorite war horse [shod] with pure silver shoes" — these are details that no one can at present either prove or disprove.[7] But whether his search ended in success or failure it continued to fascinate him, as it still does us. . . .

Being a practical man, Bowie first tried negotiation with the Lipans. If he could get permission to enter their country, he could then devote most of his time and energy to the search for the mine. He carefully cultivated Xolic, their chief, and made some headway in gaining his confidence. Xolic had forbidden any of his tribe to tell where the mine was located on pain of death by torture. He had no love for the white man, but he respected Bowie and might eventually have confided the secret to him, had he not unexpectedly died. His successor, Tres Manos, had even less faith in the palefaces, and he is said to have angered Bowie by bluntly telling him so.

There remained only one course open to Bowie. He would have to hazard encounters with the Indians. He would take a strong enough force with him so as to have some hope of standing them off. He chose only tough fighters and accurate marksmen because, of necessity, he had to limit their number. It was risky military strategy, but he was never one to let the hazards dissuade him from going after whatever he wanted. If it was a fair gamble, that was all that he asked. And the Indians were not just looking for a picturesque name when they dubbed him *El Endiablado,* "the Devil-Possessed One," or, more freely translated, "the Fighting Devil"!

In view of the Indian danger there, the Bowie brothers must have been pretty impatient to begin their explorations of the San Saba country when they set out on November 2, 1831, with such a small party. One wonders if they did not purposely seek the Governor's blessing on the project in an effort to attract men to what must have appeared to many a chimerical and foolhardy venture. Lost silver mine! Wasn't that largely an old wives' tale? Who wants his hair lifted looking for nonexistent silver? Indians had come into San Antonio wearing silver jewelry for as long as anyone could remember. Anyhow, perhaps they had got the metal from the Mexicans. . . .

Each of the Bowie boys who participated in it wrote an account of the noted San Saba fight of November 21, 1831. Rezin's story was published in 1832 in a Philadelphia newspaper. It is a good account of what Yoakum described as "a model Indian fight,"[8] and it has been reprinted a number of times since he included it in his famous history of Texas. James's account, less often seen, was made to the Mexican Governor at San Antonio. Shorter and more stilted in language, it is still a good narrative of an exciting event and is therefore given in full, as follows:

REPORT OF JAMES BOWIE.

San Antonio de Bexar, Dec. 10, 1831.

To the Political Chief of Bexar:

Agreeably to your lordship's request, I have the honor to report to you the result of my expedition from San Antonio to the San Saba. Information received through different channels in relation to that section of the country, formerly occupied by Mexican citizens, and now in the hands of several Indian tribes, induced me to get up that expedition, expecting that some benefit might result therefrom both to the community and myself. But, as my intentions were known to you and approved by your lordship previous to my departure, I deem it useless to enter into these particulars. I left this city on the 2d of November last in company with my brother, Rezin P. Bowie, eight men and a boy. Wishing, with due care, to examine the nature of the country, my progress was quite slow. On the 19th we met two Comanches and one Mexican captive (the last acting as an interpreter) at about seven miles northwest of the Llano River, on the road known as de la Bandera. The Indians, after having asked several questions in regard to the feelings of the Mexicans towards the Comanches, and receiving an assurance on my part that they were kindly disposed towards all peaceable Indians, told me that their friends were driving to San Antonio several horses that had been stolen at Goliad. I promised them that they would be protected, and they continued on their way to the city to deliver the said horses to their proper owners or to the civil authority. On the following day at sunrise, we were overtaken by the captive, who informed us that 124 Tehuacanas were on our trail, and at the same time showing us the medal received this year by his captain from the authority of this city, which was sent to us to prove that the messenger was reliable. We were then apprised that the Tehuacanas had the day before visited the camping ground of the

Comanches, and told them that they were following us to kill us at any cost. Ysayune (such was the name of the Comanche captain), having become informed of the determination of the savages respecting us, tried first to induce them to desist from the prosecution of their intention, insisting they should not take our lives, and telling them he would be mad with them if they went to attack us, but they separated, dissatisfied with each other. Ysayune sent us word that if we would come back he would do all he could to assist us, but that he had only sixteen men under his command, and thought that we could defend ourselves against the enemy by taking position on a hill covered by underbrush, which the captive was ordered to show us, adding that the houses on the San Saba were close by. The houses alluded to were the remains of those belonging to the San Saba mission, that had been long abandoned. We did not follow the Comanche's advice, thinking that we could reach our destination, as we did, before the enemy could overtake us. But once arrived we could not find the houses, and the ground upon the San Saba offering no position for our protection, we went about three miles to the north of the river, and there selected a grove wherein to encamp for the night. There was a smaller grove about fifty varas from the one chosen for our encampment, and I caused it to be occupied by three men, so as to prevent the enemy from taking possession of it, and thereby have an advantage over us. However, we passed the night without being disturbed.

On the 21st, at eight o'clock a.m., we were about to leave our camping ground, when we saw a large body of Indians close upon us, and at a distance of about two hundred varas. Several of them shouted in English: "How do you do? How are you? How are you?" We soon knew by their skins that they had among them some Caddoes, and we made signs to them to send us a man to inform us of their intentions. Just then we saw that the Indian, who was ahead on horseback, was holding up a scalp, and forthwith a volley of some ten or twelve gunshots was discharged into our camp, but without effect. At the arrival of the Indians, my brother repaired with two men to the smaller grove which was between us and the Indians, but when I saw that most of them were withdrawing and sheltering themselves behind a hill about 100 varas northeast of our position, expecting that they would attack us in a body from that direction, I went to tell my brother to come back and on our return Mr. Buchanan was shot and his leg broken. We had scarcely joined our camp when, as I expected, the Indians came from behind the hill to dislodge us, but as the foremost men, and among them the one who seemed to be the leader, fell, they busied themselves in removing their dead, and to do this they had to come closer and fight sharply, but it was at the cost of more lives on their part. This contest lasted about fifteen minutes; but when they perceived that they could not enter our camp they withdrew, screening themselves behind a hill and surrounding timber, and thence com-

menced firing upon us from every direction. While we were thus engaged, fifteen Indians, who, from the report of their firing, seemed to
be armed with rifles, concealed themselves behind some oaks in a
valley about sixty varas to the northwest. These were the severest of
our foemen, and they wounded two more of our men and several
horses. At about 11 o'clock, a.m., seeing that they could not dislodge
us with their fire-arms, they set fire to the prairie, hoping thus to burn
us or compel us to abandon our camp. So soon as the prairie was on
fire they loudly shouted, and, expecting their stratagem would be successful, they advanced under protection of the smoke to the position
they had first been obliged to abandon; but when the fire reached the
valley it died out.

Thinking the siege would be protracted, we employed Gonzales and
the boy Charles in making a breastwork of whatever they could lay
their hands upon, such as boughs and our property. From that moment
until 4 o'clock the fire slackened gradually, and the Indians withdrew
to a considerable distance. But the wind having shifted from the southwest to the northwest, the Indians again fired the prairie, and the con-
flagration reached our camp, but by dint of hard work in the way
of tearing the grass, and by means of our bear skins and blankets,
made use of to smother the flames, we succeeded in saving the greater
part of our animals and other property. We expected a furious attack
of the enemy under cover of the smoke, in order to penetrate our camp,
but the greater part of them withdrew to a pond, distant about a
half a mile from the battle field, to procure water, and those of them
that remained kept firing and removing their dead. This work on their
part went on until about 6:30 o'clock p.m., when the battle closed,
only one shot being fired by them after 7 o'clock, which was aimed at
one of our men who went to obtain water.

We had agreed to attack the enemy while they were asleep, but
when we reflected that we had only six men able to use their arms,
and that the wounded would have to remain unprotected, we thought
it more advisable to remain in our camp, which we had now fortified
with stones and timber, so as to make it quite secure against further
assault. On the 22d, at about 5 o'clock a.m., we heard the Indians
moving towards the northeast, and at day-break none were to be seen.
However, about 11 o'clock we observed thirteen of them, who, upon
seeing us, withdrew suddenly. Subsequently, in order to intimidate
them and impress them with the idea that we were still ready for a
fight, we hoisted a flag on a long pole, as a sign of war; and for eight
days we kept a fire constantly burning, hoping thereby to attract the
attention of any friendly Comanches that might be in the neighborhood, and procure some animals for the transportation of our wounded
and our camp property.

On the evening of the 29th, the wounded being somewhat relieved,
we began our march for Bexar, and on striking the Pierdenales we

observed a large Tehuacana trail, and noticed several others between that stream and the Guadalupe, all seeming to tend in the direction of a smoke that curled upward from some point down the Pierdenales. Upon seeing these trails, we took a more westerly course, and after having crossed the Guadalupe, we saw no more signs of Indians, and arrived here on the night of the 6th inst. My only loss among my men during the battle, was by the fall and death of the foreman of my mechanics, Mr. Thomas McCaslin, from a bullet that entered below the breast and passed through the loin. He was one of the most efficient of my comrades in the fight. I had, also, three men wounded, five animals killed and several severely hurt. We could make no estimate of the loss of the enemy, but we kept up a continual firing during the day and always had enemies to aim at, and there were no intervening obstacles to prevent our shot from having their full effect. We saw twenty-one men fall dead, and among them seven on horseback, who seemed to act as chiefs, one of whom was very conspicuous by reason of the buffalo horns and other finery about his head. To his death I attribute the discouragement of his followers. I cannot do less than commend to your lordship for their alacrity in obeying and executing my orders with spirit and firmness all those who accompanied me. Their names are Robert Armstrong, Rezin P. Bowie, Mathew Doyle, Thomas McCaslin (killed), Daniel Buchanan (wounded), James Coryell, Mateo Dias, Cephas K. Ham, Jesse Wallace, Senor Gonzales, Charles (a boy).

God and Liberty.

JAMES BOWIE.[9]

It is to be regretted that James Bowie did not leave other accounts of his fights with the Indians and concerning his other contacts with them. From the evidence at hand it must be concluded, however, that, except during his boyhood in Louisiana, most of his dealings with the red man were on the violent level. At least one writer mentions his negotiating a treaty in 1832 with certain tribes in Texas, but I can find no documentary evidence of any such event.[10] In a letter to the "Jefe Politico of the Department of Nacogdoches," dated August 3, 1835, Bowie does describe a "tour through the Indian villages" of friendly Shawnees and Cherokees, made for the purpose of recruiting braves to fight hostile tribes engaged in killing and plundering Mexicans and American settlers. It seems that a trader named Coffee was his particular concern because he was egging the Comanches on to commit hostile acts with promises to buy horses and anything else of value they could steal.[11]

But Bowie had little time from now on, either for expeditions against the Indians or for hunting Lipan silver. The events of his personal life had shaken him as a gale shakes a tree, had made him again the restless blade. But everything, especially his personal tragedy, seemed to prepare him for the part he was to play in the Texas Revolution, which, only smouldering until now, soon burst into flames.

Comanche chief

-- after Catlin

chapter

7

Nacogdoches and After

IT IS not my purpose either to expatiate upon the causes of the Texas Revolution or to relate any events of that Revolution that did not involve James Bowie. The Revolution broke out on October 2, 1835, with the Battle of Gonzales. All preceding battles therefore belong to the pre-Revolution period. Bowie took no part in the two earliest military actions, which occurred at Anahuac on July 2, 1832, and at Velasco on July 27, 1832.[1] But he did participate in the Battle of Nacogdoches, the main action of which took place on August 2, 1832.

Of several Mexican garrisons located in Coahuila and Texas was one at Nacogdoches, under command of Col. Jose de las Piedras, who was not far behind Col. Juan Bradburn, former commandant at Anahuac, in tyranny over the colonists. He was a Monarchist who had not declared himself in favor of the Constitution of 1824, viewed by the colonists as a bulwark of their liberties although it was far from being an ideal document. At that time Santa Anna, as head of the Republican Party, also pretended to support it, but the citizens did not know then that he was a Monarchist wolf in Republican sheep's clothing. Piedras was at least honest in his contempt for democracy.

In any event, the civil authorities at Nacogdoches thought that Piedras ought to be forced to declare himself. With the concurrence of the civil governments of certain neighboring towns, they therefore decided to force the issue: he must either come out for the Constitution of 1824 or fight. Yoakum's account of the succeeding events, in which Bowie played a prominent though disputed role, is as follows:

Accordingly, the troops from these settlements concentrated on the last day of July [1832]; and, on the night between the 1st and 2d of August, they encamped directly east of the town, and all the families evacuated the place. After a conference between the civil and military authorities, Isaac W. Burton, Philip A. Sublett, and Henry W. Augustin, were appointed a committee to wait on Colonel Piedras, and present to him the alternative agreed on. He chose to fight. The committee reported his answer to the Texan forces, then amounting to about three hundred men. They elected James W. Bullock, of San Augustine, to the command, and, at noon on the 2d of August, marched into Nacogdoches, where they manoeuvred for some time, waiting to be attacked; but, finding that the enemy did not show himself, they advanced into the centre of the town. When a little north of the *stone house,* they were suddenly charged by the Mexican cavalry, numbering about one hundred men. The latter fired and wheeled, and received a round from the Texan rifles as they retired. In this charge the Mexicans killed Don Encarnacion Chirino, the alcalde of the town. The Texans then took possession of the houses on the north and east sides of the square, and, whenever any of the enemy showed themselves, they were shot. The Mexicans made one sortie in the evening. It was commanded by a young officer who was known to be friendly to the Texans and to their cause, and who had shown his friendship for them in the Fredonian troubles of 1827. The Texans spared him. With the repulse of this sortie, the fighting ceased. During the night, Piedras and his troops evacuated the place, leaving behind him his killed and wounded, public stores, and clothing. His ammunition he had thrown into the wells.

Colonel James Bowie, who was engaged in this action, was despatched, with a few chosen men, to pass by the retreating Mexicans, and give them a warm reception as they crossed the Angelina, twenty miles distant. He succeeded in this, by taking the lower road. As the advanced guard of the enemy, commanded by Sergeant Marcos, rode into the water, and stopped to allow their horses to drink, the Americans fired on them. Marcos fell. The Americans then drew back, and the Mexican troops proceeded on their way to a house on the hill west of the river, where they passed the night. The next morning, upon a demand to surrender, Colonel Piedras turned over the command to Major Francisco Medina, who declared immediately in favor of the constitution of 1824.

The Mexican loss in this battle was forty-one killed and as many wounded, while that of the Texans was but three killed and five wounded. The prisoners, three hundred and ten in number, were sent, under the care of Colonel Bowie, to San Felipe. Colonel Piedras was placed in charge of Captain Asa M. Edwards, to be by him delivered to Colonel Mexia at Anahuac. On the way, Edwards received news of the sailing of Mexia for Matamoras; he therefore took Piedras to Colonel S. F. Austin, by whom he was forwarded to Tampico.[2]

A more detailed account of this operation is to be found in
The Papers of Mirabeau Buonaparte Lamar. Lamar, or whoever
furnished him with this account, apparently did not regard Bowie
as the leader of the forces that followed Piedras to the Angelina
River, for he wrote:

> They had no leader, and an attempt was made to chose [sic] a com-
> mander — but it failed. Thompson, however, was the most active and
> prominent actor.[3]

Of the nineteen members of the party only seven are mentioned
by name. One, a man named Luney, was apparently "hung a few
years after for murder" despite the heroism he displayed upon
this occasion! Thompson is portrayed as the one who met with
Piedras and persuaded him to capitulate, although most other accounts, including the one in Yoakum, state that it was Bowie. An
interesting detail concerning Piedras is given in the Lamar story
as follows:

> Whilst he was on the road from the Angilena to Nacogdoches, on
> being told that the Americans were only 19 strong, that . . . fought him
> at the river, and that they had not been reenforced, he wept, and said
> that it would cost him his life for the government to know that he had
> surrendered to such a small force; . . . that it was not his fault . . . , but
> that his men were so panic stricken that they would not fight . . . . [4]

Not much is known about Bowie's movements during the rest
of 1832. The wanderlust had again possessed him. He is supposed
to have accompanied Austin to the convention at San Felipe,
whether in an official or unofficial capacity is not clear. He is also
said to have been sent into the Indian country, or may have organized his own expedition to go there and retaliate upon the
tribes who had attacked him and his party on the San Saba during
the previous year. Whatever his purpose, the Indians must have
received advance word of his coming. Possibly they had already
had enough of fighting Texans because they stayed out of his way
so well that "in a tour of several hundred miles" he "never saw
an Indian."[5]

According to one of his biographers, Sam Houston accompanied Bowie on a trip from San Felipe to San Antonio in December
of 1832. In San Antonio Bowie introduced him to his father-in-
law and to the Mexican commandant, Francisco Ruiz. About this

time Houston made an abortive attempt to arrange a meeting
between certain Comanche chiefs and United States Indian commissioners at Fort Gibson, but no evidence has been found that
Bowie was in any way connected with such efforts. From his recent experiences with the Comanches, Bowie could have had little
love for them, but he was too practical not to grasp the importance
of getting them on the side of the revolutionists and away from
the influence of the Mexican authorities, who were stirring them
up to commit depredations on settlers and other provocative acts.

Bowie being a man about whom very little of a humorous nature
has been recorded, I am tempted to relate here the only known
piece of waggery in which he engaged. It may, like some of the
Crockett stories, have been born in somebody's imagination. Even
so, it is true to his character, for in it he is shown in his accustomed role of interceding in someone else's behalf. The delecta-
tion of the chronicler in relating this piece of buffoonery shows
through in almost every line:

Some time in the year 1832 a couple came to San Felipe for the
purpose of getting married. Under the Mexican laws no one but a
Catholic priest could solemnize the rite of matrimony. There being no
priest in Austin's colony, an *arrangement de convenance,* as the French
would say, but in Texas called "constitutional marriage," was adopted.
The ceremony consisted merely in the appearance of the high contracting parties before the alcalde, and the signification of their purpose to
assume the relation of man and wife until an opportunity was had of
having the religious rite properly celebrated by a priest. The couple
in this instance who were hymeneally inclined was a country lass
from "the Cole Settlement" and a "minister of the gospel" from the
mountain district of Arkansas. They put up at the house of Mrs. Payton.
Fortunately for the prospective bride, James Bowie was also a guest
of the same landlady. Bowie recognized the bogus preacher as a scamp
who had made too free with his neighbors' stables after dark, and who
had fled the country, leaving behind a disconsolate wife and several
small children.

Of course high-toned, chivalrous Jim Bowie was not the man to sit
down and see a lecherous old villain accomplish his aims.

Bowie got Joe Powell to [im]personate a priest, which, with the proper disguise, he did well. The alcalde, Mr. Christian, was let into the
secret, which he heartily approved of when Bowie had made him
somewhat acquainted with the antecedents of the prospective bridegroom. This gentleman was informed that a priest had arrived rather
unexpectedly in San Felipe, and that under the law the matter would

have to go to him, and not to the alcalde; but he was offered the consoling reflection that it would be a *de jure* marriage, such as civilized people indulge in, and not a mere "constitutional" cohabitation.

The candidate signified the pleasure that this unexpected turn of good fortune gave him with profuse smiles. The priest announced that he was ready to catechise the bridegroom *expectant*. The *padre* spoke no English; bridegroom *presumptive* knew no more of Spanish than he did of Sanscrit. Happy accomplishment of Bowie: he was master of both languages! Bowie would, then, interpret! The females of the house were separated from this interesting coterie only by a thin board partition, through which sound passed unobstructed. Women have curiosity, and they have a right to possess it; it is a commendable quality sometimes. The catechising progressed; and if the ... reader imagines that Bowie interpreted in a voice too low to pass beyond the partition, then he's wrong, that's all. The bridegroom *doubtful* soon imagined that this *padre* was a searcher of the hearts of men, and that nothing could be hidden from his ken. His wife and children were each inquired of by name, as was his equine "crookedness." The poor fellow groaned in agony of spirit. The reader may safely imagine that there were some deeply interested "women folk" on the other side of the partition. The *padre* now announced that he would confess the lady in the case, and give the gentleman another "sitting," as his was a rather tough case. But Mrs. Payton put a stop to further proceedings by incontinently ordering the old scoundrel off the premises. He left, and did not "stand on the order of his going." And when a committee of admiring friends came to present him with an elegant suit of TAR AND FEATHERS, the haunts that had so lately known him knew him now no more for ever.[6]

Bowie was home but a brief time before he decided to go to Louisiana to take care of certain business affairs. But the cholera was already raging in parts of Mexico. He did not want to leave his family in the path of the epidemic, and, for some reason, he decided they would be safer in Monclova than at San Antonio. His father-in-law and mother-in-law went with them. It was early in 1833 when he felt free to leave. Apparently his itinerary included points in Mississippi because he made and signed his will at Natchez on October 31, 1833.[7]

When he returned, it was to receive the worst blow of his life. He found that Ursula, the children, his father-in-law, and his mother-in-law had all been swept away by the cholera within a few days. From the day he received the news he was inconsolable. He got rid of all his property as fast as possible, his interest in the textile mill at a considerable sacrifice. Then he embarked on a siege of debauchery and drunkenness. Sam, his burly slave, who had returned with him from Louisiana, tried to divert him from this course, but he had no success.

"Mars Jim," he told his master sorrowfully, "you've been drunk befoh, but I ain't never seen you like *this*."

Many times he had to carry Bowie out of a saloon or cantina and put him on his horse. And nothing the slave did could please him. Bowie went dirty and unshaven, he was almost in rags, he became so haggard and changed in appearance that even his friends did not recognize him.

One day he met Sam Houston and poured out his troubles to him. Sam had once tried the road of dissipation himself. He counselled Bowie but had the good sense not to preach.

"Why don't you go back to Louisana and see your family," he advised. "You're restless, uprooted. My guess is you'll never be satisfied anywhere after your great loss. But remember this — the cause of Texas liberation is worth everything either of us can give to it."

"I will," Bowie promised.

Both men believed Texas would be freed only by revolution. Jim had long held that the "talkers," of whom he regarded Stephen F. Austin as the leader, were merely deluding themselves.

So, accompanied by Sam, he rode away from the town that no longer had any personal ties for him except memories. During late 1833 and 1834 he was on the move most of the time. Only a few references remain testifying to his presence in widely separated places. It is fairly clear that he was working to win men to the Texan cause part of the time, but as to his specific activities little is known up to the time the Texas Revolution broke out in earnest, as it did with the Battle of Gonzales. From then on to the end Bowie was irrevocably committed to the struggle.

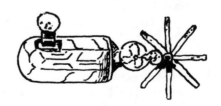

The Battle of Gonzales to the Siege of Bexar

Bowie was on other orders when the Texas Revolution opened, literally with a "bang," and so he did not participate in its first battle. The importance of that first brief encounter for the Bowie story is that it set the stage for the battle of Concepcion, in which he played an important part. A brief summary of this affray over a piece of artillery is therefore of interest.

The opening gun of the Revolution was fired early in the morning on October 2, 1835, at Gonzales, where the Texans, 150 strong, successfully repelled an equal number of Mexicans. That gun was a small brass cannon the Texans had been permitted to have since 1831 to protect the town against Indians. As part of a general plan of the Mexican Government to disarm the Texans, Col. Domingo de Ugartechea, commandant at Bexar, demanded return of the cannon on the ground that it had been merely loaned. The Texans were determined they would *never* surrender their weapons. They refused to comply.

Lt. Francisco Castaneda was thereupon ordered to go to Gonzales and, if necessary, to take the cannon by force. He arrived on September 29, 1835, and demanded to see Andrew Ponton, the alcalde, at once. He was told that official was absent and that no one knew when he would return. The Texans used this as a delaying tactic, and with the three days they gained by it, recruited men to their cause all along the Colorado River, with the rallying cry that the Mexican Government had violated the Constitution of 1824. Then, when they finally had to give Castaneda a definite answer, they told him that Ponton had returned but refused to surrender the cannon.

"I have come for the cannon, and I will not return without it," the Mexican commander replied. The "Colorado men," by now gathered in full force, expected him to attack; however, up to October 1 he had made no move, so the Texans decided to attack him.

Under command of Col. John H. Moore they crossed the Guadalupe that night. The Mexicans were encamped on a hill. Under cover of darkness, the Texans succeeded in taking up a position opposite them without their presence being detected. Then, having first painted on their cannon in large letters "Come and take it," they placed it in full view of the enemy.

At dawn, Colonel Moore sent a message to the Mexican commander demanding his surrender. When Castaneda ignored the demand, Moore gave orders to the cannoneer to open fire and to the Texans to charge. The Mexicans panicked under the attack and scattered like startled chickens. Castaneda tried vainly to rally them, but they fled in a complete rout toward Bexar where the main body of their forces was concentrated. The Texans were thus left in complete possession of the field and whatever booty the enemy had left behind. None was injured or killed. The Mexican losses, if any, are unknown.

The effect of this battle was out of all proportion to its size. The whole countryside was aroused. Boys and even old men flew to the Texan cause. Austin, with whom many had been dissatisfied because they thought him an appeaser, declared that the Gonzales affair proved the intention of the Mexicans to drive the settlers out. It was now clear that their only recourse was war. He was chosen commander in chief of all the volunteers, Sam Houston commander of the troops from eastern Texas.

On October 8, 1835, Houston issued a proclamation urging men to volunteer and promising "liberal bounties of land . . . to all who will join our ranks with a good rifle and one hundred rounds of ammunition."[1]

The Texan cause awakened interest all over the country. Companies came from five American states. New Orleans alone raised two. Added fuel was heaped upon the revolutionary fire by a decree of the Mexican Government of October 3, 1835, abolishing the state legislatures and placing everything under Santa Anna as a dictator, although that document does not mention him by name.[2]

Most of the Mexican force was concentrated in Bexar, but there was also a detachment stationed at Goliad, and these troops now began committing depredations upon the surrounding country. This was not to be tolerated, so Austin at once sent a company of men to drive them out. On the night of October 9, 1835, about forty-eight men under Capt. George Collinsworth completely surprised the Mexican garrison under Lt. Col. Francisco Sandoval and took it without loss, although one Texan was wounded. The Mexicans lost three men and had seven wounded. The invaders took twenty-four of them prisoners. The acquisition of about ten thousand dollars worth of military stores, some artillery, and some small arms was the most important result to the revolutionists of this operation.

On October 20 Austin established his headquarters about eight miles from Bexar, his next objective. He kept informed concerning activities of the Mexican troops by means of scouts and spies. Having a proper concern for the lives of his men, however, he did not immediately attack, but

... sent to General [Martin Perfecto de] Cos, who had charge of the troops in San Antonio, to see if a compromise could not be arranged. "I shall never treat with the ungrateful Texans save as rebels," was the haughty response sent by Cos.[3]

At this time Bowie, still chafing at his low military rank, was given another scouting assignment. On October 27, 1835, he received the following order from Austin:

Col James Bowie, Volunteer Aid:

You will proceed with the first division of Captain Fannin's company and others attached to that division and select the best and most secure position that can be had on the river, as near Bejar as practicable to encamp the army tonight, keeping in view in the selection of this position pasturage and the security of the horses, and the army from night attacks of the enemy.

You will also reconnoiter, so far as time and circumstances will permit, the situation of the outskirts of the town and the approaches to it, whether the houses have been destroyed on the outside, so as to leave every approach exposed to the raking of the cannon.

You will make your report with *as little delay as possible*, SO AS TO GIVE TIME TO THE ARMY TO MARCH AND TAKE UP ITS POSITION BEFORE NIGHT. Should you be attacked by a large force, send expresses *immediately* with the particulars.

S. F. Austin.
By order P W Grayson, Aid-de-camp.[4]

This order is quoted in full because the question has been raised as to who commanded the Texan troops in the ensuing battle.[5] While this order can be interpreted as placing Bowie in command, its obvious intent was that he was to initiate no military action, but only to reconnoiter and bring back information. He was to fight only if "attacked by a large force."

The report made after Concepcion states that Fannin commanded the First Division at one point, while Bowie was in charge of three companies at another. So the command was actually divided, with Fannin having under him the greater number of troops. With a tact rare in military men, he signed the report as Commandant of the First Division *below* Bowie as Aid-de-Camp!

The battle of Concepcion was fought on the morning of October 28, 1835. That Bowie was in the action from the beginning is attested by a participant named Highsmith, who told the historian, A. J. Sowell,

. . . that on the morning of the fight Bowie gave the order to "Get your guns, boys; here they come," when the Mexicans first fired on them.[6]

The Bowie-Fannin report of the battle is the most authentic; it is therefore quoted in full, as follows:

Official Account of the Action of the 28th ult., at the Mission of Conception, near Bejar.

Dear Sir, —In conformity with your order of the 27th inst., we proceeded with the division composed of ninety-two men, rank and file, under our joint command, to examine the Missions above Espada, and select the most eligible situation near Bejar, for the encampment of the main army of Texas. After carefully examining that of San José (having previously visited San Juan) we marched to that of Conception, and selected our ground in a bend of the river San Antonio, within about five hundred yards of the old Mission Conception. The face of the plain in our front was nearly level, and the timbered land adjoining it formed two sides of a triangle, both of which were as nearly equal as possible; and, with the exception of two places, a considerable bluff of from six to ten feet sudden fall in our rear, and a bottom of fifty to one hundred yards to the river.

We divided the command into divisions, and occupied each one side of the triangle, for the encampment on the night of the 27th, Captain

Fannin's company being under cover of the south side, forming the first division, and Captains Coleman, Goheen, and Bennet's companies (making in all only forty-one, rank and file) occupied the north side, under the immediate command of myself (James Bowie, aid-de-camp.)

Thus the men were posted, and lay on their arms during the night of the 27th, having [put] out strong picket guards, and one of seven men in the cupola of the Mission-house, which overlooked the whole country, the horses being all tied up.

The night passed quietly off, without the least alarm; and at dawn of day, every object was obscured by a heavy, dense fog, which entirely prevented our guard, or look-out from the Mission, seeing the approach of the enemy.

At about half an hour by sun, an advanced guard of their cavalry rode upon our line, and fired at a sentinel who had just been relieved, who returned the fire, and caused one platoon to retire; but another charged on him (Henry Karnes), and he discharged a pistol at them, which had the same effect.

The men were called to arms; but were for some time unable to discover their foes, who had entirely surrounded the position, and kept up a constant firing, at a distance, with no other effect than a waste of ammunition on their part. When the fog rose, it was apparent to all that we were surrounded, and a desperate fight was inevitable, all communications with the main army being cut off. Immediate preparation was made, by extending our right flank (first division) to the south, and placing the second division on the left, on the same side, so that they might be enabled to rake the enemy's, should they charge into the angle, and prevent the effects of a cross-fire of our own men; and, at the same time, be in a compact body, contiguous to each other, that either might reinforce the other, at the shortest notice, without crossing the angle, in an exposed and uncovered ground, where certain loss must have resulted. The men, in the mean time, were ordered to clear away bushes and vines, under the hill and along the margin, and at the steepest places to cut steps for foot-hold, in order to afford them space to form and pass, and at suitable places ascend the bluff, discharge their rifles, and fall back to reload. The work was not completed to our wish, before the infantry were seen to advance, with arms trailed, to the right of the first division, and form the line of battle at about two hundred yards distance from the right flank. Five companies of their cavalry supported them, covering our whole front and flanks. Their infantry was also supported by a large force of cavalry.

In this manner, the engagement commenced at about the hour of eight o'clock, A.M., on Wednesday, 28th of October, by the deadly crack of a rifle from the extreme right. The engagement was immediately general. The discharge from the enemy was one continued blaze of fire, whilst that from our lines, was more slowly delivered, but with good aim and deadly effect, each man retiring under cover of the hill and timber, to give place to others, whilst he re-loaded. The battle had not lasted more than ten minutes, before a brass double fortified four-pounder was opened on our line with a heavy discharge of grape and canister, at the distance of about eighty yards from the right flank of the first division, and a charge sounded. But the cannon was cleared, as if by magic, and a check put to the charge. The same experiment was resorted to, with like success, three times, the division advancing under the hill at each fire, and thus approximating near the cannon and victory. "The cannon and victory" was truly the war-cry, and they only fired it five times, and it had been three times cleared, and their charge as often broken, before a disorderly and precipitate retreat was sounded, and most readily obeyed, leaving to the victors their cannon. Thus a small detachment of ninety-two men gained a most decisive victory over the main army of the central government, being at least four to one, with only the loss of one brave soldier (Richard Andrews), and none wounded: whilst the enemy suffered in killed and wounded near one hundred, from the best information we can obtain, which is entitled to credit; say sixty-seven killed, among them many promising officers. Not one man of the artillery company escaped unhurt.

No invidious distinction can be drawn between any officer or private, on this occasion. Every man was a soldier, and did his duty, agreeably to the situation and circumstances under which he was placed.

It may not be amiss here to say, that near the close of the engagement another heavy piece of artillery was brought up, and fired thrice, but at a distance; and by a reinforcement of another company of cavalry, aided by six mules, ready harnessed, they got it off. The main army reached us in about one hour after the enemy's retreat. Had it been possible to communicate with you, and brought you up earlier, the victory would have been decisive, and Bejar ours before twelve o'clock.

With sentiments of high consideration, we subscribe ourselves,

Yours, most respectfully,

James Bowie, Aid-de-Camp.
J. W. Fannin, Commandant
first division.

General S. F. Austin.[7]

The estrangement between Austin and Bowie has been alluded to in a previous chapter. Much has to be read between the lines of the available evidence, but Bowie, apart from personal antipathy, regarded Austin as a talker and a pacificator, neither of much use in dealing with a ruthless, well-armed enemy. He and Fannin thought Austin showed poor judgment in allowing them only ninety-two men while he kept the rest of the army idle and tied up in camp. Bowie had already resigned once. On November 2 he again resigned, reiterating his conviction that the scattered parts of the army ought to be united. The Commander in Chief ignored both the advice and the resignation!

On the personal side, Bowie resented being given a series of relatively unimportant scouting, spying, and other assignments that he regarded as a waste of his military experience and knowledge of the country. Even after the creditable job he and Fannin had done in leading the troops to victory at Concepcion, Austin was chary of his praise. True, in a letter of October 28, 1835, to the Consultation, he extolled those who had won that victory, but he mentioned no one by name. And Bowie was still only a "Volunteer Aid," a rank almost as anonymous as private.[8] He was entirely justified, it seems, in expecting recognition for what he had done, in the form of a promotion. Austin may have been a bit mollified toward him because, on November 4, 1835, he gave him a temporary appointment as adjutant general during the absence of Warren D. C. Hall; but he knew little about Bowie's pride and his character as a man if he hoped to satisfy him with such an appointment. Bowie must have felt more insulted than honored. He stayed in this desk job two days, then again resigned.[9]

But what about Austin's side of this relationship? His dislike of land speculators has already been mentioned. He was convinced that they were one of the chief sources of trouble between the settlers and the Mexican Government. He was not alone in disapproving of the special privileges Bowie had secured to engage in this kind of speculation. Men prominent in the Consultation also resented or were envious of Bowie's special status. Austin may have had other reasons for disliking Bowie, but we can only speculate as to what they were. He did admit in a letter to Samuel M. Williams, dated March 21, 1832, that

A great deal of pains has been taken by *some one* to foment discord between Bowie and his connections and me, one of them has told me who he thinks it is — he thinks him to be an aspiring man, an enemy at least to both Bowie and myself — [10]

Who this "aspiring man" was Austin does not state, so it will probably always remain a mystery.

Austin may or may not have been a failure as a military leader. It is easy in the light of "hindsight" to criticize some of the
decisions of any military commander. Most of the time he seems
to have been ready to listen to the counsels of *professional* military men. One such occasion came after the battle of Concepcion,
when the Texan army, totaling about a thousand men, gathered
near the mission. Austin joined them there and on November 2,
1835, called a council of war, during which he asked for the opin-
ions of the officers as to the advisability of a direct assault upon
Bexar. All but one voted against it. The Mexican positions were
well protected by cannon. The Texans had only five artillery pieces of small caliber. The prevailing opinion of the officers, to which
he acceded, was that it would be more advisable to begin a siege
and wait "For the larger 18 lb cannon and additional reinforcements."[11]

But Austin was to have no further tests of his military leadership. The Consultation at San Felipe appointed him as one of
three commissioners to the United States on November 12, 1835,
replacing him with Sam Houston as commander in chief. Houston
was not immediately available, so Austin ordered the men to elect
a temporary commander. They chose Col. Edward Burleson. Even
though Burleson was his close friend, Bowie was hurt that he
had not been considered for the post.

The Texan forces made various attempts to lure the Mexicans
from Bexar, but General Cos was too wary for them. He, too, had
decided to sit tight until reinforcements arrived. There were
minor skirmishes between scouts and outposts of the two armies,
but these were insufficient to hold the interest of the restless men.
The volunteers cooled to lukewarm, and, of the thousand men who
had originally gathered at Concepcion, by November 14 only
about six hundred remained.[12]

It is easy to imagine the excitement created on the morning of
November 27 when Erastus "Deaf" Smith returned to camp from
a spying trip and reported sighting a party of about one hundred
Mexican soldiers on the old Presidio Road. Rumor already had it
that Colonel Ugartechea was expected soon with funds to pay
off the Mexican army, so the Texans, eager for excitement, were
more than ready to believe it was he. All of them wanted to
join the raiding party, but the cautious Burleson kept most of

them in camp. He put James Bowie at the head of a detachment of one hundred cavalry, with orders to intercept and capture the supposed train of gold-laden burros.

This was the prelude to the much-written-about "Grass Fight," which, although it turned out to be pretty much of a comic opera affair, actually did Bowie no discredit. If anyone was to blame, it was "Deaf" Smith, who failed for once to live up to his reputation as a spy. A second look would surely have shown him his error.

The real circumstances were that the Mexican cavalry horses were starving, and General Cos had sent out the party of men to cut grass for them. Yoakum summarized what happened as follows:

Colonel James Bowie . . . set out in a gallop, in advance. Shortly after, the remainder of the army, with the exception of a suitable guard, followed. They met the enemy about a mile from the town [Bexar], on their return. Bowie, with the advance, charged upon them, when they took a position in the bed of a dry branch. The movement of the Texans had been seen from the town, and the besieged marched out to defend the foraging-party, bringing with them two pieces of artillery. Just as Bowie charged the right of the foraging-party, the besieged came up on the left. Bowie now turned his attention to the latter, and for a short time the battle was well sustained. The enemy, however, retreated as they fought. The main body of the Texan force coming up meanwhile, charged the foraging-party, drove them from the bed of the dry branch, and took position in it. After the last charge, the enemy retreated yet more rapidly — still, however, continuing the fight until they reached the town, when the Texans formed in a ravine, but shortly afterward returned to their camp. The Mexican loss in this confused, running fight, was about fifty killed, two wounded, and one missing. The enemy lost about seventy head of horses, taken by the victors.[13]

There was only one Texan casualty, a soldier stunned by a ball that grazed his forehead. On the way back to camp some of the Texans stopped to see how badly off he was. The story is that he was sitting on the bank of a ravine holding his head in his hands. One John McGuffin called out, "Hello, there! What are you doing? — catching your brains in your hands?" Such was the rough humor of military men, but it turned out the man was not seriously hurt, only dazed, and he soon recovered.[14]

The Texan army was encamped in open country, without shelter, and so had little protection from the bitter winter weather. Burleson was about to give the order to move the army to some more protected spot near Goliad or Gonzales when, on the morning of December 3, 1835, three men, named Smith, Holmes, and Maverick, came into camp. They had been held in Bexar for some time as Mexican prisoners. From them it was learned that the Mexicans were not in as strong a position to ward off an attack as had been supposed. Some definite plans of assault were formulated, only to have General Burleson unexpectedly postpone them. It later transpired that he feared their plans had somehow been revealed to the enemy. The arrival of an absent guide named Arnold and of Lieutenant Vuavis, a deserter from the Mexican army, set his fears at rest. These men revealed that the discontent in the Mexican garrison was almost as great as that in the Texan camp, while their military position was even weaker than described by the three Mexican prisoners.

It was on the evening of December 4 that Col. Benjamin R. Milam rallied the men to his side with the now-famous cry, "Who will go with old Ben Milam into San Antonio?"

There seem to be only scraps of information concerning James Bowie's role in the storming of Bexar that occurred between December 5 and 9, but it is fairly certain that he took part in it. In any event, when the morning of December 10 dawned, the fierce contest was over, as evidenced by the white flag flying over the Mexican redoubt. Terms of surrender were drawn up on the following day. Around 1,400 Mexicans were conquered by about 500 Texans.

Bowie must have gone to San Felipe immediately after this battle. He was still seeking a commission as colonel at the head of his own regiment. Whether his friend Burleson encouraged him to do so is not known; but he did seek help from General Houston, who promised to try to persuade the Consultation to give him the commission. It turned out that the Consultation was occupied with weightier matters, so there was considerable delay, during which Bowie chafed and mulled over what else he could do to further his case. He had always left the "politicking" and speech-making to Rezin, but he decided it was now his turn to say his piece. He would be put off no longer. He went at once to the sessions of the Consultation and demanded to be heard. John

Henry Brown has given us the only known summary of his plea, prepared by an auditor and eyewitness:

Stepping inside the railing, hat in hand, with a dignified bow he addressed the council for an hour. He reviewed the salient points of his life, hurled from him with indignation every floating allegation affecting his character as a man of peace and honor, admitted that he was an unlettered man of the Southwest, and his lot had been cast in a day and among a people rendered necessarily, from political and material causes, more or less independent of law, but generous and scornful of every species of meanness and duplicity.

He said that he had cast his lot with Texas for honorable and patriotic purposes; that he had ever neglected his own affairs to serve the country in an hour of danger, had betrayed no man, deceived no man, wronged no man, and had never had a difficulty in the country, unless to protect the weak from the strong and evil-intentioned. That, yielding to the dictates of his own heart, he had taken to his bosom as a wife a true and lovely woman of a different race, the daughter of a distinguished "Coahil-Texano"; yet, as a thief in the night, death had invaded his home and taken his wife, his little ones, and his father-in-law; and now, standing alone of all his blood in Texas, all he asked was the privilege of serving it in the field, where his name, so frequently besmirched by double-dealing, unspeakable cowards, might be honorably associated with the brave and true.

Not an indecorous or undignified word fell from his lips — he made not an ungraceful movement or gesture — but stood there before the astonished council, the living exemplification of a natural orator.

He tarried not, but turned immediately and left the chamber, satisfied that he would receive generous consideration, and returned to San Antonio.... In that memorable December, 1835, Bowie received his Colonel's commission.[15]

Fate was hurrying him on faster than he knew toward that destiny to be forever "honorably associated with the brave and the true."

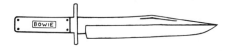

chapter

9

The Still-Restless Guns

— Bowie Enters the Alamo

J AMES BOWIE's brief association with one of two Matamoras expeditions furnishes another example of the type of frustration that dogged his military career. The circumstances require some explanation, not because of the abortive character of the expedition, but rather to show that none of what occurred was his fault.

To begin with, there was almost incredible confusion in the civil and military governments in the latter part of 1835 and early in 1836. This confusion came about largely because of a split between Governor Henry Smith and the Council of the Provisional Government. Their functions overlapped, and there was almost nothing on which they could agree. They quarreled constantly, and Governor Smith, being a man of violent temper, used abusive language to the Council. Goaded beyond endurance, its members finally impeached him.

The Council was conservative and made up mainly of men representing the "peace party," who thought open revolution was not then expedient, preferring a cautious, wait-and-see policy. They thought it possible to win over a certain sympathetic segment of Mexicans to the Texan cause. Governor Smith, on the other hand, was with the "independence" or "war party," impatient to take military action at once to secure independence. From the first, the Council decided military moves without consulting either the Governor or Sam Houston, the commander in chief. The Governor naturally regarded himself as the one to make such decisions and did so. The result was conflict and almost complete chaos. And this conflict came to a head in attempts to send an expedition to capture Matamoras, a town on the Rio Grande, considered by both factions of great strategic value to the Texans.

A Matamoras expedition had been planned earlier but was postponed when it was decided to lay siege to Bexar. After Bexar was captured, the whole matter came up again. An enthusiastic backer of such an expedition was Dr. James Grant, who had once owned, and since lost, large estates in Coahuila. He was certain of success because he believed that the Mexican Federalists opposed to Santa Anna would fly to the Texans' aid. His secret purpose was to restore the old Federalist system in Mexico in the hope of recovering these estates. In other words, he was actually not interested in the cause of Texan independence, even though he had fought in, and been wounded during, the siege of Bexar.

Joining Grant in this scheme was Col. Francis W. Johnson, who had replaced Col. Benjamin R. Milam as leader during the siege of Bexar after Milam was killed. The Council backed this expedition, probably because the troops, being steadily increased in number by new arrivals, were again getting restless for action, and it was considered good policy to keep the Texan cause actively before the public in order to obtain its continued support.

Also in favor of a Matamoras expedition, but for different reasons, was Governor Henry Smith, who appointed Sam Houston as its organizer. Houston could think of no better man to lead it than James Bowie. Accordingly, on December 17, 1835, he sent Bowie orders to recruit

. . . a sufficient number of men for the purpose, . . . proceed on the route to Matamoras, and, if possible reduce the place and retain possession until further orders.

If successful, Bowie was to

. . . annoy the troops of the central army; and reduce and keep possession of the most eligible position on the frontier . . . .

Houston stressed the importance to his plans of capturing and holding the port of Copano. He gave Bowie considerable discretion in carrying out this mission.[1]

On January 1, 1836, Bowie returned to San Felipe. On the following day he secured authority to raise a regiment of volunteers. Houston's orders were for him to begin the expedition from

Goliad, but instead Bowie stayed at the capital of the Austin colony, where he set about collecting equipment and supplies. He must also have heard of its counterplans, for he "exhibited to the Council his orders of the 17th of December, 1835, and took leave of them."[2] He then returned to Goliad, where, on January 10, he wrote Houston informing him that Doctor Grant had arrived and would leave with his own men for Matamoras on the following day.

It is not necessary to trace here all of the moves and countermoves of government factions. Suffice it to state that Sam Houston returned to Goliad, where he found most of the volunteers were for going with Grant. He complained that the army had been "stolen out from under him." Having little authority over most of them, except the loyal Bowie and some others, he disassociated himself from their acts and moved on. Then something happened that turned his interest in another direction. On January 17, 1836, he heard that Johnson and Grant had denuded the Alamo of arms, supplies, and nearly everything else vital to its defense, to outfit their foray into Mexico. He was furious. After some thought, he concluded that there was only one way to keep the enemy from seizing and making a citadel of the Alamo: to destroy it.

Again Houston turned to Bowie. He abandoned the idea of sending him to Matamoras and, instead, sent him

... with thirty men, to Bexar, with a letter to Colonel Neill, desiring him to demolish the fortifications at that place and bring off the artillery, as it would be impossible to hold the town with the force there.[3]

In a letter of January 30, 1836, to Governor Smith he expressed his fear of an attack in force on that place by the enemy and mentioned his most recent orders to Bowie. Always ready to praise him, he added that "He [Bowie] met the request [to go to the aid of Colonel Neill] with his usual promptitude and manliness."[4]

When Governor Smith learned from Col. James C. Neill of the stripping of the Alamo, he, too, became furious, and it was his insults to the Councilmen for what he regarded as their military bungling that caused them to impeach him. Even when the Council appointed Lieutenant Governor Robinson acting governor, Smith still refused to relinquish his office. The confusion in just about all branches of government continued, frustrating the entire Texan movement for the time being.

It may be added that "Johnson-Grant & Co.," as some contemptuously called them, and about sixty of their "die-hard" followers, went on with their expedition to Matamoras, even after most of the volunteers decided not to accompany them. They were later surprised by the advance guard of the Mexican army and "cut to pieces, none of them surviving except Johnson and one or two of his men."[5]

* * *

Bowie and his men probably entered the Alamo on the 19th of January, 1836. Bowie at once conferred with Colonel Neill, in command of the garrison, and persuaded him that the former mission had more strategic value than he had previously supposed. They agreed that it was in danger of being attacked, probably very soon. Bowie at once joined the forces there. It has been said that, in so doing, he "disobeyed" Houston, but this may be too strong an accusation in view of the fact that Houston always depended heavily upon his judgment.

On February 2 Bowie wrote Governor Smith concerning the crucial situation at the Alamo, the imminence of attack, the need for supplies and money — the same pleas made repeatedly by Neill, Travis, and others who hoped to make the Alamo somewhat less of a deathtrap. He concluded:

The salvation of Texas depends on keeping Bexar out of the hands of the enemy. Colonel Neill and myself have come to the conclusion that we will rather die in these ditches than give up to the enemy. The citizens deserve our patriotism, and the public safety demands our lives rather than evacuate this post to the enemy.[6]

Much has been written about Bowie's alleged bad conduct shortly after he entered the Alamo — specifically, his dissipation, his quarrels with Colonel Neill, and his "high-handed" acts. Colonel Neill was one who complained about some of these acts, but the strongest charges were made by William Barret Travis, who, as the Governor's appointee, regarded himself as in command, and by Capt. John J. Baugh, Adjutant of the Post of Bexar, in letters written to the Governor on February 13, 1836. It should be mentioned that Bowie was very popular with his men, the majority of whom despised the "regular military" as much as he. Although not a matter of record, it can be surmised that they may even have egged him on. Certainly, they would not have been reluctant to join their free-handed leader in bouts with the bottle on all occasions!

In his letter of February 13, Travis berated and belittled Bowie as being "roaring drunk all the time, . . . proceeding in a most disorderly and irregular manner . . . and turning everything topsy-turvy."[7]

Add to this that Bowie was a colonel, forty-two, with vastly more military experience than Travis, who was twenty-seven, ambitious, and resentful of any threat to his advancement, and much of the motivation for Travis' criticism becomes apparent. But we do not have to rely upon the word of Travis alone. Captain Baugh, who was not competing with the volunteer leader for command of the garrison, made even stronger accusations. He wrote that Bowie, trading on his great popularity, "seemed anxious to arrogate to himself the entire control," and had even gone so far as to confiscate goods of families moving from the town for use by the Texan volunteers. He copied into his letter Bowie's order arbitrarily releasing prisoners. Other than the antagonism of a volunteer against an army man, there is no evidence that the two were enemies. And it seems unlikely for another reason that Baugh would have made these charges had they been untrue. Take the matter of the release of prisoners. He would hardly have risked punishment, to say nothing of Bowie's anger, by quoting his order into the record inaccurately. Moreover, his details are too convincing to have been fabricated.

Baugh went on to describe how Bowie freed one Antonio Fuentes, who had been sentenced to a jail term by Judge Seguin. Seguin ordered the prisoner returned to jail. Being thus thwarted, Bowie paraded his troops in the square in noisy protest, all of them, including him, "being drunk, which has been the case ever since he has been in command." Colonel Travis, by now Colonel Neill's successor pro tempore, is pictured by Baugh as being so upset over all this that he contemplated leaving the Alamo and taking "his troops to the Medina . . ."[8] He did not go, but he must have been pretty badly upset even to consider such a move, under the circumstances.

Admittedly, this is pretty much an ex parte account, Bowie's side of it being practically undocumented. According to the authority Reuben M. Potter, Travis was unpopular with the volunteers, even though appointed to replace Colonel Neill by a governor to whom they had once sworn allegiance and given their political backing. The volunteers,

... who [now] cared little for either of the two governments, wished to choose their own leader, and were willing to accept Travis only as second in command.

Bowie had in fact taken complete command of the garrison before Travis' arrival, deriving his alleged authority from his election to full colonelcy by the volunteers. This event probably occurred on February 8 or 9, 1836, since Potter dates it "about two weeks before the enemy came in sight" on February 22, 1836.[9] So the reader can take his choice. One appeal to authority may be as valid as the other. Apparently the principals in the argument began to think so too.

As a matter of fact, Bowie and Travis were forced to agree to a split in authority. The peril was such that they *had* to get along with each other; but those who surmise that such an arrangement could not have lasted long without a showdown are probably right. Travis' and Bowie's joint letter of February 14, 1836, to Governor Smith explains clearly the division of authority agreed to. (See pp. 197-98.)

But the powder keg was never to explode. About this time something happened that forever ended their rivalry. Bowie was helping with the construction of a lookout post, or possibly a gun position on the wall, when he fell and broke either his hip or his leg. The accident occurred on or about February 21. Whether he was also suffering from tuberculosis will never be known. Apparently he kept going for a while, but on February 24 he collapsed, having come down with pneumonia or typhoid-pneumonia. His last act before this prostration, and one which infuriated Travis, occurred on February 23 — but that story is deferred to the section of this book dealing with the siege of the Alamo. In any event, Bowie's retirement to his cot in the Alamo decided the issue in favor of William Barret Travis, who thereafter became commander of all the forces in the Alamo.

But what about the positive side of Bowie's behavior during the period before he was stricken? There is at least some evidence that he was not "roaring drunk" quite "all the time." The papers of Mirabeau B. Lamar contain minutes of a "Citizens' and Soldiers' Meeting" in which he participated. It was held on January 26, 1836, and its purpose was "to draft a preamble and resolutions for consideration of the meeting." Colonel Neill presided. Bowie and his friend James Butler Bonham were two of seven members of a committee selected to draft this preamble and resolutions, Bonham serving as its chairman.

An examination of these resolutions leads one to conclude that they were largely propagandistic in nature, being intended for publication in the two Brazoria newspapers. Their contents are not profound, but they must reflect to some undetermined extent Bowie's and Bonham's thinking. The following digest may therefore be of interest:

1. They affirmed support of Governor Smith as "promoting the best interests of the country and people . . ."
2. They denounced the Executive Council as anarchical in its behavior toward the Governor and affirmed an unwillingness to submit to it on occasions where it sought to annul his acts or "embarrass" him.
3. They extended an invitation to the army under General Houston, and anyone else who cared to, to utter similar sentiments.
4. They condemned confiscation by the Executive Council of $500 supposed to have been used to pay soldiers in the garrison of Bexar.
5. They stated that the committee did not recognize appointments made by the President and Executive Council in relation to the Matamoras expedition.
6. They extended a vote of gratitude to Governor Smith.
7. They requested editors of two Brazoria newspapers to publish the proceedings of the meeting.[10]

The body of the "Preamble" also condemned the President and Executive Council for exercising impeachment power they did not have, for removing the Governor, and for reopening the land offices.

Finally, the question might be asked: Was Bowie's conduct really much different from that of the other volunteers or, for that matter, from that of soldiers of the regular army on leave? The volunteer soldier was a special breed of man — individualistic, independent, "beholden" to no one, truckling to no one, and taking orders only from someone of his own choosing. Most were hard drinkers. As one of them, Bowie represented their code. At least two volunteer companies chose him as their leader in preference to Travis. For them, freedom of choice was one of the irreducible minimums of democracy.

And they *all* knew the fate that was in store for them. An enemy was approaching in strength they could not resist for long. Hope gradually faded that they could obtain reinforcements in any substantial number. Certain death stared them in the face. They were literally trapped and they knew it, none being more conscious of it, perhaps, than the experienced Bowie.

And for Jim the town was full of ghosts. Every time he passed the Veramendi house he must have felt a twinge of pain.

Under these conditions, *understanding* is called for, not blind condemnation. Death rapped on the door, and *they all heard it!*

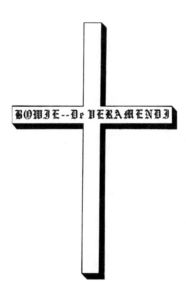

David Crockett

Courtesy of Mrs. Standish Bradford, Hamilton, Mass.

DAVID CROCKETT
From the portrait painted by Neagle in 1828

chapter

1

Crockett's Youth and Marriage

D<small>AVY</small> C<small>ROCKETT</small> was born on August 17, 1786, in a wilderness cabin on the Nolachucky River, East Tennessee, in what is now Washington County. His father, John Crockett, emigrated from Ireland and, on his arrival in America, took up farming in Pennsylvania. He was a soldier in the Revolutionary War, lived a short time in Lincoln County, North Carolina, and then moved to eastern Tennessee, at that time a part of Virginia. Davy's mother was Rebecca Hawkins, born and reared in Maryland.

Young Davy grew to manhood in the heart of the Creek country. His grandfather and grandmother were both murdered by Indians. Indians also wounded an uncle, Joseph Crockett, took his brother James prisoner, and later captured still another uncle who, being deaf and dumb, was "less able to make his escape." This uncle remained with them seventeen years and nine months. Davy's father and a William Crockett eventually found out that he was being held prisoner by an Indian trader, from whom they purchased his freedom.

There were nine children in the Crockett family, three daughters and six sons, of whom Davy was the fifth. Life on the Nolachucky was hard. John Crockett sought to improve on a really miserable existence by moving to Cove Creek, where, in partnership with a man named Galbreath, he erected a water mill. A freshet came and swept away mill and investment and nearly drowned his family, so the unfortunate father again moved, to what is now Jefferson County, Tennessee. There he opened a tavern on the road from Abbingdon to Knoxville.

Davy stayed here until he was twelve, when he decided to start out for himself. He first hired out to an old Dutchman named Jacob Siler to help him drive a herd of cattle into Virginia. After six weeks of this work, he was overcome with homesickness, ran away, and joined a teamster traveling back toward Knoxville.

He at last reached home, where he stayed until the next fall. There was no work for him, so his father sent him to a country school run by a birch-wielding backwoods schoolmaster. He had been in school only four days when he had a falling-out with another boy, waylaid him after school, and gave him a sound thrashing. Afraid the teacher would give him an equivalent or worse beating, Davy played truant. The teacher reported his absence to his father. As luck would have it, the elder Crockett already had "a few horns aboard" and was in a bad humor, so Davy was certainly in for a whipping whether he went or stayed. He hated discipline like a young colt. Then and there he made his break for liberty. The old man took after him, and Davy escaped his heavy hand and hickory only by hiding in the brush while the irate old man "passed by, puffing and blowing, as though his steam was high enough to burst his boilers."

The die was cast. Young as he was, Davy never returned home except for brief visits. He was a tough, sturdy lad and easily found employment, first as a drover with a man named Cheek, whom he accompanied to Front Royal, Virginia. Here his employer sold out his herd and paid Davy a few dollars for his services. For a while he drifted about the East. In Baltimore he engaged to work his way to London on a sailing vessel, but a wagoner who had his money and clothes refused to return them and tried to force him to go back to Tennessee. He went so far as to threaten the boy with his wagon whip. Forced to make another break, Davy waited until nightfall and set out. He had gone only a short distance when he fell in with another wagoner, this time a kind one, who not only retrieved his belongings from the thief but paid part of his fare back home.

Davy next hired out to work off a note for forty dollars held by a Quaker neighbor against his father. While on this job he had his first violent love affair, which was with the Quaker's niece. He thought that he was making good progress in his courtship, for at last she promised to marry him, and the wedding day was set. But she must have been a fickle sort. On the day he called to ask her parents' consent to the marriage he learned that she had gone back on her word, was, in fact, going to marry a suitor of longer standing on the following day.

It was a bitter blow to Davy and the first of three jiltings. He was most hurt over the last of these until he discovered that it was his prospective mother-in-law, an Irish biddy ambitious for her daughter to marry a rich man, who was the real stumbling block to his suit. He tried hard to win her favor — he called it "salting the cow to get the calf" — but she was adamant. But he had another principle, which was "Be sure you're right, then go ahead." The time to put it to the test had come. The girl, whose name was Mary (nicknamed "Polly") Finley, loved him and he loved her, so they cancelled out the maternal opposition by eloping and getting married!

With his wife's small dowry, which included two cows and their calves, and money he earned as a day laborer, Davy procured an old broken-down horse, set up a home, and began family life in earnest. His wife was a good weaver and used her spinning wheel and loom to bring in more much-needed income.

Crockett continued farming during the years 1809 and 1810. Then he heard about the opening up of the fertile Duck River country and resolved to move there. Accordingly, he loaded up his wife and baby and his belongings, set out across the mountains, and was presently settled in Lincoln County, where he remained until the close of the War of 1812.

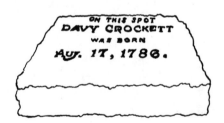

Marker, Greene Co., Tenn.

chapter

2

To the Creek Indian War

C ROCKETT HAD obtained his first rifle
some time before his move to Duck River and, roaming through
the woods hunting game to supply his table as all men did in
those days, he had already become a fine shot. A local shooting
match was held with a beef as the prize. He entered and won it,
as he did many others in later years.

But he was never contented with domestic life, being essen-
tially a man of action. The Creek war, which began with the
butchery of thirty-six whites at Fort Mimms in August 1813, gave
him the twin spurs of duty and necessity to break away. He volunteered for service in a company captained by Francis Jones,
later a congressman from Tennessee, and took part in the long
and bloody struggle against the Creeks that followed. It was a
badly managed campaign from the start, and it gave Crockett his
initiation into Indian fighting.

Winchester, not far from Crockett's cabin, was the place of mus-
ter, and before long a company of ninety men had assembled
there. After roll call they went into camp at Beaty's Spring and
remained there for two days waiting for more volunteers, who
soon collected to the number of twelve hundred. They were divided into two regiments, and the whole campaign was under
command of Gen. Andrew Jackson.

Captain Jones assigned Crockett to scout duty because of his
knowledge of woodcraft and set him the task of finding out the
position of the Creeks. Davy selected George Russell, another
young fellow and the son of Maj. William Russell, as his companion. There were twelve spies altogether, commanded by a Maj.
John H. Gibson.

They crossed the Tennessee at Ditto's Landing and marched fifty miles before going into camp in the enemy country. Any misgivings Major Gibson may have had about Crockett's youth were soon allayed, for Davy inspired the entire company with his expert woodcraft, his sagacity, and his judgment.

The major divided the force into two parties. He placed the young scout in charge of one and commanded the other himself. They were to reconnoiter the country, then return to the meeting place. Davy brought his four men back shortly after nightfall, but the major and his detachment failed to come in, so he decided to set out and try to find them. On the way they stopped a short time at a Cherokee town, then at the house of a "squaw man" named Radcliffe. Having a Creek wife, Radcliffe was safe from attack, but he warned the party that ten Creek warriors had left there scarcely an hour before. Discovery by these Indians would at the least mean a fight. Radcliffe urged them to turn back, but Davy's objective was the capture of just such a marauding band. Some of his men agreed with Radcliffe, but Davy finally won them to his way of thinking.

They went on, but they did not find the warriors. Later they came upon a camp of friendly Creeks and stayed the night with them. About ten o'clock an Indian scout returned with the news that a large war party had been gathering at Ten Islands to meet General Jackson's forces. It was vital to get this intelligence to the General, so Crockett decided to backtrack to the main camp. By starting at once they were able to reach it on the following morning.

The scout expected his news to be received with the greatest interest, but Col. John Coffee listened to him with only bare courtesy. At first he was only surprised, but when Major Gibson came in and received much more attention for reporting substantially the same facts, he became angry. Davy was forced to conclude that he had been thus discriminated against for only one reason: he had no military rank. He was so nettled by this treatment that he then and there got a permanent distaste for army red tape.

General Jackson acted quickly, however, and brought his men in by forced march the next day, their feet badly blistered by the gruelling trek. Fortunately, Coffee had time to throw up an earthwork entrenchment. Seeing it would be hazardous to storm such a position, the Indians fled, unwilling to risk a battle. Davy was one of the force of eight hundred volunteers who pursued them. They were unable to overtake the fleeing warriors but they did find and burn one of their large towns. Grain was plentiful in the Indian corn fields, but there was very little meat, so Davy set out with his rifle and killed sufficient game to keep the men supplied.

A base was established at Ten Islands, and Cherokee spies were sent out to observe the movements of the Creeks. One day one of them reported sighting a large town about eight miles distant. Col. Newton Cannon, who had replaced Colonel Coffee, immediately took five hundred volunteers and set out to attack it. As the troops approached, they were to divide so that part of them would pass around each side of the town. When the two columns met, the Indians would be completely surrounded. By keeping carefully out of sight, they succeeded in this maneuver.

Captain Hammond's company of rangers led the assault. The Indians spied the soldiers too late. They came yelling to meet the attack, but a withering fusillade sent them scampering for cover. Seeing the troops were closing in around them and there was no escape, they offered to surrender, but this was not permitted. Years later Crockett described how some of the squaws begged pathetically to be taken prisoners. He saw seven of them hanging to one man's hunting shirt. Only these few escaped the awful fate of the others when they were sent back of the lines.

Davy saw forty-six warriors enter the big log house in the center of the town. He reported this to Colonel Cannon, who immediately ordered his men to attack the building. As they closed in firing, arrows began to fly from the windows. One squaw sat down in the doorway. Using her feet against a bow to draw it, she let fly an arrow that passed entirely through and killed a volunteer named Moore. This act only served to enrage the other men, who proceeded to slaughter warriors, squaws, and children indiscriminately. They then set fire to the cabin and burned alive the warriors inside. A total of one hundred eighty-six Indians were killed or captured.

Altogether, the battle of Tallushatchee, fought on November 3, 1813, was a bloody initiation into war for young Davy. In addition, he and the other men went hungry most of the time and suffered other severe privations.

The period of enlistment was already up for Davy and the other volunteers, but the battle of Tallushatchee was only the beginning of the serious fighting. The massacre at Fort Mimms was a clear victory for the Creeks. Faced with just as complete a victory on the part of the whites, the Indians were enraged. In retaliation they planned an attack on Fort Talladega, but this was learned almost too late when an Indian runner came into camp one night and told General Jackson what was afoot. Jackson at once ordered some eight hundred of the half-starved men to prepare to march.

The volunteers had no sooner come in sight of the fort than they were almost captured by some eleven hundred hostile Creeks, who were negotiating with members of their own tribe inside, trying with threats to get them to participate in a plot to attack the whites. The friendly Creeks inside demanded three days in which to consider. At the end of that time they would make known their decision. Meantime they had sent a runner to General Jackson with news of their plight.

The Creeks outside the fort were apparently confident of victory because they did not attempt to leave the stockade. Instead, they fired from ambush and killed five of Major Russell's men. General Jackson immediately split his forces as had been done at the battle of Tallushatchee, using the same right-and-left flanking movement to encircle them. The Creeks did not discover the stratagem until the troops were already charging toward them, firing. They fell under the deadly fire like wheat before a sickle. Some were so panicked they could not collect their wits enough to fight. When the slaughter ended, four hundred warriors lay dead upon the field. The rest massed together like sheep and, by sheer weight of numbers, pushed through the soldiers' lines and escaped into the woods.

Only fifteen volunteers were lost. The soldiers buried them in a common grave, then set out on their way back to the fort. The weather had suddenly turned cold and they were suffering more than ever. They therefore proposed to General Jackson that he let them return home temporarily to procure clothing and other needed supplies. Jackson was indignant at this unmilitary procedure. He declared they would remain where they were and serve six months if necessary. The General's reply to what they considered their just demands angered the men, and, despite the menace of a cannon placed on the bridge, they left in a body, some eight hundred strong. Their comrades commanding the cannon wanted furloughs as much as anyone else, so they left their posts and deserted with them.

Davy Crockett was among those who left. It must be remembered in judging these volunteers that they had lived on squirrels and even cowhides, in addition to enduring all of the other hardships of marching and fighting. Few had any use for military regulations, and Davy was not among them. Still fewer had had any formal military training. Certainly the return in glory had been small.

Davy's distaste for war was deepened as the Creek campaign continued. His regiment was now under command of a regular army officer, Maj. Uriah Blue. The privations only increased, and for more than a month the army beat about the country in vain, finding scarcely any Indians. In the entire campaign fewer than twenty were killed. The Creeks continued to menace the settlements, but they did not attack. At last the weary soldiers filtered into Fort Strother and went into quarters. Crockett himself was at home when General Jackson met the Creeks at a place called Hickory Ground, near Fort Williams, where he signed the treaty with them that ended the war.

Davy's participation in the Creek Indian War ended his military career until he joined the forces of the Texans at the Alamo years later. He was already something of a hero, however, and a political career appeared to be a natural result of his popularity.

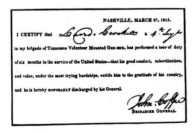

chapter

3

Davy Goes into Politics

Not long after the close of the Creek War Davy returned home to find that, under the burden of farm work, his wife "Polly" had taken sick and was on the point of death. Nor did her health improve under his care. She grew worse and died in the summer of 1815, when he had been home only two months. He was lonely and hard put to it to adjust himself to this loss until he persuaded one of his married brothers to come and live with him.

Davy remained single for some time, but presently he fell in love with Elizabeth Patton, a widow who lived nearby. She had two children of her own, but this was not as much a barrier to the progress of his courtship as was his own bashfulness. Plucking up courage, however, he at last proposed, and she accepted him. With his second wife he also acquired a well-stocked farm and a good home. But, as before, he soon became restless. Before long he moved with several neighboring farmers to the Shoal Creek country.

Shoal Creek may have had its attractions, but law and order were not among them. So many bad characters and outlaws had drifted into that part of the country that no one was safe. At last some aroused citizens got together and appointed magistrates and constables to keep order. They chose Crockett as one of the magistrates. These officials were given power to make arrests and to punish offenders, although they were without the benefit of written laws or statutes. This arrangement suited Davy down to the ground because he could hardly write his own name, and he confessed he "had never read a page in a law book" in his life. The whole procedure was based on "natural born sense," which he had in abundance. He procured a husky constable to enforce his orders and began to do business.

Davy held court in his own cabin. He did not bother to issue written warrants. He simply told the constable: "Catch that fellow and bring him up for trial." The culprit came in, dead or alive, or badly mussed up, as he chose. If Davy thought he needed a whipping, he ordered it done, or carried out the sentence himself. The Tennessee State Legislature changed this rather direct method of adjudication when Giles County came under its jurisdiction. Thereafter, it appointed magistrates by law. Davy continued to serve, but he was required to keep a record of his proceedings and to issue warrants. Because of his scant schooling he said all of this "was at least a huckleberry over my persimmon."

But new honors awaited him. He had been on Shoal Creek only five years, but his reputation had spread far and favorably. He was elected colonel of a militia regiment maintained to furnish protection against the Indians. Then, in 1821, he was asked to run for the Tennessee State Legislature. He was opposed by a man named Hogan, who had considerable experience as a politician. It turned out to be a campaign full of amusing incidents, which he relates with the relish of a true humorist, even though he was more often than not the butt of the jokes himself. Several of these are well worth retelling.

Hogan was a well-dressed, heavy-set man with fat jowls and a love of whisky, money, votes, and, above all, easy living. One day he was in his hotel room, thinking how simple it would be to defeat Crockett. His secretary, a meek-looking young man of about twenty, was transcribing a speech his employer would soon deliver to constituents of Lawrence and Heckman counties when Hogan chose to voice his contempt for the backwoodsman.

"Crockett!" he snorted. "I won't have any trouble defeating that ignorant bear hunter. Why, I'll venture he can't even write his name, and he knows less about the laws and government of this State than an Indian!"

As he warmed to his subject, the red-faced politician began to enjoy the ridicule he was heaping upon his opponent.

"I'd like to see that ignoramus get up and make a political speech!" He could no longer repress his mirth. His fat sides quaked with laughter. In fact, he had to set his toddy down on the table to keep from spilling it. "He doesn't know a tariff from a turnip seed!"

A clamor of voices in the street under his window broke into his mirth. The secretary stuck his head out to investigate.

"What is it?" Hogan queried.

"There's a group of backwoodsmen out here, sir. They want *you*," replied the secretary.

"I wonder why," said the annoyed Hogan.

He opened the door to the balcony and found himself gazing at about twenty men variously clad in buckskin or homespun. At their head was a brawny sun-bronzed hunter with snapping brown eyes and a grin on his face. He carried a long rifle.

The politician recognized him and snorted his displeasure.

"What do you want with me, Crockett? You'd best be out trying to round up some votes. You'll need them."

"That's what we came to see you about, Hogan," Davy replied good-naturedly. "Some of us Duck River boys are goin' on a squirrel hunt. We're goin' to be out two days and then have a big barbecue. The boys think we ought to make a political hunt of it."

"Why, how d'ya mean?" grunted Hogan suspiciously.

"You round up your men and the side that shows up with the fewest squirrel scalps has to pay for the whole frolic."

The portly legislator frowned, for he made it a point never to expend unnecessary effort or money on votes that he could win through oratory.

"You'll find politics is something different from a squirrel hunt," he grunted. "Why don't you stick to your 'b'ar' hunting, Crockett, and leave government to men who know something about it?"

A multiple roar of protest greeted this speech.

" 'Fraid you'll have to buy somebody a drink, Hogan?" taunted one tall backwoodsman.

"A little exercise'll take some of that blubber off'n your sides!" screeched another.

"We think a heap more of bein' a good sport than we do of oratory," yelled a third.

Hogan threw up his hands, forcing a sickly smile as he thought of tramping through the rough wilderness country that was certain to be filled with all sorts of perils and discomforts; but they had him in a corner. He could not afford to refuse the wager.

"I accept," he assented sourly, "and I'll show you I can round up squirrel hunters as well as voters, *Mister* Crockett!"

With that he stepped back into the hotel room and slammed the door after him.

At the end of two days, the two parties of hunters came into Shoal Creek settlement. One was headed by Crockett, who looked no more tired than if he had just stepped from his cabin. The other, composed of only ten men, was rather followed than led by a short, puffing man clad in a suit of dirty buckskin. It was Hogan, but he was hardly recognizable. He was covered with mud, hatless, his face shiny with sweat and coated with grime, his gray hair matted and sticking out in all directions. He limped painfully as he went to the stump that was to have been the pedestal of his oratorical victory and sat down. His own men joined in the laughter at his expense.

Rustic tables were set in a nearby clearing, and at the sound of the voices of the frontiersmen, some of their wives left meal preparations long enough to come and see what was causing all the mirth.

"You met me on my own ground, Hogan," Davy was saying in his good-natured way. "What is your tally?"

Breathless, Hogan waved weakly toward one of the men in his party.

"A hundred and twenty-six," spoke up the rifleman. He dug into a grimy buckskin sack and produced some skins.

"We'll take your word for it," Davy replied. "We got two hundred and fifty-one. I guess that means you pay for the shindig, Hogan."

Hogan could still only wave his hand in agreement. He continued to puff as he watched the other men wander over to the tables, talking. Presently, he began to think. It was plain this ignoramus in the coonskin cap had the men on his side. But suppose he was challenged to a debate on public questions? Crockett would be certain to make a fool of himself, if he accepted the dare. Whom, then, would the men follow?

Hogan joined the others. Even though he was still too exhausted to eat, he entered into the talk, took some teasing about his defeat, and bided his time until the feasting on barbecued meat and other homely victuals came to a halt. Then he mounted the stump. He had his speech well in hand. He orated for a full hour on the issues of tariff, the money question, Jackson's policies, a hundred and one things he knew Crockett had scarcely heard of. At intervals he fired questions at his "worthy opponent," demanding that he declare himself on these issues. He had the immense satisfaction of seeing Crockett remove his coonskin cap to wipe the perspiration from his forehead with his buckskin sleeve. The woodsman was not making his own law now, as he had done when he was a magistrate. He was not hunting "b'ar" or fighting Indians!

Hogan finished in a flourish of silver-tongued oratory and turned the attention of the audience to Crockett.

"I demand that Crockett tell you *his* position on these important questions. What does *he* have to say?"

Davy realized better than anyone else that Hogan now had him in a corner. He wrote as follows:

I made many apologies, and tried to get off, for I know'd I had a man to run against who could speak prime, and I know'd, too, that I wasn't able to shuffle and cut with him. He was there, and knowing my ignorance as well as I did myself, he also urged me to make a speech. . . . I found I couldn't get off, and so I determined just to go ahead, and leave it to chance what I should say. I got up and told the people I reckoned they know'd what I had come for . . . . I had come for their votes, and if they didn't watch mighty close I'd get them too. At last I told them I was like a fellow I had heard of not long before. He was beating on the head of an empty barrel near the roadside, when a traveler, who was passing along, asked him what he was doing that for. The fellow replied that there was some cider in that barrel a few days before, and he was trying to see if there was any then, but if there was he couldn't get at it. I told them that there had been a little bit of a speech in me a while ago, but I believed I couldn't get it out. They all roared out in a mighty laugh, and I told some other anecdotes, equally amusing to them, and believing I had them in a first-rate way, I quit and got down thanking the people for their attention. But I took care to remark that I was as dry as a powder-horn, and that I thought it was time for us all to wet our whistles a little; and so I put off to the liquor-stand, and was followed by the greater part of the crowd.

Needless to say, it was Davy Crockett who was elected.

While in Pulaski, Tennessee, on this campaign, Davy met Col. James K. Polk (later President) under rather embarrassing circumstances. But let Davy relate the incident:

He [Polk] was at that time a member elected to the Legislature, as well as myself; and in a large company he said to me, "Well, colonel, I suppose we shall have a radical change of the judiciary at the next session of the Legislature." "Very likely, sir," says I; and I put out . . . , for I was afraid some one would ask me what the judiciary was; and if I knowed I wish I may be shot.

But Davy's luck in other matters was not so good as it was in politics. He was suddenly faced with bankruptcy. It happened in this way. A spring freshet swelled Shoal Creek to the point where it washed out a large grist mill, distillery, and powder mill he had built on its bank. He had already used up his credit in building these structures, and the calamity left him with a large debt. He did not hesitate to sacrifice all his belongings, however, to pay off his creditors.

When the legislature adjourned, he moved his family into another, smaller cabin. He was in really desperate straits. Winter was coming on. One of his creditors who had rented him the cabin also let him have a horse, but as yet he had laid in no food. Luckily, a boat came up-river at this time, and he and his eldest son hired out to the captain as general roustabouts and stevedores in exchange for transportation to McLemore's Bluff, some money, and household provisions. He already had some corn gathered from his Shoal Creek place. Christmas was approaching, however, and he still lacked meat. To hunt he had to have gunpowder. His brother had a keg of it, but he lived six miles off. There were already four inches of snow, and two streams he had to cross were partly frozen over. In spite of this he made up his mind to hazard the trip.

Crockett made a two-day trip on foot over the frozen wilderness to his brother's place and back. The way in which he forded icy streams without wetting gun or powder, a hunt he took in below-zero weather — these exploits may have been ordinary in pioneer times, but they would not be so regarded today. "When I got home," he wrote, "I wasn't quite dead, but mighty nigh it; but had my powder, and that was what I went for."

From this point on, he was dogged by financial misfortune. None of his business ventures panned out. He seemed more successful at bear hunting than anything else, so he decided to sell some of the many bear skins he had accumulated during the winter. He got enough in return to buy some coffee, sugar, powder, lead, and salt. Then he returned home.

A week later a man came to his house and told him he had again been proposed as a candidate for Congress. Davy could not resist the urge to get into politics again. He hired a young man to work in his place on the farm and set out on another characteristic Crockett campaign. Everywhere he was hailed as the bear-hunter and wit, and he told stories and cracked jokes with the voters as he had done before, with the same success. Dr. William E. Butler, his opponent, was snowed under in the election.

Davy served for two years, 1823 and 1824. Then his ill-timed opposition to General Jackson started to swing the political tide against him. He did not vote for the General's nomination as a presidential candidate and he made no secret of it. He also opposed his Indian bill. Although he never explained his strong personal dislike of Jackson, it was probably caused by the General's treatment of him and the other volunteers during the Creek Indian war. At any rate, he could not live it down politically. Unpopular as was Colonel Alexander, his opponent, Davy must have been slightly more so, for he lost the election by two votes.

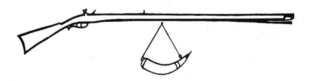

chapter

4

Davy Quits Politics

In order to make some money Davy next began cutting the timber on his land. There was a considerable demand for pipe staves in New Orleans, and he contracted to supply a large quantity. He hired men, employing some to cut the staves and others to build flatboats in which to float them downstream to market.

That was in 1826. By summer of the following year he had loaded a number of scows and was ready to launch them. He had had little or no experience either in navigating the river with these unwieldy barges or, for that matter, in building this type of craft.

As had happened with most of his business ventures, misfortune followed close on his heels. He and his crew were out only two days when they ran into disaster. They failed in two attempts to land at wood yards, although men came out with lights and tried to guide them to shore. Their boats were too heavy and the current too strong. That night, when Davy was down in the cabin of one boat, he was trapped. He relates the experience as follows:

The hatchway into the cabin came slap down, right through the top of the boat; and it was the only way out except a small hole in the side, which we had used for putting our arms through to dip up water before we lashed the boats together.

We were now floating sideways, and the boat I was in was the hindmost as we went. All at once I heard the hands begin to run over the top of the boat in great confusion, and pull with all their might; and the first thing I know'd after this we went broadside full-tilt against the head of an island where a large raft of drift-timber had lodged. The nature of such a place would be . . . to suck the boats down. As soon as we struck, I bulged for my hatchway, as the boat was turning under sure enough. But when I got to it, the water was pouring through in a current as large as the hole would let it, and as strong as the weight of the river would force it. I found I couldn't get out here, for the boat was now turned down in such a way that it was steeper than a house-top. I now thought of the hole in the side . . . . With difficulty I got to it, and when I got there I found it was too small for me to get out by my own power . . . . But I put my arms through and hollered as loud as I could roar, as the boat I was in hadn't quite filled with water up to my head, and the hands who were next to the raft, seeing my arms out and hearing me holler, seized them and began to pull. I told them I was sinking, and to pull my arms off, or force me through . . . .

By a violent effort they jerked me through; but I was in a pretty pickle when I got through. I had been sitting without any clothing over my shirt; this was torn off and I was literally skin'd like a rabbit.

Davy's political fortunes were good and bad by turns. On the eve of this second bankruptcy he was again elected to Congress. He was faced with the embarrassing problem of getting railroad fare to Washington, but one of his creditors came to the rescue and twice lent him one hundred and fifty dollars. He found himself on the tide of another wave of popularity, and it swept him to re-election in 1829. By this time the whole country was stirred by his honesty and conscientiousness at a time when political skulduggery was the rule. He filled this term, but his opposition to Jackson, who was elected to the presidency in 1828, again spelled his defeat. Among other things, he voted against the Jackson-sponsored Indian removal bill, which he pronounced a "wicked, unjust measure." When he returned home, he discovered that he had committed an unpardonable political sin. Jackson was still the people's idol. Davy was not content to admit popular opinion was against him, however, and he bitterly asserted that libel had been used, both on the stump and in the newspapers, to defeat him.

In 1834 he made a triumphal tour through the northern states. Notwithstanding his supposed disfavor, he was everywhere received with wild acclaim. The young men of Philadelphia, where he made several speeches, presented him with a fine rifle, an engraved silver-plated tomahawk, and a "butcher-knife." He moved on and was lionized to an even greater extent in Pittsburgh, Cincinnati, and Louisville.

He went on to New York, where he wound up the trip. A com-

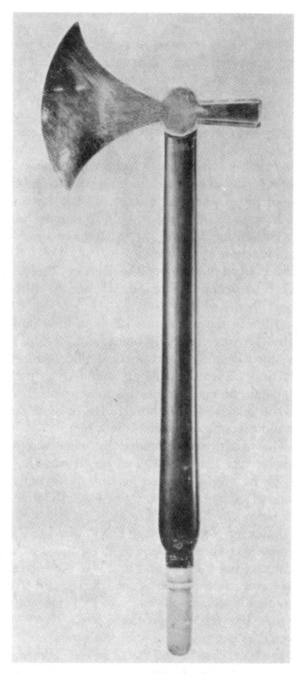

Courtesy of the Smithsonian Institution
Silver-plated tomahawk presented to Crockett

mittee of young Whigs received him cordially and put him up at the elegant American Hotel. That night he went to the Park Theater, where he saw Fanny Kemble play in the grand style. He made a speech at the Exchange. He went to Peale's Museum, where he did not appreciate the scientific value of "sticking up whole rows of little bugs, and such like varmints." He went next to the City Hall, and was there introduced to the Mayor. He fulfilled various other social engagements, had something caustic to say about the shocking social conditions in the crowded and filthy tenement district. At last he was ready to pass on to Boston, to see Harvard, and to sample New England hospitality, which included a somewhat more reserved ovation than he had received elsewhere.

Louisville marked the end of the journey. Davy stopped no more until he reached Tennessee, whence he turned "like a wearied bird" home to rest.

He found life in the wilderness lonely, a little miserable, and tedious after the excitement and homage of his trip. He thought himself destined for the highest political office, perhaps even the presidency. So 1835 again saw him a candidate for political office. In his campaign, he made use of his most colorful side, that of the backwoodsman and bear hunter. He dressed the part and carried an old flintlock rifle around with him.

This last campaign was attended by what was perhaps the most laughable incident of Davy's career. It was also marked by bitterness, for he openly accused Jackson of buying votes to defeat him and elect his opponent, a one-legged Dutchman named Adam Huntsman.

As usual during electioneering, Davy was hard pressed for money. There was an equivalent in those times as standard as wampum among the Indians, and that was the coon skin. It was passed over every saloon counter for whisky, and it was in that connection that Crockett used a pelt to bamboozle a shrewd Yankee trader, for whisky a politician must have in those days, if he expected to get anywhere with the voters.

The Colonel had just left his home in this final campaign and was headed for the Cross Roads, dressed in his hunting shirt and carrying Betsey, his rifle. When he arrived, he found that Job Snelling, whom he ridiculed as a "gander-shanked Yankee . . .

shipped to the west with a cargo of codfish and rum," had set up a shop at the meeting place, mostly for sale of liquid refreshment.

Many of the voters had already assembled. When they saw him coming, they shouted "There comes Crockett!" and "Let's hear the Colonel." The candidate wrote that he wasted no time but mounted the stump and "began to bushwhack in the most approved style." He continues:

I had not been up long before there was such an uproar in the crowd that I could not hear my own voice, and some of my constituents let me know that they could not listen to me on such a dry subject as the welfare of the nation until they had something to drink, and that I must treat them. Accordingly, I jumped down from the rostrum, and led the way to the shantee, followed by my constituents, shouting "Huzza for Crockett," and "Crockett for ever!"

When we entered the shantee, Job was busy dealing out his rum in a style that showed he was making a good day's work of it, and I called for a quart of the best, but the crooked critur returned no other answer than by pointing to a board over the bar, on which he had chalked in large letters, "Pay to-day and trust to-morrow." Now that idea brought me up all standing; it was a sort of cornering in which there was no back out, for ready money in the west, in those times, was the shyest thing in all nature, and it was most particularly shy with me on that occasion.

The voters, seeing my predicament, fell off to the other side, and I was left deserted and alone, as the Government will be, when he no longer has any offices to bestow. I saw, as plain as day, that the tide of popular opinion was against me, and that, unless I got some rum speedily, I should lose my election as sure as there are snakes in Virginny. . . . So I walked away from the shantee, . . . and not a voice shouted, "Huzza for Crockett." Popularity sometimes depends on a very small matter indeed; in this particular it was worth a quart of New England rum, and no more.

Well, knowing that a crisis was at hand, I struck into the woods with my rifle on my shoulder, my best friend in time of need, and as good fortune would have it, I had not been out more than a quarter of an hour before I treed a fat coon, and in the pulling of a trigger, he lay dead at the root of the tree. I soon whipped his hairy jacket off his back, and again bent my steps toward the shantee, and walked up to the bar, but not alone, for this time I had a half a dozen of my constituents at my heels. I threw down the coon skin upon the counter, and called for a quart, and Job, though busy in dealing out rum, forgot to point at his chalked rules and regulations . . . .

Davy thus got some of the voters in a good humor, and they were again ready to shout "Crockett for ever!" — until he had spoken a few minutes longer, when they again confessed to an overpowering thirst. Without a word Davy stepped up to the bar. But he had no more coon skins. What was he to use for money? The Crockett resourcefulness again came to his rescue. His story resumes as follows:

While standing at the bar, feeling sort of bashful while Job's rules and regulations stared me in the face, I cast down my eyes, and discovered one end of the coon skin sticking between the logs that supported the bar. Job had slung it there in the hurry of business. I gave it a sort of quick jerk, and it followed my hand as natural as if I had been the rightful owner. I slapped it on the counter, and Job, little dreaming that he was barking up the wrong tree, shoved along another bottle, which my constituents quickly disposed of with great good humor, for some of them saw the trick, and then we withdrew to the rostrum to discuss the affairs of the nation.

... I wish I may be shot, if I didn't, before the day was over, get ten quarts for the same identical skin, and from a fellow, too, who in those parts was considered as sharp as a steel trap, and as bright as a pewter button.

This joke secured me my election, for it soon circulated like smoke among my constituents, and they allowed, with one accord, that the man who could get the whip hand of Job Snelling in fair trade, could outwit Old Nick himself, and was the real grit for them in Congress.

Of course, the Colonel meant the joke secured him his district, for when the results of the election became known, it was found he had lost by 230 votes.

chapter

5

A Texan Volunteer

D<small>AVY'S</small> <small>DEFEAT</small> in the election of 1835 ended his political career, but it ushered in the most exciting and colorful period in his life, ending in a blaze of glory at the Alamo.

Crockett found it difficult to abandon his political ambitions. He had just returned from a trip on which he had been lionized in the largest cities of the nation, and he had found it gratifying to be the object of public acclaim. It was therefore natural that he should turn to other fields in which he might regain distinction and glory. The cause of Texan freedom was just the sort of thing he was looking for. But before he left for Texas, he decided to give one last speech to his constituents. Into it he poured all his bitterness and resentment, and he concluded it

... by telling them that I was done with politics for the present, and that they might all go to hell, and I would go to Texas.

With characteristic ability to cut off one phase of his life completely and begin another, he left home one chilly morning, dressed in a hunting suit, wearing a new fox-skin cap with the tail still on it, and carrying his rifle Betsey. His destination was Little Rock, Arkansas, where he arrived three days later.

At Little Rock a crowd had collected. He concluded wrongly that the people had assembled to greet him. Then he learned they were interested in a juggler who had set up a Punch and Judy show. The fiddler accompanying the show had got drunk, so the show could not proceed. The disappointed crowd was about to disperse when an old man drove up to the tavern in a sulky loaded with books and pamphlets. He turned out to be a minister and a man of wide talents. The local innkeeper was aware of his gifts and, with a sharp eye for anything that would increase his trade, urged the parson to play the fiddle for the show. But the man of God was against using his talents for such worldly purposes, and the innkeeper was hard put to it to overcome his religious scruples. He knew, however, that the owner of the show had arrived penniless and that he had a sick wife and five children.

"If you don't fiddle, the show can't go on," he told the minister. "And if it doesn't go on, you'll be responsible for sending that man, his sick wife, and his children to bed without any supper."

The minister was obviously affected.

"If I could be concealed from the audience—"

"Nothing easier," cried the other; "we will place you behind the scenes, and no one will ever dream that you fiddled at a puppet show."

Unhappily, the parson's concealment was only temporary because he accidentally knocked down the scenery and exposed himself. Unembarrassed, he mounted a chair and preached a sermon on charity. The next morning he departed.

When the Little Rock citizens discovered Davy's identity, they arranged for a public dinner in his honor. Being through with politics, he was at first reluctant to accept their invitation; but, on learning the menu was to include fat bear cub, venison, and wild turkey, he relented.

In the interval preceding the dinner he entered a shooting match with some of the town's marksmen and handily won it.

The dinner was a huge success, and Davy used the occasion to give a speech against the administration and to damn the whole "trade" of politics. The following day he tried to recruit men to accompany him to Texas, but he had no success. Some of the citizens escorted him as far as the Washita. There they again came across the eccentric parson, stranded in the middle of the river, his horse refusing to back out. He was playing his fiddle for all he was worth in order to attract rescuers. The men helped him back to shore, and to show his appreciation he fiddled for a dance. The lack of women was partly compensated for by a plentiful supply of liquor, but enthusiasm soon fizzled

out, the Little Rock escort took its leave, and Davy proceeded
on his journey. The parson accompanied him some distance and
proved interesting company because he was conversant with
politics, religion, nature, and literature — subjects concerning
which the Colonel knew little as far as books go, but about
which he displayed no little common sense.

After various minor adventures, Davy reached Fulton, Arkansas, where he presented a letter of introduction to some citizens
and was hospitably received. On the following day he boarded
a steamer for Natchitoches, Louisiana.

The passengers were a motley group: merchants, emigrants,
gamblers, outlaws, and "promoters" of all kinds. Among the
gamblers was a man who was playing thimblerig, a game in
which three thimbles and a dried pea or a small piece of cork
are used. His fingers were so nimble that he could place the pea
under any thimble without being detected. The "suckers" placed
small stakes to guess which thimble the pea was under. He was
leading on some of the more gullible players by letting them win
small bets when Davy stepped up. "Thimblerig," as he afterward called him, immediately proposed that he make a bet.

Davy despised gambling, especially such an unfair bunco
game as this, and he frankly told Thimblerig that it was "about
the dirtiest way that a man could adopt to get through this dirty
world." But Thimblerig kept urging him on, insisting that all
was fair and aboveboard, so Davy plotted to teach him and the
rustics he was robbing a lesson. He placed a bet of fifty cents.
As he expected, Thimblerig let him plainly see him put the pea
under the center thimble. Davy did not give him an opportunity
to change its location, but shoved his hand away and looked for
himself. The pea was there, so he demanded and received the
amount of his bet. Thimblerig then tried all his wiles to get
him to hazard again, but Davy refused and informed him he
had bet his first and last money on thimblerig. Thus the tables
were turned. Amid shouts of laughter, red-faced at being beat-
en at his own game, Thimblerig gathered up his paraphernalia
and retired.

True sport that he was, Davy invited the thimblerigger to the
bar for a drink. Soon they were laughing and talking as though
nothing had happened. Thimblerig forgot his defeat and laughed

heartily at Davy's witty yarns. In fact he seemed so receptive that Davy urged him to give up shell games and crime and come and help him fight for Texan freedom. In so doing, the Colonel argued, he could regain some of his self-respect. Plainly, quite a struggle went on between the gambler's good and bad sides before he came to a decision. Davy's vivid description of the moment is as follows:

He started from the table, and hastily gathering up the thimbles with which he had been playing all the time I was talking to him, he thrust them into his pocket, and after striding two or three times across the room, suddenly stopped, his leaden eye kindled, and grasping me by the hand violently, he exclaimed with an oath, "By ——, I'll be a man again. Live honestly, or die bravely. I go with you to Texas."

Davy and Thimblerig proceeded on their way from Natchitoches, but not before the Colonel had run into a second recruit to his cause. This man was in many ways even more singular than the first. He called himself the Bee-Hunter, and he had the handsome face and romantic past of a story-book hero.

This is how it happened. Davy was walking down the street at dawn one morning when he was attracted by a tenor voice at once the sweetest and most melancholy he had ever heard, singing a scrap of a love song. He proceeded a little farther in the direction from which it came and spied a tall man leaning against a sign post. He was in his early twenties, lithe yet powerful in build. His deerhide hunting jacket was tastefully ornamented with Indian beadwork, and he wore under it a clean white shirt, with a black ribbon around his neck. His boots were polished. His fur cap sat jauntily on his head, and some black curls stuck out from under it. Even his rifle shone with uncommon brilliance.

Davy continued to listen, lost in the enchantment of his voice, until the music was rudely interrupted. A fat, red-faced man, dressed in a dandified manner and wearing a beaver hat, came by giving vent to his feelings in an excited voice. He was apparently looking for someone to curse for his misfortunes, whatever they were, for he accosted the singer, called him a scoundrel, and insisted he had defamed him to certain unnamed "ladies." The young man bore the tirade in the greatest good humor until the other called him a coward. At that his face turned white.

He calmly handed his knife and rifle to Davy. Then, moving with the speed of a cat, he seized the fat man and had him lying on his back under the nearby town pump before he knew what it was all about. He continued to pump water on him until the bully was thoroughly cooled off. Then he released him. A mess of mud and water, but tactfully silent, the windy one made himself suddenly scarce.

That was Davy's introduction to the Bee-Hunter, who now reclaimed his weapons. He betrayed no surprise at Crockett's presence. In fact, he declared he knew that he was there and said that he had been trying to find him in order to accompany him to Texas. His trade was hunting bee trees and selling beeswax and honey he obtained from them. Thus he had traveled over a wide expanse of the surrounding country and knew it like a book.

Davy was pleased to have such an entertaining guide. The way the Bee-Hunter handled the bully at Natchitoches had already won his admiration. Thimblerig turned out to be an old friend of the romantic young man and was overjoyed at seeing him again.

On the following day the three of them set out on the old Spanish Road for Nacogdoches, Texas, guided only by an occasional blaze on a tree. Thimblerig resisted with difficulty the temptation to ply his thimble game among the people they met, and the Bee-Hunter carolled his romantic songs. Davy tried to win other recruits to the Texan cause, but he had little success, either on the way or at Nacogdoches.

There the Bee-Hunter had a sweetheart named Katie, and when it was time to go, the two other men were witnesses to a tearful parting of the lovers. But the call to glory and duty was stronger than love, and the singer sang a last refrain which proved prophetic:

> But home came the saddle, all bloody to see,
> And home came the steed, but home never came he.

Then he tore himself away and joined his companions.

While Davy was unable to win any more recruits, the party was joined by two hard-looking men who had once been in the service of the Lafittes at Barataria Bay. Surprisingly enough, they were themselves headed to join the Texan volunteers. But for this and their acquaintanceship with the Bee-Hunter, Davy might not have welcomed their company. Now that they were identified with the cause in which he believed, and were ready to fight for it, it mattered little to him who they were or what their past had been.

THIMBLERIG

chapter

6

Adventures along the Way

THE TRAIL to the Alamo was beset with danger and adventure for Davy and his volunteers. Once they were caught in a buffalo stampede. Chasing a large bull, Davy got lost on the prairie. He had badly winded his small mustang and so was almost as bad off as if he had been afoot. His life was in peril because the country thereabouts was infested with wolves and other predators. He looked around for a safe place to spend the night. On a river bank he found a big tree. It had blown down, but the few remaining limbs were stout and the foliage was thick enough for good cover. As he moved to climb it, he was startled by a fierce snarl. He scanned the tree for the animal concealed there. It was a big cougar and the way it licked its chops and prepared to spring told plainly that it was famished. He knew he had to shoot and shoot in a hurry. He aimed Betsey at its head and pulled the trigger. Instead of going into death struggles, the animal was only infuriated by the bullet, which had glanced off its thick skull.

He had no time to reload. The cougar growled and leaped. Davy stepped aside and, using his rifle as a club, struck it a heavy blow. He might as well have hit it with a twig. He was in for it now. The cat attacked again and sank its fangs into his left arm, tearing and ripping the flesh in a way that made him faint with pain. He next tried to blind it with his knife but missed. In maneuvering for another thrust he tripped on a vine and fell. In an instant, the animal leaped upon him again and this time began to tear at his leg.

As luck would have it, the fight was going on at the edge of a steep bank. Davy worked carefully toward the brink. As he slashed with his knife, he gradually reached the declivity and rolled down it, taking the cat with him. Fortunately, the man was uppermost when they stopped. He already had his hunting knife poised for a thrust, and he plunged it with all his remaining strength into the animal's lower neck. Its long blade entered his gullet to the hilt and pierced his heart. In comparing this with his other hand-to-claw encounters with animals, Davy wrote:

I have had many fights with bears, but that was mere child's play; this was the first fight I ever had with a cougar, and I hope it may be the last.

It is a good illustration of the toughness of his constitution that he *slept* the rest of the night, although he was forced to admit that he felt stiff and sore the next morning!

A new misfortune awaited him. He had just finished roasting a goose over a comfortable fire when a war party of Comanches rode up. His horse was gone, so he could not escape. They had been attracted by the smoke, and numbered nearly a hundred. But Davy was resourceful enough to meet even this danger. He knew how much Indians admire bravery, so he showed them the body of the dead cougar and described in sign language and what few Comanche words he knew how he had killed it. The Indians were completely won over and wanted to adopt him into the tribe! Davy declined the honor; however, the chief gave him a horse and accompanied him as far as Bexar.

On the following day he recovered his mustang, with the chief's help, and accidentally stumbled upon Thimblerig's prairie camp. With his characteristic love of a joke, Davy put the Comanches up to faking an attack on him. Poor Thimblerig was badly frightened until the Comanches rode off yelling, without doing him any harm. But Davy had to do some tall explaining before the ex-gambler joined in the laughter at his expense.

Thimblerig related all that had happened to him in the meantime and said that the Bee-Hunter had found some honey and brought in a supply. Later he had gone hunting and would soon return to camp.

When the Bee-Hunter rode in, he was weighed down with wild turkeys. There was a happy reunion, joined in by the ex-privateers, who presently came into camp, and climaxed by a feast. When the sun came up, they broke camp and soon after crossed the Colorado, headed for the Alamo.

About twenty miles from San Antonio (then Bexar) a band of twenty armed Mexicans appeared out of nowhere and rode down on them, yelling and evidently seeking a fight. One of them, a fellow with a red feather in his hair, acted as spokesman.

"Surrender or we fire!" he shouted in Spanish.

"Fire, and be d——d!" returned one of the ex-privateers in English.

The Mexicans took the advice and opened fire, but they must have been poor shots because they failed to hit anyone. When Davy and his companions returned the fire, it was to better effect. Those of the attackers who had not been unhorsed were seized with sudden panic and rode off. The pursuers gave up the chase only when they came in sight of the "independent flag flying from the battlements of the fortress of Alamo." They told the sentry who they were, and were heartily welcomed by the buck-skin-clad patriots already gathered there. As was the custom of the frontier, whisky flowed freely. All of Davy's party got drunk except the Bee-Hunter, who seldom drank and whom the Colonel characterized as "the most jovial fellow for a water drinker I ever did see."

One of the first men Davy met was Colonel William Barret Travis, in command of the "regulars." Travis introduced him to Colonel James Bowie, in command of the volunteers. While he and Bowie were talking, Bowie drew his knife to cut a strap. "I wish I may be shot," Davy wrote, "if the bare sight of it wasn't enough to give a man of a squeamish stomach the cholic, especially before breakfast."

The details of the siege belong to one of the final chapters of this book, but an appraisal of Crockett the man seems appropriate. There have been countless eulogies of the heroes who fell at the Alamo — Travis, Bowie, Crockett, and others — but Davy Crockett dominates them all in the affections of the American people, perhaps always will. The reasons are not hard to find. No man of his day captured and held the minds and hearts of his countrymen in quite the way he did. His quick wit, his droll stories, his cunning in outwitting men who were far better educated and more sophisticated than he, his innate sense of justice and fair play, his bravery — yes, even his faults — endear him to us now as they did to his contemporaries. He rightfully belongs to the company of those frontiersmen and heroes who helped to formulate, as they best expressed them, the basic aims and ideals of American democracy.

William Barret Travis

WILLIAM BARRET TRAVIS

chapter

1

Youth and Education

THE FACTS of William Barret Travis' ancestry are meager, and the circumstances and place of his birth to some degree matters of controversy. A Travis family resided on Jamestown Island, Virginia, as early as 1637, perhaps earlier, while other Travises lived in the general vicinity of Williamsburg. As far as I know, however, the connection of the Virginia Travises with William Barret Travis is only conjectural, although a distinct possibility.[1]

William's father, Mark Travis, Sr., was born at Cambridge, Edgefield County, South Carolina, on September 6, 1783, and his mother, Jemima Stallworth, was of Irish descent on her mother's side. Other natal data concerning her are not readily available.

An early farmer in this region, Mark Travis apparently amassed a considerable estate in land, stock, and slaves. In politics he was a "Nullifier" and in religion a "Missionary Baptist," according to Thomas McAdory Owen, the Alabama historian. He was married on January 1, 1808.[2] William Barret Travis, first of nine or ten children, was born on his father's farm on August 9, 1809. Except during his childhood, none of his brothers and sisters, except perhaps Mark Travis, Jr., seem to have shared importantly in his life. He had two, possibly as many as four, other brothers and four or five sisters. The record is confused on the number of each.

Mark Travis, Jr., seems to have been the only child except William who rose to relative prominence in adulthood. Born on May 18, 1827, in or near Old Town, Alabama, he studied medicine while yet a youth and participated with distinction in the

Mexican and Civil Wars, at one time being elected a general of militia in Alabama.

The controversial points in William's birth situation are whether he was born in North or South Carolina and whether he was a foundling, left at the gate of the Travis farm by some unknown person and adopted by Mark Travis. The first point has been definitely settled in favor of South Carolina. The foundling story, apparently based on a confused local tradition, was perpetuated by the writer Cyrus Townsend Brady.[3] It, too, has been pretty well exploded. Whether William's second name was ever "Barr" rather than Barret seems unimportant.

In the absence of any but the barest facts regarding William's boyhood, we can infer much from the circumstances in which he lived. His parents were sturdy, industrious pioneer types, not given to frivolity. Being religious, and having so many children to keep in line, they were undoubtedly strict disciplinarians. An uncle, Rev. Alexander Travis, an educator and long a prominent Baptist "pillar" in Alabama, would have made certain that his brother's children had proper religious instruction. Like the others, William joined the Baptist Church at an early age.

In his early boyhood William received instruction in the three R's, chiefly at home. Then he attended a school at Red Banks in the Edgefield District, where he met James Butler Bonham, who became and remained his fast friend.

To anyone knowing the severe discipline of these frontier schools, it will come as no surprise that a student revolt was staged at the Red Banks school. At least one writer states that Travis was one of the ringleaders in this affair, which led to his departure, if not actual expulsion.[4] It is interesting to speculate upon whether young Bonham participated, as he probably did, and also what kind of punishment each received when he arrived home. Travis' parents revered education and coveted it for their children, and in those days parents usually took the part of the teacher when their children got into difficulties at school. It would have been young Travis' triumph, greater than any he later achieved in the court room, if he pleaded his case eloquently enough to escape a trip to the woodshed. More likely, both boys got a "tanning." They must have laughed ruefully over it in later years. That old tyrant of a schoolmaster! Anyway, it taught the two budding revolutionists hatred of oppression and love of freedom.

What young Travis really looked like nobody knows. The only authentic adult portrait of him hardly seems to agree with the extant descriptions of him as a large, well-built, florid-faced man. It portrays him rather as thin-faced and almost slight of build; but it is only waist-length, giving little idea of his height. There seems to be a certain look of immaturity about him, so the portrait may have been painted some time in his late teens or early twenties. While we can only speculate about his appearance as a maturer man, we may perhaps deduce from this portrait, from later word-of-mouth descriptions, and from the known tendency of tall adolescents to turn temporarily into "bean poles," that his large frame later filled out considerably. Certainly, he had fine facial features and was intelligent-looking.

In 1818, or possibly as late as 1820, the Travis family moved to Conecuh County, Alabama, where they settled on a farm just outside Evergreen, the county seat. His uncle, the beloved Baptist preacher already referred to, had previously moved to this region, where he had set up the Evergreen Academy. The Travis children attended this school. Whether William was among those who completed the course, the record does not show.

The next information about him is that he was sent to a school in neighboring Monroe County that had achieved some repute for its mentor, a "Professor" McCurdy. He must have graduated from this school, for he was presently teaching school in both Monroeville and Claiborne, Alabama, at the same time entering the law office of Judge James Dellett of Claiborne as an apprentice. He seems to have been competent in both pedagogy and law, for he supported himself adequately by teaching and passed the bar examination some time in 1829, when he was only twenty years old.

During this period he also had his one serious youthful romance — one that ended tragically for him — but that belongs to a succeeding chapter. We turn first to an admittedly fanciful reconstruction of one of the most inspiring events that occurred in his youth.

Whether Travis actually *saw* General Lafayette on his visit to Alabama in April 1825 is unimportant. Certainly, he had the *op-*

portunity. And if he did not, he must have heard about and been inspired by all of the details, which were on everybody's lips. Few can now realize the furor created all over this country by the General's visit. And the more one knows about Travis and his devotion to the cause of liberty, the more certain he feels that no event of his young manhood could have moved him more deeply than the advent of the great Frenchman to Alabama.

Did Young William Meet Lafayette ?

Gʀ‌ENERAL LAFAYETTE's triumphal tour of this country brought him to Alabama in April 1825. The beloved Frenchman, revered by Americans only less than George Washington himself, had come to America in response to an invitation in the form of a resolution of Congress, arriving in August of the preceding year. Beginning with a reception, celebration, and ovation in New York City on August 17, 1824, he was received everywhere with greatest honors. Every locality of the country sought to be included in his itinerary, and there was anxiety all over the western and frontier areas that he might avoid some places because of travel or other difficulties. As it happened, such great exertions were made everywhere to lessen the rigors of travel between cities, to protect him, and to attend to his comforts that the sixty-eight-year-old traveler stood up very well wherever he went, although his long trip was by no means free of hardships and accidents.

Apparently no one exerted more effort to lure Lafayette into Alabama than its governor, Israel Pickens, who sent an escort to the banks of the Chattahoochee to meet him after he had traversed Georgia. Special barges were in readiness to take him on board, and a party of Creek Indians led by their personable chief, Chilly McIntosh, added to the color of the gathered throng, which included distinguished citizens, some Alabama militia under General Taylor, and a contingent of the curious. For some reason, the Indians, usually apathetic toward paleface dignitaries, greatly revered this companion of George Washington, perhaps because he was a great warrior from across the ocean. And English-speaking McIntosh could converse easily with Lafayette, for he was educated and a gentleman. And, contrary to their usual stoical behavior, his untutored tribesmen shot game for the General's table, protected, and even entertained him!

Governor Pickens seems to have prepared well because the General somehow got through the rough, often roadless country in his fine carriage, although delays in his trip across Georgia put him behind schedule. The first big "blowout" for him in Alabama was held at Montgomery, near which he was met in an elaborate ceremony by the Governor and his party, on April 3, 1825. Every facility of the small town was utilized to feed, house, honor, and entertain the distinguished guest. Beloved by everyone, refusing to see almost no one, particularly his old military comrades, whatever their rank, the old man must have been taxed almost to the limit of his strength; but he loved it all, and no welcoming speaker ever gave a more graceful or better-phrased speech than he did in acknowledging the honors heaped upon him.

Flanked by accompanying boats of every size and description, a steamboat next bore Lafayette down the Alabama River to Selma. There he received the same clamorous ovation that had greeted him everywhere else, and it was Judge James Dellett who delivered the welcoming speech, the same Judge Dellett to whom young Travis was later apprenticed. Travis, like everyone else, undoubtedly knew about Lafayette's approaching visit. He or members of his family would have learned of it, if not from Judge Dellett, then from other friends or acquaintances. The most *unlikely* eventuality is that he did *not* attend one of the receptions given him. Travis might have seen him at Selma, Cahawba (then the capital), or even at Claiborne, although the General had to cut short his visit to the last-named town because he was so far behind his schedule.

This is one of those instances in which common sense and probability will have to supplant documentation. Both Montgomery and Selma were within fifty miles of Greenville, and Claiborne and Monroeville, where Travis taught, less than a hundred miles away. I submit that Travis' local and state pride, his love of country and the libertarian principles for which Lafayette stood and for which he fought, make it most unlikely that he missed seeing him, particularly since the traveler visited towns so close to the Travis farm.

The reader may protest that this is not historical fact. Let us say it is a fact we are permitted to infer from *other* facts. Much of history is based on flimsier stuff. And if young Travis did not actually shake Lafayette's hand, who is to say that his heart, like the hearts of his compatriots, did not beat faster just knowing the great French-American patriot was on his home soil? It *could* have had no other effect than to strengthen his love for the cause of American freedom, so lately won, and his future identification with any struggle against oppression.

Mobile was Lafayette's last stopping point in Alabama. As that State's largest city, it was able to stage the most sumptuous reception, and did so. Governor Pickens, proud of how perfectly his plans had functioned throughout the stay of his guest, accompanied him until he boarded the queen of river steamers, *The Natchez,* bound for New Orleans and other western points.[1]

chapter

3

A Marriage Is Blessed and Blighted

MANY WRITERS have speculated upon the circumstances of Travis' sudden departure from Alabama for Texas, when his prospects for a brilliant law career in his home State were so bright. Although the cause of the Texan revolutionists must have been one that had already enlisted his sympathies, it was not the driving reason. All agree it must have been his tragic marriage.

As a bright young man and a good student, William Travis may have been encouraged to take up the law, or he may have decided to do so without advice from anyone. In any event, he succeeded in making a connection with Judge James Dellett to study under him. This type of "law school" was the only one available in frontier states at that time, but it was a practical one that soon proved a man's fitness or unfitness for the profession. The Judge was a first-class lawyer and a fine man, and Travis must have been flattered that he thought enough of his potentialities to accept him as an apprentice. The opportunities for lawyers on the Alabama frontier were excellent and an open door to a political career.

But Travis had to support himself while preparing for the bar, so he engaged to teach school at both Monroeville and Claiborne. He was by now a well-set-up, handsome youth and is said to have attracted feminine eyes wherever he went. He looked over the field but was in no hurry to choose a wife, or so he believed. He knew what he wanted from life, where he was going, and what kind of woman he wanted to accompany him on the journey.

To the school girls who shot admiring glances at him, he was "Professor" Travis — every male teacher was so addressed in those days. He took care to keep his relations with them strictly formal, until Rosanna Cato became one of their number. She was a lovely girl in her late teens, the daughter of a prominent family of the area. Travis fell hard, and he was determined to have her, despite competition from other swains. He was encouraged because she seemed to be equally smitten with him. He must also have been acceptable to her family because there is no record that any of the Catos objected to the match, and he had no trouble at this time even with her critical brother, William.

The two were married on October 26, 1828. By that time Travis was able to give up teaching. He set up his own law office, passing the bar examination shortly after the ceremony took place, probably some time early in 1829. The two were very happy. Clients began to pour in. They established a fine home, made friends, became quite prominent in the social life of the town. He had always known that Rosanna was attractive to other men. And, like many a young husband, he discovered to his dismay that his bride did not lose that attractiveness immediately after their marriage.

Here the mystery deepens. Whether Rosanna's family unjustly accused Travis of being overly jealous, or whether she really gave him cause to believe her unfaithful, nobody knows. No writer has yet furnished any facts as to actions of the young bride that her husband might have condemned, or the name of any other man with whom she may (or may not) have been involved. There seems to be absolutely no evidence upon which a conclusion as to her faithfulness or unfaithfulness can be based. On August 8, 1829, a son, Charles, was born, and later a daughter, Isabelle.

Whatever the cause of the split-up, Travis must have felt that the wounds were too deep to heal, because one day after making provision to turn over to his wife most of his worldly wealth, including a sizable bank account, he left town with a train of emigrants on their way to Texas by way of New Orleans and Nacogdoches. Except for the clothes on his back and a few necessities for the trip, he had little to show for his hopes, his dreams, and his years of effort that he had not had when he came to Alabama in 1818. He was accompanied by a faithful Negro family servant named Ben.

No one can have his life wrenched out of joint as Travis did without being made deeply unhappy and unsettled. He must have lain awake many a night wrestling with himself, with the hurt and pride that would not let him return, longing to see his family, and wondering how much of the wreck of his marriage was his own fault. *Was* he overly jealous? If he seemed so, why couldn't she understand that it was only because he loved her so much? She knew the way he felt. Why, then, like Caesar's wife, didn't she always conduct herself so as to be above reproach? He turned it all over in his mind a thousand times. . . .

He must have been a moody companion for the other emigrants. They undoubtedly wondered why he continued to ride beside the wagons in moody silence day after day. On the frontier were many whose hearts and minds were full, many who were going to Texas or who had no destination, who were running away from themselves, from their troubles, or from the law. It was impolite, sometimes even "unhealthy," to ask personal questions. How could they know the tears were for his lost happiness, for his small son, Charles, for tiny Isabelle, who had hardly even learned to recognize him when he left . . . yes, even for Rosanna . . . perhaps for her most of all. . . .

The records show that immediately upon his arrival in Texas, Travis took out headrights. The turmoil of his mind as to his marital status is reflected in the two different applications he made in April 1831. In one he denoted himself a bachelor, in the other, a widower. The moral rigidity of the Baptist and his pride would not allow him to forgive Rosanna or return to Alabama. He gritted his teeth and determined to stay in Texas.

If one account can be credited, he saw his wife only once thereafter. This story has it that late in 1835 Rosanna, bringing the two children, met him in the lobby of a hotel, possibly at San Felipe. There she proposed that they forget the tragic past, reunite, and begin life anew, but, almost in the same breath, threatened him with a divorce suit if he did not agree to her terms. Travis is portrayed as having been cold and adamant, although deeply moved by the sight of his children. Allegedly, he walked out without giving her an answer.[1]

That this meeting ever took place is doubtful. The remaining facts of their subsequent relationship are few, there being many unfilled gaps in the story. In any event, Rosanna returned to Alabama with the children, sued for and obtained a divorce. Ironically, Judge James Dellett, Travis' personal friend and former legal mentor, acted as her lawyer.

There is in existence a letter dated September 6, 1834, from Rosanna to Judge Dellett, thanking him for offering his legal services to her in obtaining the divorce. It was written, not from Texas, but from Natchez, Mississippi, whence she had moved and where, so she writes, she came expecting to meet Travis, when it was hoped some arrangement could be made about the custody of Charles. According to her, Travis failed to keep the appointment. After a long self-justification of her own conduct, coupled with protests of her innocence of any wrongdoing, she reveals that her brother William wrote Travis demanding to know his future intentions toward her, to which she alleges Travis replied that he wished the separation to be permanent. Her only admission that she could have had anything to do with their estrangement is contained in the following statement:

I endeavored to preform [sic] my duty as a wife with the most undeviating integrity and faithfulness and if anything occurred to dissatisfy him with me it was the result of my ignorance as to what was my duty as a wife, or I would have performed it to his entire satisfaction.[2]

Needless to say, one cannot and should not try to read anything into such a statement.

The court awarded to Travis the custody of Charles and to Rosanna the custody of Isabelle. Travis at once made arrangements for someone else to take care of his son. The presumption is that he continued to support the boy as long as he lived.

Rosanna Travis, now again Rosanna Cato, remarried. Travis never did, and the reader of most of the existing brief biographies of him is left to speculate upon his attitude toward women after the wreck of his marriage. Was he a one-woman man who never again looked at another woman? Did he turn his back on women permanently because of bitterness toward Rosanna? There is evidence to the contrary. It is to be found in a somewhat neglected record referred to as his "private journal" or "diary." Here it will be called his diary.

Travis kept this diary from August 30, 1833, through June 26,

1834. The entries in it could hardly be more factual or brief. Their nature suggests that he used this journal of his professional, financial, and personal activities largely as an aid to his memory. He avoided editorializing, particularly as regards anything political or concerning his strictly personal affairs and feelings. He seems to have been exercising a lawyer's caution, in case the diary should fall into the wrong hands!

At first glance, a reader might decide that this diary could contain very little of interest to a biographer, particularly one trying to discover anything about his love life. But should he dig a little deeper he may conclude, as I have, that *nobody* can keep a diary for long, no matter how prudently, without revealing much about himself. Some of the entries in the Travis diary are all the more stimulating to the imagination because they leave so much unsaid. One can read as much or as little as he likes into the passages quoted below. Let his conscience be his guide!

There are twenty-one entries in the diary in which Travis mentions writing to Rosanna or to her brother, William, receiving letters from them, and other mostly routine matters of their relationship. They extend over almost the entire period covered by the diary. None suggests that there was bad feeling or even friction between Travis and Cato; however, the diary ends in June 1834, and Cato could have written after that time the letter to Travis that Rosanna referred to in her previously quoted letter to Judge Dellett. But if there was any animosity between Cato and Travis, it is odd that there is no mention of it in the diary or in any of the Travis correspondence that is readily available. In late 1833 their relationship must still have been fairly cordial because Cato asked of him a favor for a friend, which Travis readily granted and recorded in his diary:

[Oct.] 11th [1833] . . . Recd letter from Wm. M. Cato introducing J. B. Johnson — and agreed he would refer to me to get credit — &c[3]

In only one other place does he refer to his correspondence with Cato, except to mention writing to him or receiving a letter from him. In his entry for February 10, 1834, Travis' mention of "papers" may indicate some legal or business relationship, the nature of which can only be guessed at:

. . . Recd one [meaning a letter] from Wm. M. Cato and papers — [4]

Papers of both families could, of course, contain evidence of the friction that is supposed to have existed between them.[5]

The only entries in the diary worth quoting that relate to Rosanna are as follows:

[Sept.] 3rd [1833] Recd letter from R. E. Travis — malo [bad] . . . . Wrote to R. E. Travis — [6]

[Nov.] 1st [1833] . . . — endorsed $10 Bill to R. E. Travis[7]

[Jan.] 9th [1834] . . . Recd letter from R. E. Travis, answered same. She is willing to give up my son Charles to me. I directed him to be sent to Brazoria to the care of Mrs. Long —[8]

[Mar.] 3rd [1834] . . . — Engaged Wm. P. Huff to bring out Charles Edward Travis who is now in N. Orleans with his mother — [9]

[Mar.] 24th [1834] . . . — Heard from Charles &c.[10]

[April] 20th [1834] . . . Arrangement to wait till divorce is effected — & then — á casar con ———[11]

All of these entries except one are somewhat prosaic and self-explanatory. But the excerpt from the entry for April 20, 1834, is of considerable interest because it shows that Travis was contemplating divorce possibly as long as a year before Rosanna's divorce suit was granted, and that he had definite plans to remarry. With the Spanish portion translated, this entry reads as follows:

. . . Arrangement to wait till divorce is effected — & then — to marry

———

This passage naturally poses the question: Who was the lady Travis intended to marry? Amelia Williams wrote, apparently on good authority, that she was a Miss Cummins of San Felipe.[12] But there information about her seems to end.

So it is clear that Travis did not permanently languish in the guise of the wronged husband, eschewing the company of women. To be sure, many of his relations with them appear to have been only "dates" to take them to some fandango, or were merely casual flirtations. But the reader will see, from the passages quoted below, that not *all* of them may have been of that character. To assuage the wrath of Texans who may misinterpret my motives and accuse me of wanting to smirch the good name of Travis, I make no judgments and offer no comments on the following excerpts from the diary. The entry for April 20, 1834, is repeated for the sake of completeness:

[Mar.] 13th [1834] ... Gave R. a breast pin — & took lock of hair &c.[13]

[Mar.] 14th [1834] Took ring from R. swam horse over creek by canoe —[14]

[Mar.] 20th [1834] ... Borrowed Grey horse of Eaton & went to Mill Creek — swam twice — good Ducking — Narrow escape — tengo buena Fortuna en el amor de la senorita —most[r]ó una carta à ella sobre el conducto de la mujer de antes — &c.[15] [Translation of Spanish portion: I am very lucky in my suit of the girl — I showed her a letter about the behavior of women in olden times — &c.]

[Mar.] 21st [1834] Horse loose — could not be caught &c Spent day pleasantly — In la sociedad de mi inamorata — [16] [Translation of Spanish portion: in the company of my loved one —]

[April] 20th [1834] ... Arrangement to wait till divorce is effected — & then — a casar con ——[17] [Translation of Spanish portion: to marry ——]

[May] 7th [1834] ... — went to Mill Creek — joyously reced ——[18]

[May] 31st [1834] ... went to Mill Creek on Huff's hors [sic] — Hell — L-v-e triumphed over slander &c — staid all night at C.'s.[19]

[June] 21st [1834] ... staid all night at Chriesman — pretty country — Miss J ——.[20]

[June] 22nd [1834] ... Adventure with Miss T —— &c —[21]

[No. 114.]   AN ACT
                  To Divorce Rosanna E. Travis from her husband Wm. B. Travis.

SEC. 1. *Be it enacted by the Senate and House of Representatives of the State of Alabama, in General Assembly convened,* That in pursuance of the decree of the Circuit Court of Marion county exercising Chancery jurisdiction pronounced and entered at the fall term of said Court, A. D. 1835. The bonds of Matrimony heretofore solemnized and subsisting between Rosanna E. Travis and William B. Travis be dissolved and that the said Rosanna E. Travis be henceforth divorced from her said husband William B. Travis.

Approved, Jan. 9, 1836.

--from Alabama Session Laws

chapter

4

"Buck" Travis at Anahuac

Before narrating some of the early events of the Texas Revolution in which Travis participated, it is necessary to describe the situation that was causing so much friction between the Texans and the Mexican Government.

Increasing American emigration into Texas and a growing movement for its annexation by the United States naturally aroused resentment in Mexico. A Mexican law of April 6, 1830, had prohibited further immigration. In spite of this there were 20,000 Americans in Texas by 1831, and they continued to pour in. Our Government had already tried to purchase Texas twice by 1830. The first offer, amounting to $1,000,000, was made through our minister, Joel R. Poinsett, in 1827; the second, amounting to $4,000,000, was made in 1829. Both were rejected. President Jackson and his successor, Van Buren, were both enthusiastic supporters of annexation.

With the growing friction between the two countries and the awakened sympathies of Americans toward the Texan cause, the Mexicans also had good reason to fear an invasion. Nor could they fail to observe the aggressive, determined character of the American settlers, the majority of whom were of Anglo-Saxon stock, traditionally successful as pioneers and colonists.

The Mexicans, and indeed the Spaniards, on the other hand, have never been adept either at colonization or in dealing with colonists. Their treatment of primitive peoples was characterized by harshness, cruelty, and lack of understanding long before the *conquistadores* came to the Americas. But even a small amount of insight into the breed of men pouring into Texas would have told them that tyranny was the worst possible way to deal with

149 –

them. They should also have remembered that only a short time before, men like these had fought and won the American Revolution. And, in a very real sense, the Texas Revolution was a continuation of that war, transplanted to the Southwest.

But the Texans were by no means united. A war party advocated taking over Texas by force. It was opposed by a more numerous and clamorous peace party that favored caution and opposed the use of armed force against the Mexican Government. Anastasio Bustamente, the President of Mexico, hated Americans and adopted an oppressive policy toward them. One of the most abhorred Mexican laws required collection of high duties on all imported goods. But even worse, from the colonists' viewpoint, was the kind of men he appointed to enforce this law. As military commandant for the district in which Anahuac was located he appointed Juan (formerly John) Bradburn, a renegade Kentuckian who had no respect for the country he had left and probably no love for Mexico. He was also contemptuous of everything smacking of democracy and justice.

Bradburn had built a fort at Anahuac in the early '30's. It was occupied by about 120 *presidarios*, or convict soldiers, whom Bustamente had allegedly sent there to enforce collection of customs. But the very presence of these lawless and evil men indicated some ulterior purpose, which was undoubtedly to provoke the settlers into committing revolutionary acts, which would, in turn, enable Mexican officials to take severe measures against them. Indeed, the record shows that the soldiers provoked quarrels with civilians in the towns, roamed through the countryside stealing pigs, chickens, and anything else they could get their hands on, and preying upon women.

In all of this the *presidarios* were abetted by Bradburn, who also seized every opportunity to harass the colonists and to deny them their rights. Some of his highhanded acts against the settlers were as follows: he thwarted attempts to organize a court district and to perfect land titles; he prevented Libertad's being made the county seat and arbitrarily designated Anahuac instead, contrary to the wishes of the settlers; he compelled servants to work for him without compensation; he declared martial law without authority or adequate reasons; he harbored runaway slaves; he collected exorbitant duties on imported goods; and he closed all Texan ports except Galveston, an act that provoked one of the first strong protests of the colonists against his tyranny.

Travis, lately arrived, was at first just an observer of some of these outrages, but, as we shall see, it was only a short time before he was one of the leaders of the militant opposition. And it did not take him long to perceive that in dealing with Juan Bradburn civilized, honorable, legal methods were useless.

Obviously, Anahuac was not a town that would have been preferred by the average quiet, peaceful, liberty-loving immigrant. Why, then, did Travis choose to settle there? Dr. N. D. Labadie, a fellow townsman, wrote that Travis and Patrick C. Jack, another lawyer, went there because Anahuac offered them the best opportunities "to perfect themselves in the Mexican language and laws."[1] If so, Travis undoubtedly found perfection difficult to attain. He had to learn a new body of law and a legal and court system that had little in common with those he knew. He could master the language, and he was flexible enough to adjust himself to almost any situation, but one doubts if he ever accustomed himself to Mexican cynicism toward the law. Almost all American frontier towns had their outlaw elements, but never before had he encountered such widespread venality and lack of *respect* for the law. It must have been one of the elements of his distrust of Mexicans, expressed later on several occasions.

Travis could also observe that Anahuac was fast becoming a focal point of events in the struggle of the Texans to win their freedom. And the Jack boys and others must soon have filled him in on conditions in and around the town, particularly with relation to Bradburn and his oppression of the settlers.

Although the record is not clear, Travis may have taken an indirect part in a brush of the colonists with Bradburn in December 1831. It seems that Bradburn and Col. Domingo de Ugartechea, the Commandant at Velasco, had issued an order to close all Texas ports except Galveston. On December 16 a large meeting of citizens was held at Brazoria to decide what to do about this arbitrary blockade, as well as other matters. There Dr. Branch T. Archer made an inflammatory speech in which he advocated immediate and direct resistance to the Mexican Government. His views prevailed, and he and a George B. McKinstry were commissioned to call upon Bradburn in the name of the colonists and to demand instant rescission of the order. At the same time they were empowered to back up their demand with a threat of force, if necessary.

Archer and McKinstry at once went to Anahuac and met with the Commandant, who at first blustered and refused to grant the colonists' request. As Foote describes the incident, the two men stuck firmly to their guns:

> Bradburn saw plainly that he had to deal with men who would not be trifled with, and in the end yielded a sort of grumbling, graceless consent . . . and announced a rescission of the hated order. After which, Dr. Archer and his associate returned to Brassoria, reported the result of their mission, and admonished their rejoiced fellow-citizens to the exercise of continued firmness.
>
> . . . It was during the stay of Dr. Archer at Anahuac, at this period, that he first saw the heroic Travis . . . . Travis agreed to station himself permanently in the vicinage of Anahuac, to exercise a vigilant observation in reference to the movements of Bradburn . . . and to make a faithful report from time to time of the result . . .[2]

Bradburn's next outrage was not long in coming. He had given in on one issue, but a few days later he placed under martial law all of the country over which he had jurisdiction within ten leagues of the coast.

Things were already at the boiling point, but an event now took place that brought to an even higher pitch the antagonism between the settlers and Bradburn, the first in which Travis was directly involved. It occurred in late 1831 or early 1832, and is described in detail by Capt. Creed Taylor, an officer in the Texas Revolutionary Army, who wrote as follows:

> . . . One afternoon in 1831 while four *presidarios* of the garrison were prowling around, they entered the house of a settler, and finding the husband away and the wife alone, attempted . . . [to rape her,] the brave woman beating off her assailants until timely help chanced to come. The woman fought with the fury of a demon and her loud screams attracted the attention of a small party hunting in the vicinity, who rushed to the scene. When they reached the house they found the door securely fastened on the inside and a terrible struggle going on within. Without a moment's hesitation they seized heavy timbers, broke open the door, and rushed upon the demons. Three of the miscreants fled and escaped. The fourth, who according to the lady's testimony was the ring leader, was knocked down and securely bound. As news of the affair spread, a posse gathered at the scene. All were

highly wrought and some of them wanted to hang the wretch to the
nearest limb . . . . But wiser council prevailed — the prisoner was a soldier of the republic, and such a course would be an insult to the flag;
the Mexican authorities would use it as a pretext to inflict greater
tyranny against the colonists. [One wonders if this "wiser council" was
that of Travis. It seems probable.] But they would inflict such punishment as would serve as a warning to his thieving, cut-throat comrades.

A bucket of tar was procured and a heavy coating was applied to
the culprit from head to foot. Then, with her own hands still bleeding
from the effects of her terrible fight, the lady ripped open her feather
bed and the trembling wretch was given an ornate dressing of feathers.
He was then mounted astride a rail, and in this garb and manner
was carried through the settlement and village, and finally turned
loose near the fort with a message for Bradburn to the effect that should
such another outrage be committed or attempted by his convict gang,
the Texans would rise to a man, and that not even a *pelado* [bum]
would be left to black the commander's boots.

Among those concerned in this embroglio was . . . Bill Travis, and
with him chanced to be such other patriotic and daring fellows as
Patrick C. Jack, Sam T. Allen, and Monroe Edwards . . . . When Bradburn learned of this affair he flew into a towering rage and swore that
every one concerned in the matter would be arrested for insulting the
flag by outraging a soldier of the government, and sent in chains to
Vera Cruz for trial before a military court.

The arrest of Travis and his comrades was the spark that set off
the flame.[3]

Later, when Colonel Piedras demanded of Bradburn his reasons for arresting Travis, Jack (the second time), and others, the
Commandant stated that Jack was arrested because of his "contemptuous letter" concerning the above-related incident, in
which he demanded the seizure and punishment of two of the
ringleading *presidarios*. At that time Bradburn also gave some
"reasons" for arresting Travis, Monroe Edwards, and Samuel T.
Allen, all of them undoubtedly trumped up to justify his actions
to his superior officer, hence undeserving of credence. All of these
matters are briefly described in Patrick Jack's account of the 1832
troubles at Anahuac, which somehow became a part of the Lamar papers.[4] But Jack was arrested once previous to this time,
under the circumstances described below.

Having made the Commandant back down on the matter of
closing the ports, the Texans decided to try the same strategy
again. Probably some time early in May 1832 they appointed

Patrick Jack as head of a committee to protest against paying the exorbitant customs duties. He did not get to see Bradburn because the Commandant found out about his projected visit and had him arrested and imprisoned aboard an American vessel anchored in the channel. This time crusty old Judge Williamson called upon the Commandant and laid down the law, refusing to leave without his promise to release the prisoner. Bradburn finally agreed.

A noisy group of well-wishers, one of them undoubtedly Travis, greeted Jack as he stepped on shore, handing him a rusty old sword as a mark of honor and acknowledgment of his continued leadership. Bradburn, who must have been suffering considerably from frustration by this time, again waxed furious and full of threats. Next time . . . just wait until *next time!* He had not long to wait.

The affair that brought matters to a head between the Texans and Bradburn concerned some slaves and occurred in late May or early June 1832. The story, as told by Dr. N. D. Labadie, a participant, began with another of Bradburn's arbitrary acts. It seems he made a practice of holding runaway slaves, on one pretext or another. Naturally the owners became incensed when he would not return their property. And Bradburn could get away with this high-handed conduct because ownership of slaves was prohibited by Mexican law. He may have collected rewards on some, harbored others, even induced a few to run away. Those he could make no money on he freed, after causing as much annoyance as possible to their owners.

The specific incident referred to was his seizure of three slaves who tried to take advantage of his offer of freedom. A certain William M. Logan of Louisiana called upon Bradburn and claimed them as runaways belonging to him. Bradburn temporized, telling Logan that he would have to procure a document from the Governor of Louisiana certifying that they were his.

A man of some patience, Logan secured the necessary document and presented it to the Commandant. Again Bradburn found excuse for delay, pretending that he would have to examine the certificate for validity, asking Logan to return the next morning. Logan did so, when Bradburn told him that he could not give up the slaves because they had enlisted in the Mexican army and "asked for the protection of the Mexican flag," which he, pious patriot that he was, was obliged by law to afford them.

Travis, who had been giving legal advice to Logan, again perceived the utter folly of trying to deal openly and honestly with Bradburn. He advised Logan to go to Liberty and stay there. Then he set about trying his own secret strategy against the Commandant, although his part in the following events can be only surmised.

One morning a few days later there was much commotion within the fort, and several mounted soldiers rode out. Rumor had it that a hostile force had been discovered only a few miles away. Confusion reigned most of the day, and that night all of the soldiers were kept under arms. Scouts were again sent out, but nothing happened and no one could find out any details. After a week of this reconnoitering, none of them reported so much as even sighting a hostile force. Bradburn had apparently been deceived. Was someone just trying to worry him? If so, who was it? He was determined to get to the bottom of the story. According to Doctor Labadie,

He called the officer of the guard, and finally the sentinel, whose answers gave a clue to the whole of the excitement, about which we had been in profound ignorance. The sentinel said that, during one dark, rainy night, same week previous, a tall man, wrapped in a big cloak, had advanced towards him, that he hailed him, when he answered, "Amigo," and handed him a letter, which letter, being directed to Bradburn, was handed to him the next day, and it was this that caused Bradburn's alarm. The letter stated that a magistrate on the Sabine was organizing a company of 100 men to cross the Sabine for the purpose of taking the three negroes by force, to whom he had given protection. The letter purported to be written by a friend, in order to give him timely warning. It was signed "Billew." Now the query was, who was the tall man covered with a cloak, who handed the letter to the sentinel? It was supposed to be Travis, and Bradburn doubtless believed the ruse was played ... to make him give up the slaves. A day or two after, while Travis and [Patrick C.] Jack were in their office, a guard of thirteen soldiers appeared at the door, and took them to the quarters as prisoners, without any explanation of the cause.[5]

Incidentally, no one has pointed out that the first four letters of "Billew" spell one of Travis' nicknames. Was Travis "Billew"? Since he was oftener called "Buck" than "Bill," we can only surmise that he was the writer of this mysterious letter.

Doctor Labadie has written the fullest account of conditions within the prison, the subsequent arrests, and the attempts to free the prisoners. Whether Travis was waging a campaign to worry Bradburn is not known, but one morning a note was found in the prisoners' laundry, addressed to "O.P.Q.," who was asked "to have a horse in readiness at a certain hour on Thursday night." The ruse, if that is what it was, worked so well (or so badly!) that the Commandant decided to rush the building of a large brick kiln near Anahuac in order to have a tighter jail. Within a week it was ready, guarded by two large cannon, and the two prisoners were conducted to it, Bradburn finding it necessary to guard the transfer with the *entire garrison of soldiery* headed by an escort of cavalry!

Doctor Labadie relates that he was able, by standing on the fence of his nearby property, to see the prisoners in transit, to greet Travis, and to promise him that help would soon come. Thinking of their "possible fate," he was moved to tears.

Nor was Bradburn satisfied with two prisoners. That night he gave a ball to which he invited four other men who had aroused his suspicions, including the doctor. Somehow Doctor Labadie learned that Colonel Morgan, James Lindsey, and two others were to be arrested. All five men attended the ball, at the height of which they received a signal from a friendly soldier in on their plans, and all escaped except Doctor Labadie. Great must have been Bradburn's chagrin when he, too, slipped through the cordon of guards around the house.

Bradburn's almost insane suspicion next settled upon Monroe Edwards, rumored to have been the intended recipient of the note from "O.P.Q." Edwards was warned of his danger, but he chose to ignore the warning, and on the following night his store was surrounded by soldiers, who placed him under arrest.

Judge William H. Jack, Patrick Jack's brother, naturally shared the excitement over these arrests prevalent throughout the Austin Colony. He went to the prison, demanded to see his brother, and asserted that he would not leave until he had done so. Although threatened, he persisted, and his demand was finally met. What he said to the prisoners is not a matter of record, but when he returned to town, he promised his friends that he would soon bring help to effect their release.

Bradburn finally arrested seventeen Texans in all, and the feeling against him grew progressively more intense. News that the prisoners were receiving cruel treatment from the soldiers surprised no one. Bradburn heaped fuel on the blaze of indignation by threatening to send them to the dungeons of San Juan de Ulloa, where they would be tried by a military tribunal and would almost certainly be condemned to death.

Judge Jack kept his promise to bring help. He and others recruited men for fifty miles around the town, to the number of one hundred and fifty. They met near the Trinity River and chose Col. Francis W. Johnson as their leader. Then they marched to the fort and confronted Bradburn, asking that the prisoners be given civil trials and promising at the same time to abide by the court's decisions. The Commandant scornfully refused their request, in fact declined to have any further dealings with them.

In this tense situation, the Texans were unexpectedly handed a bargaining pawn when they happened upon and captured some of Bradburn's soldiers, who had been sent out to look for *them!* They returned with the captives to the fort, surrounded the stronghold, and repeated their demand for release of the prisoners. Bradburn was forced to recognize that he no longer held all of the trump cards. He therefore agreed to treat with them, if they would retire six miles from the fort and deliver up *their* prisoners. The Texans agreed, provided Travis, Jack, and the others were released on the following day, in exchange for the soldiers. Bradburn agreed to this condition.

Doctor Labadie wrote that he pleaded with the men in vain for a simultaneous exchange of prisoners because he had no confidence in Bradburn's promise. He was right, for some time elapsed after they had freed the Mexican soldiers, but Travis and his companions did not show up.

The facts are that Bradburn had not only gone back on his word but was improving the time by stealing some of the revolutionists' ammunition and stores that had once belonged to Travis. He also sent urgent requests to Col. Jose de las Piedras, commandant at Nacogdoches, and Col. Domingo de Ugartechea, commandant at Velasco, to come to his aid. He was clearly bent upon egging the Texans into action, for he now sent them a letter in which he asserted that *they* had broken the agreement, and he boasted that he would confiscate their property and that of all of the other rebels.

Bradburn certainly accomplished his purpose. His letter infuriated the Texans. On June 13, 1832, they held a meeting at which they drew up a paper, since famous, called the Turtle Bayou Resolutions. In this document they condemned the tyrannical and unlawful conduct of President Bustamente, declared their adherence to the Constitution of 1824, and sent out a call to all Texans to come to their aid.

Volunteers continued to pour in until they were between two and three hundred strong. They congregated at the ranch of Taylor White, who had been furnishing the men with supplies free for more than a week. In order to be on something of an equal footing with Bradburn, the leaders decided to procure some cannons, and they dispatched John Austin to Brazoria for that purpose. When he arrived there, Colonel Ugartechea would not allow him to take the cannons, going so far as to open fire upon his boat with guns of the fort. The result was the battle of Velasco, fought on July 27, 1832, during which Ugartechea was defeated and forced to capitulate.

The main body of Texans, who had since congregated at Liberty, thus waited in vain for their artillery to arrive. Then one of those unexpected things happened which gave a favorable turn to their plans. They were on their way to storm the fort at Anahuac when they learned that Colonel Piedras was approaching with a considerable body of troops and some Indians, who later deserted when they learned they were expected to fight Texans.

Johnson sent some men to parley with Piedras. The deputation set forth their grievances, especially as related to Bradburn's acts of tyranny, and explained the situation. Piedras was, at least on this occasion, a reasonable man, perhaps made more so by the prospect of having to face a (to him) unknown number of Texans. He agreed not only to release the prisoners but to rid them of Bradburn. He kept his word to the letter, for he promptly ordered the Commandant's arrest, stripped him of his command, and sent him packing on his way to Mexico City via New Orleans. He evacuated all of the hated *presidarios*, and on July 2, 1832, he released the Texans — and thereby hangs a tale seldom repeated since it was committed to paper by Doctor Labadie.

The doctor wrote that Bradburn was so afraid Travis might seek revenge for his cruel treatment that he demanded of a Lt. Juan Cortinez that he furnish him with a guard. Cortinez probably took delight in disobeying this "order" of his ex-commander. The account continues:

> He [Bradburn] hid himself in corn-cribs and the woods for two weeks, and at last he was piloted to New Orleans by some by-ways. When there, great excitement prevailed, as all these doings were known, being reported there as fast as they occurred. He found it necessary to ask the people of New Orleans, through the newspapers, to suspend their opinions for a few days, till he should recruit from the fatigues of his journey, promising them he would lay before them the whole proceedings in Texas. Meanwhile the Mexican consul chartered a vessel and sent him off to Vera Cruz.[6]

A Lieutenant Montero, who was particularly cruel to Travis, also got a bad case of jitters and hid out in the Double Bayou woods with Bradburn for a time before the ex-commandant found it safe to proceed on his way to Louisiana.

Travis never afterward had any faith either in the Mexican Government or in the collective or individual character of Mexicans. When he was their prisoner and they had the upper hand, they were cruel.[7] Once he was free, they remembered how he had stood up to them, and the threats of vengeance he had made. Nor could they forget the steely look in his eyes as he spoke. The poltroons ran off into the woods, admitting both their guilt and their cowardice. It was lucky for them that he did not catch up with them!

And even though Anahuac and the surrounding country were again quiet, Travis and Patrick Jack must have had enough of the town, for in October of 1832 they left for San Felipe, no less determined than before to continue their efforts to promote the cause of Texan freedom.

chapter

5

Citizen and Lawyer

THE DEPARTURE of Bradburn and his soldiers from Anahuac, so far from giving the war party a shot in the arm, had the opposite effect. Revolutionary activity thrives on resistance, even persecution, and now the enemy was removed. The hated anti-immigration law was repealed, and the zeal for collecting taxes and duties seemed momentarily to have gone out of the Mexican officials. People were comparatively prosperous. The climate was the kind in which the peace party could thrive, and its conservative viewpoint came to dominate. Even the imprisonment of Stephen Austin, soon to occur, did not arouse people to the point where they favored going to war to free him. Biding its time, the core of the war party remained true to its ideals, but it took little overt action during the 1833-34 period.

How Travis was chafed by the apathy of the conservative elements is revealed in his correspondence. He regarded himself as at least one of the leaders of the war party, and a fair case has been made for the thesis that he may have envisioned himself as a potential "George Washington of a new country."[1] Instead of playing a prominent role in the events of 1833 and 1834, however, he was compelled to sit on the sidelines while others garnered the glory.

The separation of Coahuila and Texas, which the Mexican Government had promised to bring about, now became a focal issue. In March and April 1833 a convention was held at San Felipe, to which such important men as Stephen Austin, Sam Houston, David G. Burnet, Branch T. Archer, and James B. Miller were delegates. A committee was appointed to draft a constitution, and the resulting document contained provisions for such democratic rights as trial by jury, a free press, and direct suffrage; but it excluded religious liberty, which it was taken for granted the Mexican Government would never assent to, even though Santa Anna had recently been elected President on a platform including opposition to the Church party. Another committee, headed by David G. Burnet, drew up a memorial listing strong reasons for the separation of Texas from Coahuila. This committee appointed Stephen Austin, William H. Wharton, and Erasmo Seguin to present the memorial to the Mexican authorities.

For some reason only Austin went to Mexico City, but after waiting months for a reply to the memorial, he wrote despairingly to Texan officials that nothing could be expected from the Mexican Government, and he advised them to set up a separate Texan government, with or without its permission. This letter was seized as traitorous, and he was arrested and imprisoned in Mexico City. For the first fifteen months he was kept in solitary confinement. After innumerable delays — and he seems to have been held chiefly as a hostage for the continued good behavior of the Texans — he was released on July 13, 1835.

To pacify Austin and other Texans who were incensed over his imprisonment, Santa Anna made a few minor concessions to them and engaged in considerable democratic double talk in order to hide his real intentions. At the same time he was pushing with all speed his plot to make himself an absolute ruler. He proceeded to demolish the "republic" he had set up and to destroy every vestige of freedom. Also, with the same lack of foresight as his predecessor, he tried later to crush the revolutionists by force.

In Travis' diary there are a few references to his participation in the affairs of the *ayuntamiento* of San Felipe, the municipal corporation that governed the town. Its chief officer, the alcalde, was roughly equivalent to the mayor of an American town. He was at first disappointed that he was not asked to serve in a more important capacity than secretary to that body. He later changed his mind, as these excerpts from his diary indicate:

[Febr. 5, 1834]: . . . — I have been elected secretary of the Ayuntamiento — to-day — I think — I cannot accept —
[Febr. 6, 1834]: . . . accepted the office of Secretary of Ayuntamiento

& that body assigned me a salary of $400 for this year — Copied Resolution of Ayuntamiento for Robertson —[2]

In other entries in his diary, covering the period from February 7, 1834, through June 1, 1834, he mentions copying out and certifying acts and resolutions of the *ayuntamiento*, keeping its records, arranging for meetings, and like matters. On April 27, 1834, he records that he was "appointed a member of the central committee" and, on the following day, that he was one of the nominees "recommended for political chief of the Department of Brazos." These are the only other entries relating to his serving in any political capacity.

As previously pointed out, Travis kept the diary largely for convenience, as a sort of combined ledger and journal of his legal and business activities. It is not a source book for his deepest thoughts and preoccupations. It was only in letters to trusted friends that he could express himself freely. Perhaps this is why he mentions Austin's imprisonment in the diary, but nothing about his participation in drawing up a petition asking for his release.[3] But Austin was not released until July of 1835, so this petition may have been drawn up after Travis terminated the diary.

What kind of a lawyer was Travis? Unfortunately, it is only to this diary that we can turn for an over-all picture of his legal activities in Texas. But only brief references are made to most of his cases, so the diary is actually of little practical use in this connection. It is assumed that the court records of San Felipe were destroyed along with the town, which, according to a note in the front of the diary, was burned "by order of Genl Houston in 1836."

Being the capital of Austin's colony, San Felipe offered good opportunities to lawyers. Travis handled a wide variety of cases, taking in what must have been considered high fees for those times. He could hardly make a social call on a friend without having legal business thrust upon him. Much property was changing hands, and many of his cases involved settling up estates. He wrote all sorts of legal documents, translating many into Spanish or English for the alcalde.

It was not a lack of good lawyers that caused people to bid for Travis' services. He had such eminent colleagues as Robert

M. Williamson, Thomas J. Chambers, Patrick C. and William Jack, and Luke Lesassier. But he was popular in spite of the competition, probably because he took all cases that came his way and did almost everything else asked of him. But, young as he was, he was also respected for his professional competence by men in and out of the profession. It must have given him considerable personal satisfaction, for example, that Col. Abner Kuykendall asked him to take his son, J. Hampden Kuykendall, as an apprentice when there were so many of his older and more experienced colleagues to choose from. Young Kuykendall began living with him on May 10, 1834, and before a month was out his mentor was buying him shoes and clothes, taking him to the doctor, and in general acting as a father to him. Under date of June 18, 1834, Travis wrote in his diary

Old Abner Kuykendall dangerously stabbed by Clayton —

On the following day he noted that the old man was recuperating.[4] There the entries concerning Travis' relationship with both men cease.

The diary does show, for the period it covers, that Travis operated his law office alone. Patrick C. Jack was no longer his law partner. Actually, Jack did not settle in San Felipe until early March of 1834, if the following entry is correct:

[March] 14th [1834] . . . — P. C. Jack has settled in San Felipe —[5]

The only mention in the diary of any professional collaboration by the two men was made during the previous month. Under date of February 19, 1834, Travis wrote that

. . . Jack requested me & Baker to attend to his cases —[6]

Jack may, of course, have had a law practice in San Felipe before he moved. Travis refers to him often in his diary but nowhere in such a way that it can even be inferred that he was his law partner during their early residence in San Felipe.

One writer, Amelia Williams, maintained that Travis and Willis Nibbs established a law partnership shortly after Travis came to San Felipe.[7] If so, the diary is singularly lacking in evidence of it, for in it I could find no mention of Nibbs. This is peculiar for several reasons. Travis, in common with other lawyers, was constantly exchanging legal paper of some kind with his colleagues, lending them money or borrowing from them, and meeting them under all sorts of conditions. All of these matters he faithfully recorded, if there was any kind of professional, business, or even social relationship between them.

The two lawyers closest to Travis were Robert M. Williamson and Luke Lesassier. Besides being a close personal friend, Williamson thought enough of Travis to employ him professionally. Under date of June 16, 1834, Travis noted

Williamson retained me in favor of his claim to Maylam's [Milam's?] Colony — & will give me a League of Land — & retains me to represent the Alabama Company about 11 League grants in case Robertson attacks them.[8]

Williamson had become alcalde of San Felipe on January 1, 1834, and could arrange to have Travis paid in land instead of money, a common practice. The two borrowed freely from each other. On March 20, 1834, Travis wrote that he sold him a bay horse for $100 in discharge of a note; on April 17 that the alcalde "fined me $5 — for contempt, etc."[9] If he felt any particular irritation over the fine, he kept it to himself.

Luke Lesassier, who served as alcalde prior to Williamson, was another close friend of Travis. The two were often in each other's company. The alcalde had power to appoint attorneys in certain kinds of cases, and he threw much legal business Travis' way. Travis was frequently at Lesassier's house, traveled with him, and on one occasion gave him a trifling present, which the alcalde returned in kind:

[Nov.] 8th [1833] ... Gave Lesassier a looking glass — & he gave me one in return[10]

The following entry, under date of December 17, 1833, shows that, on at least one occasion, he and Lesassier collaborated on a case:

Jesse H. Cartwright retained me & Lesassier to defend him against claim of his wife from whom he has separated.[11]

As far as I know, there is extant only one detailed account of a Travis court case, a case that one witness called a "farce." But four of Travis' distinguished professional colleagues were also involved, and, if the trial was somewhat of a legal fiasco, it was not because of the incompetence of any of them. It was just that they might as well not have started the legal machinery at all. A clever amateur in the law pulled the rug out from under them, so there was nothing left to decide!

This trial and the events leading up to it were summarized by a Mrs. Dilue Harris from a journal kept by her father, Dr. Pleasant W. Rose, at whose farm the trial was held. According to Mrs. Harris the proceedings took place in April of 1834. Two neighbors, whom she designates as "Mr. A —— and Mr. M ——" got into an altercation when Mr. A —— accused Mr. M —— of branding (in effect, stealing) one of his yearling cattle. Mr. A —— then went to Harrisburg and put in a complaint against Mr. M —— to John W. Moore, the alcalde. The court that came to the Rose farm to try the case included Judge David G. Burnet, later elected first President of the Texas Republic, and Alcalde John Moore. The lawyers were William B. Travis, Patrick and William H. Jack, and Robert M. Williamson. A number of men, many of them interested or curious neighbors, congregated and camped on the farm. Travis must have been a personal friend of the Roses, for the account continues:

Mr. W. B. Travis took supper with our family. He and several of the gentlemen from Harrisburg were going after the trial to San Felipe, and father decided to go with them. Mr. Travis said he would assist father to locate land. The land office was at that place, . . . where all public business was transacted. . . .

The next day the men began to arrive early. . . . Mr. M ——, the accused, was the first man on the ground, and by one o'clock there were twenty-five or thirty people present. Mr. Moses Shipman came early. . . . He . . . was horrified that one of the neighbors should be accused of stealing. He said that if M —— was found guilty he would be sent to Anahuac or San Antonio, and probably to Mexico to work in the silver mines. He said he would much rather have paid Mr. A —— for the yearling than to have a family left destitute in the neighborhood.

. . . The trial began at eleven o'clock, and the defendant plead not guilty. A —— proved that a yearling with M ——'s mark and brand was sucking his (A——'s) cow. W. B. Travis was attorney for M——, and Patrick Jack for A——. After argument on both sides, the jury pronounced the defendant guilty. W. B. Travis gave notice of an appeal. Judge Burnet granted the accused a second hearing. Mr. Ben Fort Smith proposed to the court to adjourn till everybody present should have dinner. He got A—— to one side, bought the cow and yearling, sent A—— home, and when the case was called again there was no evidence against M——. Mr. Smith claimed the cow and year-ling. He said the branding had been done through a mistake and the de-fendant was discharged. Judge Burnet admonished him to be more careful in the future. . . . All the men in the neighborhood were rejoiced at the way it terminated.[12]

An amusing sequel to this was that Travis and Patrick Jack suggested that a dance be given to celebrate the happy ending, but Mrs. Harris' mother, who was of a strongly religious turn of mind, opposed their suggestion and said she would rather hear a sermon. A Mr. Woodruff, although Bibleless, was accordingly prevailed upon to preach. Afterward they sang some hymns. Thus were Travis' and Jack's and everyone else's desire to have a social good time frustrated by one determined woman.

Travis promised to send Mrs. Rose a Bible and the men went their various ways, he, Mr. Rose, and Mr. Williamson proceeding back to San Felipe. Travis could not find a Bible in San Felipe, but he sent the Rose girls a couple of religious books, as he noted in his diary under date of June 10, 1834:

Bo't two little books of J. B. Miller & sent to Dr. Rose's daughters —[13]

We have already had a glimpse of Travis the citizen and Travis the lawyer. But perhaps we might see what his much-neglected diary reveals about his personal life. It has already shown us that he was far from the lonely recluse, embittered against women because of his shattered marriage. But what about his social and private life, his interests, his pleasures, his tastes, and his hobbies? In a life about which we know relatively little, such matters assume an importance they would not otherwise have.

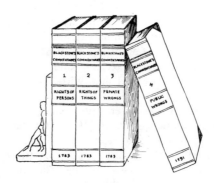

chapter

6

The Cautious Diarist

Tᴀᴀᴠɪs' ᴅɪᴀʀʏ has been shown to reveal his attitude toward women and that he was already thinking of remarrying before he and Rosanna were divorced. It also tells us something about his social life, his personal code and habits, his hobbies, and his interests.

What about his social life? According to his diary, it consisted mainly of calls on personal friends, an occasional visit to a saloon, attendance at fandangos or balls, and participation in religious services. Apparently he was the prime mover in some social events. On December 23, 1833, he wrote that he ". . . made arrangements for a Ball on a new plan — signed subscription &c. S. H. Jack is to write tickets — ."[1] Two days later, after attending the ball, he recorded: "Ball &c — fine enjoyment &c — ,"[2] while on the following day he wrote he had "Paid Ball Bill to Connell $2.50."[3] On December 26 his entry includes "Went to party to Major Lewis's — ."[4] On the 28th, it was "Miss Cummings &c went to party at Townsend's &c &c."[5] On the 31st he "— went to wedding of A. C. Westall & Miss E. Henrie —."[6] These were social events of the holiday season. He recorded no others until May 6, 1834, when he wrote that he had

Bot of Somerville $1. worth of sugar & coffee for fandango of C. B. Stewart, one gallon whiskey for Do. — Went to fandango, lost $1 — which I owe —.[7]

If he spent a relatively small proportion of his time on social matters, it was not because he was antisocial. San Felipe was a small frontier town, where public social events were uncommon. Nor does the diary contain a complete account of his social activities. He referred to few matters that did not relate to his legal or

167 —

business activities, unless they involved some expenditure of money, or the contracting of a debt.

One facet of almost every man's social life on the frontier was the saloon. Probably no men except ministers and a few teetotalers completely eschewed this stronghold of male socialization. Travis mentioned none by name, and when he patronized one, he seems to have done but little drinking. He mentions buying whisky by the bottle or the drink only a few times, and beer, once. He sometimes played faro or monte and faithfully wrote down the sums won or lost. It is interesting to note that he lost most of the time. During the period of September 2, 1833, to June 7, 1834, the only time he mentions gambling to any extent, he won only three times. On September 21 he lost $27.25[8] and on November 7, $34.[9] His total winnings were about $25, his total losses about $120. Having read thus far in the diary, one cannot escape the conclusion that he was conservative in money matters. He was not the sort of man with whom gambling is a passion, or who would continue to play in the face of steady losses. In any event, the diary ends on June 26, 1834, so we shall never know whether or not he gave up the pastime permanently.

Another phase of business that came pretty close to gambling was horse trading. Travis constantly referred to it but, oddly enough, did not mention one of the commonest forms of frontier gambling, which was betting on horse races. He made a few trifling election bets, and here the known story of his "gambling" ends.

The diary also throws some interesting light upon Travis' religious life. He was brought up a "hard-shelled" Baptist, and it can be assumed that he remained one all his life; but he did not share the narrow-mindedness of many Protestants, who regarded the dominant Catholic Church with suspicion and distrust, although the Mexican law compelled the settlers to pay it a certain outward respect as the only authorized religion of the country. On October 30, 1833, Travis noted down "preaching &c"[10] — by which he undoubtedly meant he attended church services of some kind. This is confirmed in the entry for the 31st, where he wrote that he "Sent Parson David Kincad [Kincaid?] $2."[11] On June 14, 1834, he "Dined at Connell's with priest — &c,[12] and on Sunday, the 15th, "Lent Padre Jaen $2.00."[13] On the following day he "Borrowed Cot of Connell for Padre Jaen who moved to my house —,"[14] and on June 17, he "Became responsible for Padre Jaen's board at Gay's ——."[15]

We have already noted that Travis procured and sent to Dr. Rose's daughters two small religious books, but he was unable to find a Bible for their mother in San Felipe. He may have been responsible for the distribution of considerable Sunday school literature among the colonists; if so, he does not record other examples. There is evidence, however, that he attended a Methodist camp meeting held west of the Trinity in September 1835.[16] He may have attended other such "protracted meetings."

In assessing Travis' acts of charity one should remember that the value of money in the 1830's was much higher than it is today. When he notes on May 3, 1834, that he "Bo't $5. worth in Huff's store & gave to Dearborn for charity,"[17] he actually gave goods that would probably cost several times as much today, even allowing for inflated frontier prices. All of his acts of kindness did not involve money. He often gave freely of his time, abilities, and sympathy. On September 6, 1833, for example, he sat up with a dying man and, after his death, went on to take care of the funeral arrangements.[18] He made many loans to friends, often with only their word as security, and as often borrowed on the same basis. If clients were in financial straits, he often waived legal fees. He mentions lending his kitchen, and once or twice his house, to friends. And he allowed destitute men to sleep in his office. Further, he acted as a purchaser and supplier of goods to innumerable people, often waiting a considerable period for payment, sometimes in vain. He served as go-between in all sorts of deals. He seemed available to anybody. He served Indians, colored, whites, and in a few instances, Mexicans. And, much as he distrusted Mexicans, there is no evidence that he did not want them to receive justice the same as anyone else.

There are some entries in his diary showing that Travis gave small sums of money to children. The following are some examples:

[Sept.] 1st [1833] . . . — gave Whitesides Boy 25 —[19]
[Sept.] 15th [1833] . . . — gave Dorthea, a little girl 6 1/4 —[20]
[Mar.] 5th [1834] Gave Boy 50 —[21]

[Mar.] 12th [1834] ... — gave girl 18 3/4 — Boy 12 1/2 for Bait —[22]
[June] 5th [1834] ... Gave Boy Jared 6 1/4 — Indian 6 1/4 cts —[23]

On other occasions he paid boys to perform personal services and to run errands. Fifty cents must have seemed a large sum to them:

[Mar.] 4th [1834] ... Gave Boy 50 cts for bringing saddlebags &c —[24]
[Mar.] 23rd [1834] ... — Paid boy 50 for cleaning horse — Boots &c —[25]

But apparently he went much further in helping two boys. They may have been waifs, children of the poor, or children of slaves:

[Febr.] 7th [1834] ... Sent Boy Jared to Huff's to stay — I find him clothes — Mrs Huff boards him.[26]
[Mar.] 7th [1834] ... — Sent Peter to Gay's to board — made arrangements with Mrs. Townsend to board & clothe him for his spare time &c —[27]

His love for children obviously prompted these acts, but he may, perhaps unconsciously, have been responding also to a deep personal need. In doing for the children of others he may have felt less keenly his separation from his own.

A man of Travis' education and refinement would need some contact with books. Having few of his own except law books, he prevailed upon the generosity of a Mrs. Townsend, who had a private library of unusual size for the frontier, although it must have run heavily to novels, if the list of books she lent him is indicative. Other books of more serious import he borrowed elsewhere. But too much significance should not be attached to his choice of reading matter. His law practice was heavy. He must therefore have had little time to read. When he did so, it probably was largely for recreation.

The first and heaviest reading he mentions in the diary is *The History* of Herodotus, dealing with the westward thrust of the Greeks into the Persian empire. In the nonfiction field he also read an anonymous work, first published in London in 1831, titled *Court and Camp of Bonaparte*, later published in this country (1837) as part of "Harper's Family Library." He read P. C. Headley's *Life of Empress Josephine*, four unnamed volumes of Febrero, the "*Spectator* & Bolingbroke study of History."[28] The work by H. St. John Bolingbroke was undoubtedly his *Letters on the Study and Use of History,* first published in London in 1752. The following are the only other nonfiction works he refers to: A. Green, *Yankee Among the Nullifiers;* Eliza Leslie, *Pencil Sketches, or Outlines of Character and Manners* (both American works); and an almanac of unspecified date. In the field of fiction he had a strong predilection for current historical novels by the best-known writers. Of the American novelists he read James Kirke Paulding's *The Dutchman's Fireside,* which deals with the New York scene at the time of the French and Indian War, and *Westward Ho!,* which represents the worst tendencies of the American romantic writers and may have been intended to burlesque the type.[29] Travis also read Jane Porter's *Scottish Chiefs,* Catharine Maria Sedgwick's *Hope Leslie; or Early Times in Massachusetts,* and *Wacousta,* an early popular work of the Canadian writer, John Richardson. This is a frontier romance of the life and times of Pontiac. All of the remaining novelists whose works he read were English or Scottish. These authors and the titles of their novels are as follows: Disraeli's *Vivian Grey;* Sir Walter Scott's *The Black Dwarf, Guy Mannering,* and *Rob Roy;* and Tobias Smollett's *The Adventures of Ferdinand, Count Fathom.* One cannot help but note the heavy preponderance of melodramatic romance in these works, but, as stated above, the choice was probably rather restricted.

Fishing was also one of Travis' favorite hobbies. He refers to the sport a number of times. Swimming was probably more of a necessity than a pleasure. On one occasion he swam Mill Creek in obvious furtherance of amorous interests:

[Mar.] 20th [1834] . . . Borrowed Grey horse of Eaton & went to Mill Creek — swam twice, good Ducking —Narrow escape — Tengo buena Fortuna en el amor de la senorita — (I am very lucky in my suit of the girl)[30]

Still another hobby was gardening. He wrote of obtaining and setting out pepper and cabbage plants and of getting seeds. On one occasion he wrote that he "Gave Joseph Greer counsel about potatoes."[31]

Travis records no occasions on which he fought anyone and only one when he resorted to physical violence, which was repugnant to him. Under date of June 11, 1834, he wrote that he "whipped *old Jack* for getting drunk — ,"[32] and on December 14, 1833, that he "Had a fight with John R. Jones about our ac/ts &c —."[33] "Old Jack" must have been a slave. Not knowing the circumstances or the severity of the punishment, we are in no position to judge Travis harshly for this action. His "fight" with Jones was undoubtedly only verbal.

A reader of the diary will wonder about the state of Travis' health at the time because he makes a number of entries showing purchase of medicines. Unfortunately, he seldom specifies what they were or why he was taking them. The burden of evidence is that he was as healthy as any vigorous man could have been whose profession forced him to stay indoors much of the time, although he spent as much time outside as he could. And the time came soon enough when he had to be outdoors most of the time. The revolutionary movement could not stay dormant long under the provocations of Santa Anna. And, ironically, the Texans' next brush with the Mexicans occurred at Anahuac. With his bitter memories of that place fresh in his mind, Travis could be expected to take a major part in any action to recapture it from the Mexicans.

chapter

7

More Trouble at Anahuac

IN JANUARY 1835 the Mexican National
Congress decided to set up a central authority over the Texas
part of Coahuila and Texas. It was an obvious attempt to grind
down the Texans, and, with characteristic clumsiness, that government chose an area of greatest irritation to the Texans: the reopening of the customhouses, including the one at Anahuac, from
which the Texans had driven Juan Bradburn in humiliating defeat in 1832. As a result of the Texan ports having been free since
that time, a contraband trade valued at an estimated $270,000
had developed. The Mexicans also wanted to regain this lost
revenue.

Toward the end of January one Capt. Antonio Tenorio arrived
in Anahuac with a detachment of thirty-four soldiers to re-es-
tablish the customhouse and reopen the fort. These were *presidarios* or convict soldiers like their predecessors.[1] Tenorio's job
proved to be no bed of roses. He had all sorts of difficulties from
the start — with paying, provisioning, and arming his troops; with
desertions; with bribery and other forms of resistance against
the tariff by traders and merchants; and with troubles resulting
from his own bungling.

And even without the bitter precedent of a Bradburn, the settlers had reason to complain. Collection of customs at the ports
was done unevenly and with the usual corruption. The irritation
of having to pay at all was bad enough; but some traders were
allowed to smuggle goods in free, some to pay only nominal duties, while others were forced to pay the full tariff. By way of illustration, at the customhouses in Galveston and Anahuac the law
was fully enforced, while at Brazoria only tonnage duties were

collected.[2] The angry citizens of Anahuac protested against these inequities in various ways, depending upon how much they had at stake, their own feelings, and their political beliefs. The resistance men openly refused to pay any duties, but the conservatives paid them and urged compliance with the revenue law. The *ayuntamiento* of Liberty reflected what was perhaps the prevalent attitude when, on April 17, 1835, that body issued a proclamation urging compliance until such time as the National Congress could change the law, a forlorn hope at best.

On May 4 someone set fire to some lumber Tenorio had procured to rebuild or repair the fort. The radicals were blamed for this deed. Captain Tenorio complained that they had also helped five Mexican deserters to escape, had bribed officials, and had engaged in smuggling activities. The nonconforming Texans may have been guilty on some but not all of these counts. The tension mounted.

Even though they had little faith in peaceful processes under the circumstances, the Texans decided to meet and determine what course to pursue. Accordingly, on May 4, 1835, twenty, or possibly as many as twenty-five, of them gathered at the house of Benjamin Freeman and framed a memorial to Governor Augustine Viesca asking him to support repeal of the tariff. Their dependence upon his backing disappeared with the bad news that he had been deposed and imprisoned. This highhanded act only heaped fuel on excitement that was already spreading like a brush fire on a dry day.

The blaze was bound to hit a human powder keg. That man was Andrew Briscoe, a prominent merchant and a close friend of William Barret Travis. And thereby hangs a tale, the story of the second action at Anahuac.

Young DeWitt Clinton Harris of Harrisburg came to Anahuac on June 10, 1835, to purchase some dry goods of Andrew Briscoe. He had only just concluded his business when he was told that he could remove none of the goods until he paid customs duties on them. But his own words, from a letter dated August 17, 1835, to a correspondent in Waterloo, New York, tell best what occurred:

... This [paying the duties] I was determined not to do, if I could avoid it. The evening previous to my intended departure there were several guards placed around Mr. Briscoe's store, to see that nothing was removed. About eight o'clock a young man came to the store and asked Briscoe for a box to put ballast in; this Mr. Briscoe gave him, and he placed it on a wheelbarrow filled with brick and started for the beach; after he left the store I observed to Mr. Briscoe that we could now ascertain whether my goods would be stopped or not. Shortly after, we heard the young man calling for Mr. Smith, the interpreter. Mr. Briscoe and I then walked up to the young man, and found that he had been stopped by the guard. Mr. Smith soon came up and informed the guard of the contents of the box; this appeared to satisfy him, and the box was taken to the beach, Mr. Briscoe and I going with the young man. After the box was put in the boat and we were about returning, ten or twelve Mexican soldiers came on us and ordered us to stand. Mr. Briscoe and I were taken prisoners. As we were ascending the bank a young man named Wm. Smith came down the hill, and when within ten feet of us was shot down, the ball passing through the right breast; (he is recovering). Mr. Briscoe and I were then put in the calaboose, where I remained until next day at 11 o'clock, when I was liberated, Briscoe still being detained. I immediately came to Harrisburg and made statements of the facts, which were sent to San Felipe . . . .[3]

This "statement of facts" young Harris sent directly to Travis, suggesting that the two were friends.[4]

The shipment of dry goods remained in Briscoe's store. Then Tenorio made an issue of something actually having no connection with the matter at hand. That was the ballast box. He was always ready to misinterpret every act of a citizen as an attempt either to thwart his authority or to make him look ridiculous. He wrote to Colonel Ugartechea on June 25, 1835, that "when the [ballast] box was opened, it was found to be full of mere rubbish.[5] If this had been Tenorio's only grievance against Briscoe, we could dismiss the incident by saying that he lacked a sense of humor; but Briscoe had been a ringleader in arranging for a meeting at Harrisburg on June 4, at which an "agreement" was presented to the citizens to meet again on the 6th, elect officers, and march with a small company of men against Anahuac. This document also set forth the grievances against the Mexican Government for the way the customs laws were being administered. It was signed by Briscoe, young Harris, and some fifty-four others, a number of whom later withdrew.

If the men of Harrisburg were in the vanguard of resistance against paying customs duties, Anahuac citizens remained in a state of indecision on the issue up until late June. But on the 21st of that month something occurred that erased the doubts of many waverers as to the intentions of the Mexican Government toward the colonists. General Cos, who had been charged with subduing Texas to Santa Anna's will, sent some dispatches to Captain Tenorio informing him of certain military plans to station Mexican troops strategically throughout Texas and, eventually, to beat down the revolutionists. The courier carrying this and other dispatches had the bad luck to fall into the hands of some members of the war party when he arrived in San Felipe. There, where the sentiment for war was strong, the contents of the dispatches were rapidly disseminated, and they gave considerable comfort to the beleaguered adherents of that party.

On June 22 a meeting was held at San Felipe and a resolution adopted to make Travis the head of a company of volunteers, whom he was to recruit himself. He was then to attack and capture the garrison at Anahuac. According to young DeWitt Clinton Harris' letter quoted in part above, an "order" — presumably from the leaders of the war party — was sent on the 24th of June "for the Mexicans to be disarmed . . . ."

Travis' account of what followed is contained in his letter of July 6, 1835, to Henry Smith. In it he revealed that certain men at Anahuac had also asked him to head this mission. The following is part of his account:

> . . . I had [also] been invited to go to Anahuac for the above purpose by several of my friends, who are the principal citizens of that place, and who were suffering under the despotic rule of the military.
>
> Under these circumstances, I set out for Galveston Bay, raised a volunteer company of twenty men on Buffalo Bayou and San Jacinto, and being elected captain of the company, I proceeded to Anahuac in the sloop "Ohio," with a six-pounder mounted on board. We landed on the 29th, took possession of the place, and commenced active offensive operations. On the morning of the 30th the troops, about forty in number, capitulated, delivered us sixty-four stands of arms (muskets and bayonets), and agreed to leave Texas immediately under parole, never to serve against the people of Texas. I sent them bag and baggage on board the sloop, and they are now on the march without arms to La Bahia.
>
> This act has been done with the most patriotic motives, and I hope you and my fellow citizens generally will approve it or excuse it.[6]

A number of details given in other accounts are omitted by Travis. It seems that about 4 P.M. on the afternoon of June 29, after the *Ohio* had anchored in the channel off Anahuac, the men took the six-pounder and rowed ashore. When Captain Tenorio sent a messenger to ask what they wanted, Travis demanded that he surrender the fort, together with all its arms and equipment. Tenorio delayed some time, then said he wanted the night to think it over. Some accounts say that Travis gave him an hour, but at least one eyewitness wrote that terms were not negotiated until the following morning, agreeing with the Travis version. This anonymous participant in the attack also related that the Travis forces, presumably on the evening of the 29th, pursued the Mexican soldiers

...for about six hundred yards and drove them from the quartel... into the woods. Night was now advancing. Our cannon was leveled at them and one round fired on them which was not returned.[7]

It was after this, then, that Tenorio verbally surrendered and requested a cease-fire until morning, when he would meet Travis at the customhouse to discuss terms. This participant estimated the Travis forces at about twenty-seven, the Mexicans at over fifty, of which the Texans took seven prisoner during the night. Young Smith, the interpreter wounded at the outset of the trouble, was the only casualty on either side. Another detail of the surrender terms omitted from the Travis account was that the Mexicans were allowed ten or twelve stands of arms and ten cartridges each in order to protect themselves from Indian attack on the march to Bexar. Needless to say, one of Travis' first acts on investing the fort was to release his imprisoned friend, Andrew Briscoe.

Five days after Tenorio capitulated, the sloop *Ohio*, bearing the Texans and their prisoners, arrived at Harrisburg, where a Fourth-of-July celebration was in progress. They were too late for some of the festivities, but not for a barbecue. The ball was put off until the night of the fifth. One of the amusing sequels to the whole affair was the conduct of Captain Tenorio, who, with his men, was allowed to remain and rest for a few days before continuing on to Bexar. Tenorio was apparently a man of great charm and fine manners, and is said to have acted as if he were the hero of the occasion instead of a defeated commandant! At the ball, he was especially gallant to Mrs. Kokernot, a handsome French widow. Not really vicious like Bradburn, he resembled in type the combination petty officer and official frequently satirized in comic opera. Some time later he proceeded with his men to San Felipe, where he was somewhat lionized, and so did not reach Bexar until September 8th.

Travis' exhilaration over his revenge on Bradburn did not keep him from enjoying the holiday season. Among other social events, he attended a fandango. But, even amidst that gaiety, he sensed that his action at Anahuac had put him in an unfavorable light with many Texans. A number of them, some of whom he counted as friends, eyed him coldly. The hope he expressed in his letter of July 6 to Henry Smith that "you and my fellow citizens generally will approve it or excuse it" shows that he was then aware of this undercurrent of censure. But he realized what a hornet's nest he had stirred up only after he returned to San Felipe a short time later.

chapter

8

Same Story — Different Ending

THE REACTION of the majority of settlers was clearly against Travis' taking of the garrison at Anahuac. In his Journal, Ammon Underwood described the fears of many Texans as well as anyone living at the time. He wrote that

... much of the Community in this section of the Country are highly excited against the conduct of the party and the course of those few, who were the leaders of the expedition, on account of the threatening aspect of the government against the Colonies, as they have been preparing for some time an expedition against us .... [1]

Mrs. Dilue Harris, another contemporary, attributed the lack of approval to the older citizens who, because they "had families with all they possessed in Texas, wished rather to pay duties to Mexico than to fight."[2] Another group, the land speculators, feared an upset in the *status quo* might invalidate their land titles. Still others felt that Travis had acted without proper authorization. An unidentified writer, whose notes are included in the *Lamar Papers,* went so far as to assert that he received

... an express from the authorities at San Fillipe [sic] countermanding what had been ordered; but ... refused to obey the countermand, and proceded on to reduction of the place.[3]

Travis and no one else, as far as I can discover, mentioned such a countermanding order. If it was as informal as his original "orders," which were actually in the form of a resolution adopted by the meeting at San Felipe, then who is to say that they were binding upon him in the same way as military orders? It will also be remembered that Travis, in his letter quoted above, wrote that certain friends at Anahuac had only "invited" him to seize its fort. Obviously, under the circumstances he had to formulate his own plan of action; and, having acted arbitrarily to a degree we cannot now determine, he must have realized that he made himself, to that same degree, vulnerable to criticism.

Travis was probably most hurt when the *ayuntamientos* of a number of nearby towns passed resolutions condemning what he had done. They not only disavowed responsibility but declared that he had acted counter to the wishes of the people. Some of these resolutions were printed and given wide distribution, others only posted in public places.

In his own version of what happened at Anahuac, Travis plainly stated the authority for his action and his own motives. He was, above all, honest. It is therefore difficult to believe that he would not have told a straight story to his close friend, Henry Smith. In a letter to him, dated July 6, he wrote:

> I have only time to say that I returned last evening from a successful expedition to Anahuac. On the 21st ultimo resolutions were adopted here [at San Felipe], recommending that in connection with the general defence of the country against military sway, the troops at Anahuac should be disarmed and ordered to leave Texas. In addition to that I had been invited to go to Anahuac for the above purpose, by several of my friends who are the principal citizens of that place, and who were suffering under the despotic rule of the military.[4]

He protested that he acted from "the most patriotic motives," and, as already mentioned, expressed a hope that his action would be excused, if not approved.

Whether the resolution of a town council and the invitation of several prominent friends constituted adequate authority for taking this military action was, and still is, debatable. Although Travis had expressed some doubts about it himself, nevertheless his conscience was clear. Sensitive as he was to public opinion, after being battered by it he could still write:

> I am determined, for one, to go with my countrymen: Right or wrong, "sink or swim, live or die, survive or perish," I am with them![5]

One of Travis' next acts is difficult to understand. It may have been dictated in part by this loyalty to his countrymen; however, before judging him harshly one should keep in mind that the government's intention to arrest the leaders of the war party was already a widespread rumor. Rotting in jail, he would be as powerless to advance the revolutionary cause as he had been in 1832. At any rate, he wrote a letter to Colonel Ugartechea on July 31, 1835, expressing a strong desire to "make amends" for the attack on Anahuac, and, in the interest of achieving a "peaceable termination" to the difficulties between the Texans and the Mexican Government, he offered to open a correspondence with him by which "this good understanding may be brought about . . . ."[6] Making such an appeal to one who was the actual source of much of "the despotic rule of the military" must have gone cruelly against the grain; but Travis was a man of strong principles, and no action he ever took proves this more conclusively. He received no answer to his proposal, a double humiliation. But he was prepared to eat more humble pie because he wanted so intensely to square himself with his fellow citizens.

He first "very reluctantly" published a "card" in the *Texas Republican*, at the urgings of some friends, notably Nibbs and Wharton. The substance of this card was that he would follow with an explanation of his motives at a later date. There is no record that he did so, but we are certain that his supporting evidence included the resolutions adopted by the *ayuntamiento* of San Felipe at the June 21 meeting. This is made evident in his letter of August 5, in which he exhorted Henry Smith as follows:

> Do consult with J. A. Wharton as to what is best, and do it according to your united judgment. If that pledge in the card could be gotten over, I should feel satisfied to say nothing; but as I do not see how that can be done, suppose you publish the resolutions, with a dozen lines of explanatory remarks in my name. At all events let what is published be short and not in the tone of an apology, as I feel that I have none to offer.[7]

He had had time to think more maturely about his conduct, and he gave his friend the results of that thinking:

> I know I acted by the consent and approbation of the political authorities. I know that the people here all favored the measure, and I went into it believing it to be right and that it would meet the approbation of all — and, as you say, time can only determine whether it was a good or bad measure.[8]

He then continued in a tone of manifest resentment:

I was only an individual actor in the business. I joined the volunteer company which had collected for the purpose of taking Anahuac and was elected its commander without my knowledge or solicitation. I see no reason why I should be singled out as the responsible person. Indeed, most men in this part of the country are satisfied with my course, and the public generally will be, I think, when they reflect on the matter, knowing the facts. Conscious that I have not intentionally erred, I bid defiance to any who may be disposed to persecute me, and feel assured that I have numerous friends to sustain me in it.[9]

He apparently planned to publish anonymously "some articles . . . upon the affairs of Texas," according to another letter to Smith, dated August 24, 1835. Whether these articles were to concern the Anahuac affair is not clear. Apparently they were not printed, may, indeed, never have been written.

On September 1 Travis again wrote Henry Smith, this time transmitting the explanation promised in his original card. He also directed Smith to follow it with some previously sent documents which, he judged, "can better exhibit my motives than a volume from me."[10] Neither letter nor documents were published, but certainly the explanation is worth quoting here, even though previously printed. It is as follows:

To the Public:

The undersigned published a card some time since, stating that he would give the public his motives in engaging in the expedition to Anahuac which resulted in the capture of the garrison of that place on the 20th of June last. Circumstances beyond my control have hitherto prevented me from redeeming the pledge therein given. I will now do so in a few words.

I refer the public to the following documents to shew what were my motives in that affair. At the time I started to Anahuac, it seemed to be the unanimous opinion of the people here that that place should be reduced. The citizens about Galveston Bay, who had formed a volunteer company for the purpose sent to this place for aid. The Political Chief approved the plan and presided at a meeting of about 200 persons who adopted the resolutions which appear below.

Being highly excited by the circumstances then stated, I volunteered in that expedition, with no other motives than of patriotism and a wish to aid my suffering countrymen in the embarrassing strait to which they were likely to be reduced by military tyranny. I was casually elected the commander of the expedition, without soliciting the appointment. I discharged what I conceived to be my duty to my country to the best of my ability. Time alone will shew whether the step was correct or not. And time will shew that when this country is in danger that I will shew myself as patriotic and ready to serve her as those who to save themselves have disavowed the act and denounced me to the usurping military.

San Felipe, September 1st, 1835.

W. Barrett Travis.[11]

With Travis, if the motives were pure, the logic was correct, and the act helped the Texan cause, how *could* it be wrong? Every instinct told him he had done the right thing. At least one writer has propounded a theory that Travis wanted to become the leader of the Revolution, and that it was to further his military ambition that he thrust himself forward as leader of the attack on Anahuac. This thesis, like many another, can be proved mainly by inference, if at all. Travis' subsequent military career shows that, while he had a laudable desire to advance in rank and to be placed in a branch of the service where he thought he could do the most good, he never pushed himself, perhaps never even envisioned himself, in the role of supreme military leader. He was, in fact, entirely willing to accept Austin and Houston successively as commanders in chief. He once wrote Austin expressing strong sentiments of confidence in his military sagacity.[12]

Travis was neither the irresponsible paladin nor the power-seeker, the professional military man with a thirst for advancement at any cost, nor the glory-hunter. Actually, this second action at Anahuac was insignificant, militarily. It was important chiefly because it served to crystallize the issues and because it disillusioned the appeasers who, up to that moment, had believed anything could be gained by trusting the Mexican authorities. This disillusionment was hastened by several events that took place early in September.

The first of these concerned a chance meeting of Travis with a strange Mexican who arrived in San Felipe one day from San Antonio. He said he was a friend of Stephen F. Austin, who would soon be released from prison and allowed to return home. If he was an emissary of the Mexican Government, sent to frighten the Texans, as some surmised, he certainly was a talkative one. He revealed that a large body of Mexican soldiers was to arrive between the 12th and 15th of the month to garrison certain Texan towns. According to Travis' account in his letter of August 31,

1835, to Andrew Briscoe, two hundred men were to be stationed at San Felipe, "Temoxtitlan [sic], and Nacogdoches . . . and . . . Anahuac." They were sworn to arrest all who had any part in the two raids on Anahuac and the one at Velasco, and with the aid of certain Texans, they were to "overrun the people and keep them in vile submission."[13] The aroused Texans would have jailed the garrulous visitor, but there was no jail in San Felipe, and no one had the time to guard him.[14] In any event, the burden of his talk was soon circulated. Taken alone, it was sufficient to turn the tide against the peace party and in favor of the war party.

In this same letter to Briscoe, Travis also wrote that "the Mexican or Tory party . . . are routed horse and foot." It was the first time in two months he was not "ashamed to tell what was going on." The people had not only turned overwhelmingly to the revolutionists, but were clamoring for a convention which, it was decided, would be held at San Felipe on September 12. Travis was right in his prediction that it would mark the "last expiring struggle" of the "Tories" and "submission men." In another letter written on the same day, he exulted in the following terms:

The devil has shown his cloven foot and his lies will be believed no longer. "Heaven's hangman will lash the rascals round the world!"[15]

As the loose-tongued Mexican had predicted, Stephen F. Austin was released, and, fortuitously, he arrived in Texas just before the convention opened. (It was held at Brazoria, rather than at San Felipe, as originally planned.) The main item on the agenda was whether to fight Mexico. Austin attended the meeting and, having become disillusioned himself concerning the pretended aims of the Mexican Government, came out strongly for armed action. He was wildly acclaimed, and his strong backing served to throw practically all of the remaining "die-hard" Texans into the ranks of the war party. From then on the peace party dwindled rapidly. Some of the "submission men" were even forced to leave San Felipe, chiefly because they were involved in a plot to arrest Travis and other moving spirits of the Revolution.

Dr. James H. C. Miller, the Political Chief, was one of these plotters. In a letter of July 25, 1835, to J. W. Smith, he outlined a scheme to arrest Travis and others. As the highest local civil authority, he could order their seizure. He then planned to turn them over to the military authorities. For some reason he did not carry out the plot during his incumbency, but he urged Wiley Martin, his successor, to do so.

But it was General Cos who finally acted. He sent an order to Colonel Ugartechea to require the Political Chief to arrest the revolutionary leaders. If Martin did not promptly make the arrests, Ugartechea was to take soldiers and do so himself. Perhaps Cos correctly estimated the character of Wiley Martin, for it turned out Martin had a strong sense of self-preservation and no appetite for the job. He told Ugartechea, or one of his aides who served him with the requisition to make the arrests, that the wanted men had disappeared and that he knew nothing of their whereabouts!

It is doubtful in any event that the war party would have allowed the arrests to be made. In an August meeting they had adoped a resolution to the effect that they would deliver up no citizen to the Mexican military authorities for trial, no matter what he was accused of.

News of the cowardly plot spread, and Dr. Miller, Wiley Martin, and Thomas J. Chambers, another "submission man," were driven out of the capital of the Austin Colony by the new coalition.

There is no evidence that Travis fled to avoid arrest, but he was not waiting around, and he hastened to volunteer his services to the Texan Army.

chapter

9

Scouting and Recruiting to Duty at Bexar

TRAVIS GAVE up a seat in the Consultation called for October 15, 1835, to join the Texan Army scouting service. This was some time in September. There is no record that he participated in the Battle of Gonzales, which occurred on October 2, or in the Battle of Concepcion, which took place on October 28. In the Consultation of November 3, 1835, Henry Smith was elected Governor, and Sam Houston was made Commander in Chief of the army, replacing Stephen Austin.

On October 27, 1835, Austin ordered Travis to

... raise a volunteer Company of Cavalry of not less than fifty or more than Eighty men — each man to be armed with a double barrell gun or Yager and brace of pistols. Without the Consent of the Capt. not more than one tenth of his Company shall be permitted to volunteer in the proposed corps.[1]

How much progress Travis made at this time in raising the volunteer company of cavalry is not a matter of record. He was not solely occupied with recruiting because he and his men captured about three hundred Mexican horses while on a scouting expedition. This occurred early in November near San Antonio. Austin must still have been Commander in Chief, for on November 11 he copied into his Order Book a lengthy combined letter and order in which he thanked Travis for accomplishing this feat, even though he had since learned the animals were "all very poor, being the refuse horses" of the Mexican army. Being "useless to us here," he ordered Travis to "drive them to the neighborhood of Seguin's Ranch," there to put them to "good pasture where they will recruit." If this did not work out, he was to do as he thought best. Austin was a bit inconsistent because he also ordered Travis to "bring in to headquarters as many of the horses as are fit for active service,"[2] after having already pronounced them "useless."

Austin must have been worried about Ugartechea's movements at this time. Fearing that he might intercept Fannin, who had been sent out with a small force, or Travis with the *caballada,* he sent a lengthy order to Col. Edward Burleson on November 15. Burleson was to intercept the Mexican colonel before he could overtake either; however, in a postscript, he added that Travis

... has this moment arrived without accident having secured the Cavy-ard [sic] by sending it beyond the Guadaloupe. He heard nothing of the enimy.[3]

Austin must also have been confused as to dates because two days later he wrote that Travis had returned to camp on the 16th with "six horses and four prisoners — the horses were sold at auction by the Quarter master."[4]

There is little detail in all of this about Travis' actual movements in capturing the horses. His own account shows that the affair involved somewhat more than would be surmised from reading the bare report of his superior. The following is from his letter of November 16, 1835, to Austin:

... On the evening of the 5th Inst. I left the camp at head Quarters as a volunteer under the command of Capt Briscoe, who had been despatched on a Scouting expedition to the westward of San Antonio. On the third day after Capt B. Set out, he concluded to return to camp from the Laredo Crossing of the Medina. Feeling Satisfied that much good might be done to the Service by a detachment's going farther west on the Laredo road, I proposed to take command of a small detachment of 12 men, who volunteered to go with me upon such an expedition. I accordingly set out on Sunday the 8th Inst. & camped at Salinas's Ranch, on the Atascosas on the first night. On the next day, I took up the line of march towards Laredo, and after having travelled about five miles, I discovered the trail of the public cavallada, which had been sent off from Bexar, about 8 days before. Having pursued the trail for several miles, along the Laredo road, we came to where the party with the cavallada had encamped about two days before, after which the trail became much fresher, & we pursued with renewed confidence of success, at a brisk pace until we arrived at the Macho, about 50 miles from San Antonio, where the Soldiers with the horses had evidently encamped the night before. I then made the best disposition I could, of the Small force I had, to attack them wherever I should find them, & pursued them with great caution until after night, when being informed by my guides that we were within two or three miles of San Miguel Creek, at which they must have encamped with the cavallada, as there was no other water on the road within five Leagues; & thinking it not prudent to attack them in the night, (as I understood they were 20 strong) & we would thereby lose the advantage of our superior marksmanship; & fearing that the cavallada might *Stampede* & be lost, I encamped for the night without water & without shelter from the cold or rain which was falling upon us. On the morning of the 10th, at day break I marched to attack the enemy with all speed. I found them encamped in a very advantageous position amidst some oaks on the west bank of the San Miguel about 70 miles from St. Antonio & seeing two of their men out collecting the horses, I ordered my men to charge into their camp on horse back, with a view to divide them as I supposed their force to be superior in numbers to our own. I accordingly rode up to their encampment at the head of my men at a full gallop, took them completely by surprise & they surrendered without the fire of a gun. Two of them escaped — we took five prisoners, six muskets, two swods [sic] & 300 head of gentle Spanish horses including ten mules. Having despatched a courier to advise you of the capture, I had the horses &c, collected immediately, & started with them & the prisoners to a point on the St. Antonio river about 35 miles below Bexar, where I arrived safely with them on the 4th day after I left the San Miguel. From thence agreeably to your superior orders I sent the cavallada under convoy of six faithful men to Gonzales, where they will probably arrive to-morrow. I have nothing further to add, than that during ten days of arduous service, my men have had to mount guard every night, & to be on fatiguing duty during the day, without any other food than meat without salt; & that most of them have conducted themselves with a heroism & firmness worthy of the great cause of liberty in which they are engaged, & the satisfaction they enjoy of having rendered some service to their country, more than compensates them for the fatigues & privations they have undergone in a bleak wilderness, amidst cold & rain.

    I have the honor to remain

Your excellency's
obt. sert
W. Barret Travis[5]

Travis is supposed to have distinguished himself during the storming of San Antonio by the Texans under Burleson, between December 5 and 10, 1835. The record is not clear as to just how he was employed at this time, but being on detached duty, it must have been as a scout. One writer has questioned — perhaps others have too — whether Sam Houston acted wisely in keeping

Travis and Fannin on recruiting duty when both had so clearly proved their military competence.[6] It was a matter of some surprise to me that Travis, so far from objecting to such assignments, seems to have welcomed them, or at least preferred them to others. In his letter to Henry Smith of January 29, 1836, for example, he wrote as follows:

... I hope your Excellency will take my situation into consideration, and relieve me from the orders which I have heretofore received, so far as they compel me to command in person the men who are now on their way to Bexar. Otherwise I shall feel it due to myself to resign my commission. I would remark that I can be more useful at present, in superintending the recruiting service.[7]

But Travis did not continue long in his first recruiting assignment. He was raised to the rank of major of artillery in December, but he immediately declined the promotion.[8] He preferred the cavalry, if he was to be taken off detached service, so he requested the Governor to make him a lieutenant colonel in that branch, a request that was authorized by the General Council on December 20, 1835. Governor Smith presented him with his commission four days later. He was thus in a position to go to the relief of Col. James C. Neill at San Antonio, and was so ordered some time in January 1836. The Governor disregarded his request to have this order revoked.

Travis had a momentary temptation to join an expedition to take Matamoras, which he heard was in preparation. Two men named Johnson and Grant had organized this quixotic enterprise. What Travis did not know at the time was that they had stripped the Alamo of weapons and supplies to outfit it. San Antonio, with Colonel Neill and only sixty men to defend it, was thus rendered all but indefensible against any attack in force by the enemy.

Travis first declared his intention to join the expedition, then decided against it.[9] He may have had in mind joining another expedition to Matamoras that Fannin had under consideration. Of course, our old friend the writer who sees nothing but selfish ambition in Travis' every act thinks he turned away from both expeditions because he saw no opportunity to lead either![10] Is it not more likely that he felt he was more needed at the Alamo? And then there was the matter of his orders. ...

Just how competent was Travis as a military man? Certainly the Governor had confidence in him as a soldier or he would not have chosen him to go to Colonel Neill's relief. Austin had also expressed satisfaction with the efficient way in which he carried out his orders. But perhaps the best evidence of official respect for his military judgment was a request from "an honorable member of the [General] Council" for his "views on the organization of an Army for the defence of Texas." His reply to that request is dated December 3, 1835. In it he outlined his plan for the kind of military organization he believed could repel the Mexican armies. Capt. J. W. Fannin had set forth his views in a letter concerning the Regular Army; Travis therefore addressed himself "more particularly to the subject of the organization of volunteer corps." It would be some time, he stated, before a regular army could be trained and equipped; meantime, he envisioned this volunteer army as filling the breach. Specifically, his plan was as follows:

That a law be passed, authorizing the executive to accept the services of, or raise, at least a Brigade of volunteers to be composed of two Regiments of from five to Eight hundred men each, to be subject while in service to the orders of a Brigadier General, who should be subordinate to the Commander in Chief of the regular army. That the field officers of the volunteer Brigade should be appointed by the Governor & council & the company officers elected by the companies, respectively. That there should be three Battalions of Infantry & one of Cavalry. That the Battalion of cavalry, should be composed of four companies of 40 rank & file & twelve officers or three companies of 60 rank & file each & the necessary number of officers. That cavalry should be commanded by a Lt. Col. who should be subject alone to the orders of the commander in chief for the time being. Here allow me to remark that I have been a little surprised that the Convention should have overlooked the establishment of a Cavalry Corps, for I consider that such a Battalion as I have indicated, is indispensible to the service of Texas during the present struggle. Do you wish to get information of the movements of a distant enemy? It must be done by cavalry. Do you wish to escort expresses? Guard Baggage while on the road? Charge a defeated & retreating enemy? Cut of[f] supplies of the enemy? Harrass an invading army by hanging upon his rear or forming ambuscades in his front? Do you wish to carry the war into the enemie's country as has been indicated? Do you wish to take him by surprise, or perform, any other movement requiring celerity & promptness? All these things must be done by cavalry and cavalry alone. In a word, all

the brilliant military exploits, which have ever been performed in time
& which we read of in the history of nations, have been accomplished
by celerity of movement, & promptness of action. You must have well
organized cavalry, before your armies will ever move quickly —
That the arms of the cavalry should be broadswords, pistols & double
barrelled shot guns or Yaugers. That the infantry should be armed as
other infantry in the service, except flanking companies — Perhaps the
volunteer infantry would be more effective armed with rifles or yaugers
— That the volunteer Brigades should be mustered for twelve months
unless the war should sooner be brought to a close and should be
subject to *regular discipline* & the *rules & articles of war*. A mob can do
wonders in a sudden burst of patriotism or of passion, but cannot be
depended on, as soldiers for a campaign —[11]

As will be seen from this excerpt, Travis thought that volunteers could not be relied upon over the long haul, but this view
was not based on prejudice alone. He had only recently tried to
raise a volunteer corps, but had been forced as late as January
29 to admit to the Governor that he had failed to recruit anything like the hundred men requested. Furthermore, he had
seen volunteers desert by dozens after every battle, most recently after the siege of Bexar. But one feels certain that their conduct at the Alamo removed this bias from his mind. There he
must have seen the true worth of those same sharp-shooting volunteers, such as Davy Crockett and his Tennessee boys, who
stuck in the face of certain death, when, perhaps, they did not
feel as strongly bound to as men under discipline of the regular
army.

On January 28, when Travis wrote Governor Smith "... I
have done every thing in my power to get ready to march to the
relief of Bexar," he had assembled barely enough horses and provisions for the thirty men he had recruited, who were "all regulars except four." He painted a gloomy picture of the prospects,
what with divided authority, lack of confidence in the strife-
torn government, and the desperate need for money, supplies,
and equipment. Nevertheless, he resolved to go on, and to obey
his orders, no matter under what adverse conditions. He enclosed
a list of men "who deserted on the roads from Washington & San
Felipe to this place." By "this place" he meant the camp at Bur-
man's on the Colorado, from which he was writing.[12]

And so, with his little band, he set out for San Antonio to reinforce the sixty men under Colonel Neill at the Alamo.

chapter

10

The Settling Doom

O<small>N</small> J<small>ANUARY</small> 6, 1836, Col. James C. Neill, in command of the Texan forces at San Antonio, wrote a letter to Governor Henry Smith and the General Council that was to split them and their adherents into warring camps and to affect directly the already desperate military situation. He described with stark realism the military plight of the garrison: the need for 100, or even 200, more soldiers than the 104 stationed there; their ragged and destitute condition; the need for medical supplies; and, above all, the lack of money. Two hundred men who had volunteered to protect the town had already deserted. He could not guarantee more would not follow unless they, the Governor and the Council, would "ameliorate our condition."

Governor Smith received the Neill letter on January 9. The subsequent events have been related elsewhere in this book: how he excoriated the General Council and blamed it for the state of military unpreparedness; how the insulted Council impeached him and recognized the Lieutenant Governor in his place; and how they succeeded in stripping him of much of his power. As Reuben M. Potter put it, Governor and General Council

... repudiated each other, and each claimed the obedience which was generally not given to either. Invasion was impending, and there seemed to be little more than anarchy to meet it.[1]

On January 14 Colonel Neill wrote Sam Houston for the third time about the same matters he had dealt with in his letter of the 6th to the Governor, protesting that

Fourteen days has expired since I commenced informing my superior officers of my situation, and not even an item of news have I received from any quarters.[2]

— 192

But, unknown to Colonel Neill, Houston wrote Governor Smith on January 17, enclosing his letter and informing him that he had ordered the destruction of all fortifications in Bexar. The Alamo was to be blown up and abandoned, for his conclusion was that "it will be impossible to keep up the station with volunteers."[3]

As has been related in the biography of Bowie, Houston ordered him to carry out this destruction of the Alamo. Bowie arrived there on January 19. He must have been influenced from the first by Colonel Neill, who was all for holding the fort. The two got on well together, at least for a time. In his letter of February 2 to the Governor, Bowie had nothing but praise for the commander, with whom he was "laboring night and day laying up provisions for a siege, encouraging our men, and calling on the Government for relief."[4] They had "come to the solemn resolution that we will rather die in these ditches than to give up to the enemy."[5] There was, however, another reason that Houston's evacuation order could not readily be carried out. They had too few draft animals to move the heavy artillery.

On January 23 Colonel Neill wrote the Governor requesting a writ by which the volunteer army could elect and send two delegates to the convention at Washington, Texas, assuring Smith of their support. He later received a letter describing the repudiation of Smith by the General Council and wrote him on January 27 expressing his astonishment "to find your body in such a disorganized situation." He alluded to an indignation meeting held by the soldiers on the 24th, at which they had censored the high-handed actions of Johnson and Grant in outfitting the Matamoras expedition with supplies and equipment from the Alamo.

Colonel Neill's great discouragement at this time is obvious. One can hardly blame him for requesting leave to go home, even if he had not had the excuse of illness in his family.

As has already been pointed out, Travis felt equally hopeless about the possibility of defending the Alamo, even before his departure for that place. In his letter of January 28 to the Governor he had described the extreme urgency of the situation. Of his own personal efforts he wrote as follows:

I have strained every nerve. I have used my personal credit and have slept neither day nor night since I rec'd orders to march — and with all these exertions, I have hardly been able to get horses and equipment for the few men I have.[6]

He arrived at the Alamo with his men early in the morning on February 3. Crockett came in around February 8, with twelve of his "Tennessee boys." Bowie arrived on January 19, with thirty soldiers from Goliad and accompanied, some say, by James Butler Bonham.

Bowie had thus been with Colonel Neill for two weeks prior to Travis' arrival, if not actually sharing the command, then coming pretty close to it. Travis' replacement of Colonel Neill upset that relationship, and something happened immediately to square the two off against each other.

The situation was as follows. Travis did not assume the command until around February 13, but some time before Colonel Neill left on the 11th, the volunteers got wind of the replacement. Like all volunteer forces of the time, they reserved the right to elect their own colonel, and so balked at having one chosen for them. Reuben M. Potter has given us the best account of what followed:

> The volunteers . . . wished to choose their own leader, and were willing to accept Travis only as second in command. They were, therefore, clamorous that Neill should issue an order for the election of a Colonel. To get over the matter without interfering with Travis's right, he prepared an order for the election of a Lieutenant-Colonel, and was about to depart, when his men, finding out what he had done, mobbed him, and threatened his life unless he should comply with their wishes. He felt constrained to yield, and on the amended order James Bowie was unanimously elected a full Colonel. . . . His election occurred early in February, 1836, about two weeks before the enemy came in sight; and Travis, who had just arrived or came soon after, found Bowie in command of the garrison, and claiming by virtue of the aforesaid election the right to command him and the re-enforcement he brought. They both had their headquarters at the Alamo, where their men were quartered, and there must have been a tacit understanding on both sides that conflict of authority should as far as possible be avoided. This, however, could not have continued many days but for the common bond of approaching peril.[7]

In Travis' slightly differing version, he stated that *he* issued the "order for the election," and he goes on to tell why he did "not solicit the command of this post." The matter of his friction

with Bowie, briefly dealt with in one of the preceding chapters
on Bowie, was so fundamental, however, that it all but drove him
from the Alamo. In all fairness, then, Travis' side of the controversy should be given. This can best be done by quoting one of
his letters to the Governor. Fortunately, he received strong confirmation of his statements in a letter written by Cap. John J.
Baugh. The Travis letter of February 13 is in part, as follows:

> My situation is truly awkward and delicate. Colonel Neill left me in
> command, but wishing to give satisfaction to the volunteers here and
> not wishing to assume any command over them, I issued an order for
> the election of an officer to command them with the exception of one
> company of volunteers that had previously engaged to serve under me.
> Bowie was elected by two small companies, and since his election has
> been roaring drunk all the time, has assumed all command & is pro-
> ceeding in a most disorderly and irregular manner — interfering with
> private property, releasing prisoners sentenced by court-martial & by
> the civil court & turning every thing topsy turvy. If I didn't feel my
> honor and that of my country comprometted [?compromised], I would
> leave here instantly for some other point with the troops under my
> immediate command as I am unwilling to be responsible for the drunk-
> en irregularities of any man.[8]

Captain Baugh, in his letter to Governor Smith of the same
date, threw some additional light on why the volunteers objected
to being commanded by Travis. Apparently it was not that they
had any personal objection to him, but because he was a "regular officer," a reason born of the depths of their contempt for any
regularized military service. The rest of Baugh's letter is worth
quoting in full, although one should remember that he, like Travis, seems to have had some prejudices against volunteers. It is
regrettable that there are no Bowie letters in existence giving his
side of the controversy. The pertinent parts of the Baugh letter
are as follows:

> An election was ... ordered by Col Travis and Bowie was elected
> without opposition. None but the volunteers voted and in fact, not all
> of them. The consequence was a split in the Garrison. Col. Travis as
> a matter of course, could not submit to the control of Bowie, and he
> (Bowie) availing himself of his great popularity among the volunteers
> seemed anxious to arrogate to himself the entire control.
> Things passed on in this way yesterday and today until at length
> they have become intollerable. Bowie as commander of the volunteers,
> has gone so far as to stop carts laden with goods of private families

removing into the country. He has ordered the Prison doors to be opened for the release of a Mexican convicted of theft who had been tried by a jury of 12 men among which was Col. Travis and Col. Bowie himself.

He has also ordered and effected the release of D. H. Barre, a private in the Regular Army attached to the Legion of Cavalry, who had been tried by a Court Martial and found guilty of desertion and actually deliberated [?liberated] him from Prison with a Corporal's Guard with loud huzzas: But the most extraordinary step of all and that which sets aside all law, Civil and Military is that which follows

Commandancy of Bejar
Feb. 13th 1836

Capt of Corps —

You are hereby required to release such Prisoners as may be under your direction for labor or otherwise.

James Bowie
Commander of Volunteer forces of Bejar.

Under this order the Mexicans who had been convicted by the civil authorities and the Soldiers convicted by Court-martial and some of whom had been placed in the Alamo, on public works were released.

Antonio Fuentes who had been released as above said presented himself to the judge under the protection of Capt. Baker of Bowie's volunteers and demanded his clothes which were in the Calaboose, stating that Col Bowie had set him at Liberty, whereupon the judge (Seguin) ordered him remanded to prison, which was accordingly done. As soon as this fact was reported to Bowie, he went in a furious manner, and demanded of the judge a release of the prisoner, which the Judge refused saying that "he would give up his office and let the Military appoint a judge." Bowie immediately sent to the Alamo for troops and paraded in the Square under Arms in a tumultuously [sic] and disorderly manner. Bowie, himself and many of his men being drunk which has been the case ever since he has been in command.

Col. Travis protested vigorously against these proceedings to the Judge and others, and as a friend to good order and anxious to escape the stigma which must inevitably follow he has drawn off his troops to the Medina where [he] believes he may be [as] useful as in the Garrison, at all events save himself from implication in this disgraceful business.

I have ventured to give you this hasty sketch of passing events, in justice to myself and others who have had no hand in these transactions.[9]

Subsequent events make it obvious that Travis never carried out his threat to draw "off his troops to the Medina," but he was really vexed with Bowie.

Above and *verso:* Letter of Travis and Bowie to Gov. Henry Smith, of February 14, 1836, describing the "very destitute situation" of the garrison and the division of military authority between the two men.

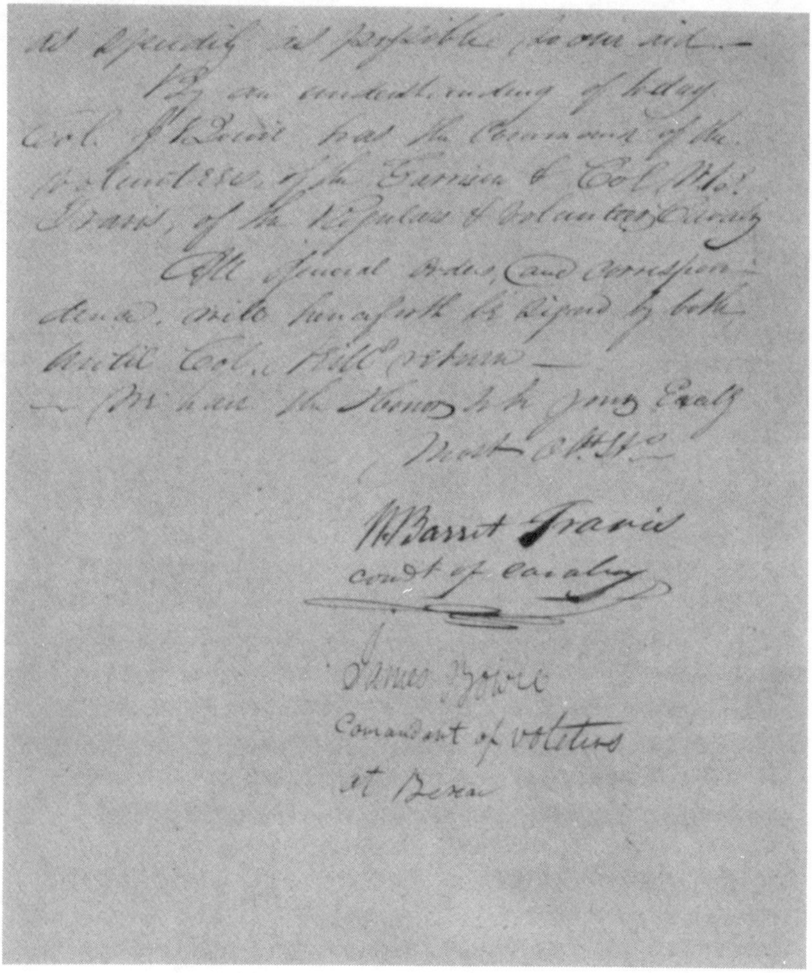
as speedily as possible for our aid.—
By an understanding of today
Col. J. Bowie has the Command of the
Volunteers of the Garrison & Col. W. B.
Travis, of the Regulars & Volunteer Cavalry
All general orders, and correspon-
dence, will henceforth be signed by both
until Col. Neill returns—
—We have the Honor to be your Excy
Most Obt Sts

W. Barret Travis
comdt of Cavalry

James Bowie
Comandant of volunteers
at Bexar

Reproduced by permission of the Director,
The Bancroft Library, University of California

We have no details concerning the Travis-Bowie "truce" negotiations, during which there must have been an exchange of salty words, some unprintable! But we do have evidence that such a truce was entered into, in the joint Travis-Bowie letter reproduced on the preceding pages. It will be noted that the pronoun "we" is used all the way through it. The most significant part of the communication is contained in the last two sentences, as follows:

> By and understanding of today Coln J. Bowie has the command of the volunteers of the garrison, and Col. W. B. Travis of the regulars and volunteer cavalry.
>
> All general orders and correspondence will henceforth be signed by both until Col. Neill's return.[10]

This was not the end of the feud, but they were to have only one more clash before illness forever removed Bowie from the scene as an active participant in the defense of the Alamo.

A number of writers have remarked upon the seemingly desultory nature of the training, preparations, and morale within the Alamo, in view of the expected Mexican attack. In the light of what has already been written here, the reasons for this state of affairs are not hard to guess. The forces were literally destitute of the commonest needs. More than half of them were volunteers who had been foraging for themselves and their horses ever since their arrival. They had not been paid. The town and countryside were fast becoming depleted of food, including beef cattle. Small wonder, then, that Travis and others who tried to institute daily drill met with little success. The truth is that many of the privates were hard pressed just to stay alive. They were actually able to perform little or no work in constructing the fortifications, so much of it had to be done by officers.

There was no feeling of extreme urgency. Most of the men, including Travis, gave little credence to rumors of impending attack, at least in the near future. Mexicans were constantly spreading old wives' tales, few of which had any basis in fact. In his book Dr. John Sutherland stated that most people believed Cos's defeat would make Santa Anna think twice before following in his footsteps.[11] Others felt that Cos had been disgraced by accepting such terms and that Santa Anna would be angered into swift retaliation, rather than being intimidated. In any event, these rumors flew thick and fast every day, and the Texans paid little attention to them.

The subject of warnings is especially interesting because it is possible that Travis received reliable intelligence of the Mexicans' approach as early as February 16, 1836. It came about in this way. One of his Mexican friends was Judge J. M. Rodrigues, with whom Travis was in almost daily contact on his way to and from the Alamo. It seems that Rodrigues received a definite report on the 15th from one Rives, his wife's cousin, that a large force of Mexicans was on its way. Rodrigues at once warned him, but Travis was not disposed to believe the Rives report.

Rodrigues relates in his *Memoirs* that he continued to warn Travis, who finally told him secretly that, regardless of the truth or falsity of the rumors, he and his men were going to hold the Alamo as long as they could, even if they all died trying. There is the interesting possibility that Travis *did* believe this intelligence but pretended not to in order to keep from worrying his men unnecessarily. It is also possible that he did not want to run the risk of mass desertions from the depleted garrison, or to increase the alarm among the citizens.

One of Rives' reports clearly in the class of untenable rumors concerned Santa Anna. Rives avowed that he saw the general in disguise on the night of February 21 at a fandango given by some Texans on Soledad Street. He also insisted that he knew Santa Anna by sight.

The time pattern is such that the Mexican leader *could* have attended the ball, except for certain factors that make it very unlikely that he did so. He could have learned through his spies that the ball was to be given on the night of the 21st. What better time to attack the garrison than on the morning of the 22nd? But it rained heavily that night, and the Medina, on the bank of which Santa Anna and his men had camped, rose so high that crossing it was practically impossible. Santa Anna had many bad qualities, but he was not stupid. Even if he had been able to attend the ball in disguise, it is unlikely that he would have risked discovery and capture. Too, it would have involved some risk, discomfort, and danger of a disastrous accident while making the crossing. If Rives, the self-constituted "intelligence offi-

cer," went this far, Travis can be excused for placing little re-
liance on his reports![12]

But the report brought in by Blaz Herrera, a cousin of Juan
Seguin, on the evening of February 20 was harder to ignore. On
the 18th Herrera had actually observed Santa Anna crossing the
Rio Grande with about 5,000 troops. Travis called together his
chief aides to hear Herrera's story. Even with this startling and
seemingly authentic news, some of them considered it on a par
with other Mexican "yarns" and therefore entitled to little serious
consideration. So the meeting adjourned without reaching any
decisions.[13]

But, with the increasing departure of the Mexicans from the
town and surrounding country, Travis must have concluded before long that so much smoke must denote fire. On the morning
of the 23rd he placed a sentinel on the roof of the church, with
orders to ring the bell if he sighted the enemy. He then went to
his room, but he had scarcely sat down when he heard the bell
ringing and the sentinel crying out that he had sighted Mexican
troops.

Travis joined Doctor Sutherland and others gathered in front
of the church. He decided to send out scouts at once to see if they
could get a line on the strength and location of the approaching
Mexican forces. Doctor Sutherland and John W. Smith volunteered their services. They had ridden only a short distance from
town when they came upon the force of Mexican cavalry numbering a possible 1,500. While they were returning, the doctor's
unshod horse slipped on the rain-soaked ground and fell on him,
injuring his legs; but with Smith's help he managed to remount,
and the two returned safely.

Travis was at last convinced. He immediately moved his headquarters into the Alamo, together with all of his men who had
been stationed or were, for other reasons, outside the improvised
citadel.[14] He then wrote to Gonzales for help. The ailing Doctor
Sutherland again offered to act as his courier and was again accepted. Travis also sent a similar letter by another messenger to
Fannin at Goliad.

The garrison was in a bad way when it came to supplies. There
was very little on hand to eat. Their cattle, which they had been
accustomed to driving in for slaughter as needed, were now cut

off. They had very little corn and practically no coffee, sugar, or salt. As luck would have it, they obtained both corn and beef merely by chance. Then they set to work in earnest on some of the neglected defenses.

The few letters Travis wrote from the Alamo between February 24 and March 3, 1836, are of inestimable value for the Texan side of the Alamo story during the siege. Everything about them is of interest, even notations made on them by messengers, and this applies particularly to his most famous letter, written on February 24 and addressed to "The People of Texas and all Americans in the world." There are many regrettable gaps in the Travis story, but if one letter can epitomize the man, this must be it. Perhaps it tells us all we *need* to know about William Barret Travis and, for lack of other evidence, all we *can* know of the thoughts and feelings of the men under him, for whom he was really writing.

"Here they come!"

"Give Me Help, Oh My Country!"

T RAVIS' FIRST official message from the Alamo was addressed to Judge Andrew Ponton and others in Gonzales, and was as follows:

Commandancy of Bexar
Feb. 23, 3 o'clock p.m., 1836
To Andrew Ponton, Judge, and the Citizens of Gonzales:
    The enemy in large force is in sight. We want men and provisions. Send them to us. We have 150 men and are determined to defend the Alamo to the last. Give us assistance.
W. B. Travis,
Lieut-Col. Commanding.
P. S. Send an express to San Felipe with the news — night & day —
Travis.[1]

Governor Smith immediately had this letter printed as a handbill, followed by a strong "Appeal to the People of Texas" in which he gave his own summary of the desperate circumstances at the Alamo. He so far misjudged the situation, however, as to state that the men there might be able to hold out as long as thirty days. It is difficult to understand such an estimate because, by now, he must have been aware of their desperate lack of almost everything. In any event, he made a strong appeal to *"all* who are able to bear arms" to "rally without a moment's delay to the aid of your besieged countrymen." His handbill was dated February 27, 1836.

Reference has already been made to Travis' letter of February 23 to Colonel Fannin. Knowing that Fannin had a sizable force at his disposal at Goliad, he must have counted heavily on his help. According to Yoakum, Fannin received the dispatch on the 25th, and was able to set out on the 28th

... with three hundred men and four pieces of artillery, leaving Captain Westover in command at Goliad ... But he had only proceeded two hundred yards, when one of his wagons broke down, and, having but one yoke of oxen to each piece of artillery, he was compelled to double his teams in order to get them ... across the river. Besides, his only provisions consisted of a tierce of rice and a little dried beef. A council of war was therefore held, when it was determined to return to Goliad, which was accordingly done.[2]

Fannin has been blamed by some for this decision, but it must be remembered that he had his own rendezvous with fate in the person of General Sesma, who, by the 29th, was already marching to meet him.

Thirty-two men recruited from Gonzales entered the Alamo on March 1 under command of Capt. John W. Smith, bringing the total number of Texans in the fortress to slightly over 180.[3]

Although it was followed by others in the same vein, Travis' letter of February 24, 1836, "To the People of Texas & all Americans in the world" is certainly his most famous. Although reproduced in facsimile and many times printed, it is well worth repeating in full because it portrays its writer at his best, and it puts in its most eloquent form the pathos of the doomed garrison:

Commandancy of the Alamo —
  Bexar, Feby. 24th 1836 —

    To the People of Texas & all Americans <u>in the world</u> —
  Fellow Citizens & Compatriots

I am besieged, by a thousand or more of the Mexicans under Santa Anna — I have sustained a continual Bombardment & cannonade for 24 hours & have not lost a man — The enemy has demanded a surrender at discretion, otherwise, the garrison are to be put to the sword, if the fort is taken — I have answered the demand with a cannon shot, & our flag still waves proudly from the walls — <u>I shall never surrender or retreat.</u> Then, I call on you in the name of Liberty, of patriotism & & everything dear to the American Character, to come to our aid, with all despatch — The enemy is receiving reinforcements daily & will no doubt increase to three or four thousand in four or five days. If this call is neglected, I am determined to sustain myself as long as possible & die like a soldier who never forgets what is due to his own honor & that of his country —

<u>Victory or Death.</u>

William Barret Travis
Lt. Col. Comdt

P S The Lord is on our side — When the enemy appeared in sight we had not three bushels of corn — We have since found in deserted houses 80 or 90 bushels & got into the walls 20 or 30 head of Beeves —

Travis[4]

Not all of the notes on the cover and other portions of this letter have, so far as I can determine, been accurately published, and they are of more than passing interest. On the back is an endorsement, apparently made by Travis himself:

> To
>   The People of Texas
>   and
>   All Americans[5]

Also:

Send this to San Felipe by Express
Night & day ———[6]

Another note on the back of the letter was made by "L. Smither," obviously Lancelot Smithers, one of the messengers from the Alamo. Amelia Williams states that he left the Alamo on February 23, 1836, and then quotes a letter of February 24 "To All the Inhabitants of Texas," which he must have taken to Nacogdoches. But he also wrote the following note on the back of the Travis letter, which may actually have been taken from the Alamo by other hands:

N b [Nota bene?] I hope that Everyone will Rondivis at Gonzales as soon [as] posible as the Brave Soldiers are suffering do not neglect this powder is vary scarce and should not be delad one moment.

L. Smither[7]

Amelia Williams does not quote quite correctly the additional endorsement by Albert Martin, another messenger, as I find it. It is as follows:

Since the above was written I heard a very Long Canonade during the whole day. Think there must have been an attack made upon the Alamo. We were short of ammunition when I left. ——— ——— all the men you can ——— ———.

Albert Martin[8]

Still another fragmentary statement by an unknown hand is worth including. As nearly as I can decipher the writing, it is as follows:

When I left there was but 150 determined to ——— die. Tomorrow
——— ——— ——— with what men I can ——— ——— at all events.
Col. Almonte is there. The troops are under the Command of Gen
Seisma.[9]

In his letter of February 25, 1836, to Sam Houston, Travis described the action since the siege began on the 23rd and lauded
the conduct of several men, although he felt "that it would be
injustice to discriminate." He must have had only scant hope,
even this early, of receiving reinforcements. He concluded:

Do hasten on aid to me as rapidly as possible, as from the superior
number of the enemy, it will be impossible for us to keep them out
much longer. If they overpower us, we fall sacrifice at the shrine of our
country, and we hope posterity and our country will do our memory
justice. Give me help, oh my Country! Victory or Death![10]

The last of his official letters from the Alamo Travis directed
"To the President of the Convention" on March 3, 1836. After
reviewing the action since February 25, which he thought they
ought to be aware of from his letter of that date to Sam Houston,
he summarized the succeeding events to date, describing the
gun emplacements and encircling "entrenched encampments" of
the enemy, who had continued to keep up a steady but almost
wholly ineffective bombardment, with no loss of life to the Texans. He made the by now routine statements about his efforts to
procure reinforcements and the failure thereof, and concerning
their other most pressing needs, particularly for ammunition. He
reiterated his strong belief in the importance of the battle being
fought there:

... This neighborhood will be the great and decisive battle ground.
The power of Santa Anna is to be met here or in the colonies; we had
better meet it here, than to suffer a war of desolation to rage in our
settlements. A blood red banner floats from the church of Bexar, and
in the camp above us, in token that the war is one of vengeance
against rebels; they have declared us as such, and demanded that we
should surrender at discretion, or that this garrison should be put to the
sword. Their threats have no influence on me or my men....[11]

In a letter of March 3 to a friend (not identified in the *Houston
Telegraph and Texas Register* for March 24, 1836, where it was
printed) Travis repeated practically all of the material in this
last official letter. He may have written other letters, but most of

them have been lost or destroyed. One interesting exception is a note, written on a piece of wrapping paper, that survived by a miracle long enough to fall into the hands of an editor. Which newspaper first printed it is not known. The *Texas Monument* for March 31, 1852, published at LaGrange, Texas, picked it up from the *Victoria Advocate*. The comments, as well as the letter, seem worth quoting:

Messrs. Editors: — Among the most interesting reminiscences of 1836, which I have seen, is a note addressed by Col. Travis, from the Alamo, to a gentleman in Washington county, who had charge of his son. It ran thus

"Dear Sir: — Take care of my little boy. If the country should be saved I may make him a splendid fortune. But if the country should be lost, and I should perish, he will have nothing but the proud recollection that he is the son of a man who died for his country.

"Yours, &c.,
"Wm. B. Travis."

It was written on a scrap of yellow wrapping paper, and seemed to have been done in great haste. The paper is torn and ragged, and the date quite effaced. It was transmitted by that last courier who brought the news that "the summons to surrender had been answered with a cannon shot, and the flag of Texas still waved on the walls." When the courier was about to depart on this dangerous errand, the hero snatched a hasty moment from ... his ... post, to dispatch this last note on his private business. . . .

R. Monon.

Goliad, Jan. 29, 1852.[12]

And so the last thoughts he had time to commit to paper concerned his son. But he must also have been thinking of his little daughter, who probably had a place of special affection in his heart. In May 1835 he had made a will. In it he bequeathed equal shares of his estate to each of his children, but he also specified that, in addition, anything coming to him from his father's estate should go to his daughter.[13]

Travis had long known, but perhaps only now fully realized, that he and his men were doomed. But there was no turning back. And now that he had lost all hope that help would arrive, he somehow felt relieved.

"God help us!" he said softly. It was not merely an exclamation. It was a prayer.

The Siege

This painting portrays the siege just before investment of the church. There is no historic basis for the white flag shown flying from the fort.

THE MISSION of the Alamo, named the Mission of San Jose when it was founded on the bank of the Rio Grande in 1703, was relocated and renamed three times before it was moved to its present location in 1744 and rechristened by its present name. The church, only one of the mission buildings, was in the form of a cross, with stone walls five feet thick and twenty-two and a half feet high. The main part of this structure was roofless at the time of the siege. The windows were high above the ground, and the front had the usual relief carvings and statues. The doors were of heavy oak.

Adjoining the church on the left arm of the cross was the convent yard, about a hundred square feet in area, with walls sixteen feet high and three and a half feet thick. At the southeastern corner of this yard was a sally port, defended by a small redoubt. The convent and hospital building was of adobe, two stories high and eighteen feet wide, and extended along the west side of the yard 191 feet. It was divided into one long hospital room and a number of small cells.

The main plaza extended before the church and convent, with one side toward the river. It was somewhat over two acres in area and was enclosed by a wall eight feet high and slightly less than three feet thick. On the southern end of this plaza were a prison and some barracks.

These constituted the important structures of the Mission, which was isolated from the town by the San Antonio River, except for a cluster of miserable *jacals* on the river's east bank.

The *acequias*, or canals, supplied water to the Mission.

It takes no military expert to conclude that such a place would be impractical as a fort.

The complete story of what went on during the siege of the Alamo is not, and never can be, known. And, in connection with an event so important in Texas history, it might be expected that many conflicting stories would be told about the details by

RENDEZVOUS AT THE ALAMO

witnesses and alleged witnesses, and that is exactly what occurred. Faced with these many varying accounts, the events and statistics of which often differ radically, the wise historian will choose one that is generally conceded to be freest from error. With a few dissenting voices, that choice is the account of Capt. Reuben M. Potter, who was living in Matamoras at the time of the siege, who knew many of the high-ranking Mexican officers, and who embodied his careful investigations in his famous work, *The Fall of the Alamo*, first published in 1878.[1] In part, beginning with the advent of the Mexican forces into San Antonio, Captain Potter's article is as follows:

The main army of operation against Texas moved from Laredo upon San Antonio in four successive detachments. This was rendered necessary by the scarcity of pasture and water on certain portions of the route. . . .

The advance from Laredo, consisting of the dragoon regiment of Dolores and three battalions of infantry, commanded by Santa Ana[2] in person, arrived at San Antonio on the afternoon of February 22. No regular scouting service seems to have been kept up from the post of Bowie and Travis, owing probably to division and weakness of authority, for, though the enemy was expected, his immediate approach was not known to many of the inhabitants till the advance of his dragoons was seen descending the slope west of the San Pedro. A guard was kept in town with a sentinel on top of the church, yet the surprise of the population was so nearly complete that one or more American residents engaged in trade fled to the Alamo, leaving their stores open. The garrison, however, received more timely notice, and the guard retired in good order to the fort. The confusion at the Alamo, which for the time being was great, did not impede a prompt show of resistance. In the evening, soon after the enemy entered the town, a shot from the 18-pounder of the fort was followed by a parley, of which different accounts have been given. According to Santa Ana's official report, after the shell was thrown, a white flag was sent out by the garrison with an offer to evacuate the fort if allowed to retire unmolested and in arms, to which reply was made that no terms would be admitted short of an unconditional surrender. Seguin, however, gave . . . a more reliable version of the affair. He related that after the firing a parley was sounded and a white flag raised by the invaders. Travis was not inclined to respond to it; but Bowie, without consulting him, and much to his displeasure, sent a flag of truce to demand what the enemy wanted. Their General, with his usual duplicity, denied having sounded a parley or raised a flag, and informed the messenger that the garrison could be recognized only as rebels, and be allowed no other terms than a surrender at discretion. When informed of this, Travis harangued his men and administered to them an oath that they would resist to the last.

The officers obtained a supply of corn, and added to their stock of beef after the enemy entered the town. On the same day a well, which a fatigue party had been digging within the walls, struck a fine vein of water. This was fortunate, for the irrigating canal, which flowed past the foot of the wall, was shortly after cut off by the enemy. The investment had not yet commenced, nor was the firing ... renewed that evening, and the few citizens who had taken refuge in the fort succeeded in leaving it during the night, if not earlier.

On the night of the 22d of February the enemy planted two batteries on the west side of the river, one bearing west and the other southwest from the Alamo .... They were the next day silenced by the fire of the 18-pounder of the fort, but were restored to activity on the following night. On the 24th another body of Mexican troops, a regiment of cavalry and three battalions of infantry arrived; and then the fort was invested and a regular siege commenced, which, counting from that day till the morning of the 6th of March, occupied eleven days. By the 27th seven more besieging batteries were planted, most of them on the east side of the river, and bearing on the northwest, southwest, and south of the fort; but there were none on the east. As that was the only direction in which the garrison would be likely to attempt retreat, Santa Ana wished to leave a temptation to such flitting, while he prepared to intercept it by forming his cavalry camp on what is now called the Powder House Hill, east of the Alamo.

During the first few days occasional sallies were made by the garrison to obstruct the enemy's movements and burn houses which might cover them. The operations of the siege ... consisted of an active but rather ineffective cannonade and bombardment, with occasional skirmishing by day and frequent harassing alarms by night, designed to wear out the garrison with want of sleep. No assault was attempted ... till the final storming took place. The enemy had no siege train, but only light field pieces and howitzers; yet a breach was opened in the northern barrier ... near the northeast angle, and the chapel was the only building that withstood the cannonade firmly, as the balls often went clean through the walls of the others. ...

... The first sight of the enemy created as much confusion with as little panic at the Alamo as might be expected among men who had known as little of discipline as they did of fear. ... Yet amid the disorder of that hour no one seemed to think of flight; the first damaging shock, caused by the sight of the enemy, must have been cured by the first shell that he threw ....

The conflict of authority between Bowie and Travis, owing probably to the caution in which neither was deficient, had luckily produced no serious collision; and it was perhaps as fortunate that, at about the second day of the siege, the rivalry was cut short by a prostrating illness of the former, when Bowie was stricken by an attack of pneumonia, which would probably have proved fatal, had not its blow been anticipated by the sword. This left Travis in undisputed command.

The investment was not too rigid to admit of the successful exit of couriers by night, and one or two had been sent out, since the enemy appeared, with letters to Colonel Fannin at Goliad, asking for aid. On the 29th of February it was resolved to send an officer, who, in addition to bearing despatches, might make his own influence and information available .... Captain Seguin was recommended by most of the officers; for, as he was of Spanish race and language, and well acquainted with the surrounding country, it was thought that he would be more likely than anyone of his rank to succeed in passing the enemy's lines. Travis wished to retain him in the garrison; but at a council of war, held on the night of the 29th, he yielded to the wishes of the majority. That night Seguin and his orderly, Antonio Cruz Oroche, prepared for the sally. Another of his Mexican recruits, named Alexandro de la Garza, had already been sent as a courier to the Provisional Government. Having no horse or equipments for himself, the Captain requested and obtained those of Bowie, who was already so ill that he hardly recognized the borrower. To him and the rest Seguin bade what proved to be a last adieu, and sallying from the postern on the northern side, took the high road to the east. As might be expected, the rank and file had begun to look with jealousy on any departure from within . . .; and when Seguin produced the order . . . to pass him and his orderly out, the sentinel at the postern began a rude comment; but a few words from the Captain, intimating that his errand was one which might bring safety, at once soothed the rough soldier, who bade him God-speed.

The road which the two horsemen took passed near the cavalry camp of the enemy, and where it crossed their lines was stationed a guard of dragoons, who were then resting, dismounted. Seguin and his man rode leisurely up towards them, responding in Spanish to the hail of their sentinel that they were countrymen. They were doubtless taken for Mexican rancheros of that neighborhood, and seemed to be riding up to report; but, when near enough for a bold start, they dashed past the guard at full speed. The hurried fire of the troopers was ineffective, and before they were in the saddle the fugitives, who were both well mounted, were far ahead. The latter then took to the bush and made good their escape. The next day Seguin met an officer from Fannin's post, who informed him that his mission would be wholly unavailing, and advised him to join the camp then forming at Gonzales, which he did.

On the following night, the 1st of March, a company of thirty-two men from Gonzales made its way through the enemy's lines, and entered the Alamo never again to leave it. This must have raised the force to 188 men or thereabouts, as none of the original number of 156 had fallen.

On the night of the 3d of March, Travis sent out another courier with a letter of that date to the government, which reached its destination. In that last despatch[3] he says: "With a hundred and forty-five men I have held this place ten days against a force variously estimated from 1,500 to 6,000, and I shall continue to hold it till I get relief from my countrymen, or I will perish in the attempt. We have had a shower of bombs and cannon-balls continually falling among us the whole time, yet none of us have fallen. We have been miraculously preserved." As this was but two days and three nights before the final assault, it is quite possible that not a single defender was stricken down till the fort was stormed. . . .

In stating the force of the garrison during the previous ten days, Travis did not include the little re-enforcement which had come in only two days before; yet, as he mentions but 145, while the garrison is known to have numbered 156 when the enemy appeared, he must have rated eleven as ineffective or absent. A part of them may have been counted out as departed couriers, and the rest had perhaps sunk under the fatigue of duty. Had there been any wounded, he would probably have referred to them.

On the 4th of March Santa Ana called a council of war, and fixed the morning of the 6th for the final assault. The besieging force now around the Alamo, comprising all the Mexican troops which had yet arrived, consisted of the two dragoon regiments of Dolores and Tampico, which formed a brigade, commanded by General Andrade, two companies or batteries of artillery under Colonel Ampudia, and six battalions of infantry, namely, Los Zapadores (engineer troops), Jimenes, Guerrero, Matamoras, Toluca, and Tres Villas. These six battalions of foot were to form the storming forces. The order for the attack . . . was signed by General Amador, as Chief of Staff. The infantry were directed at a certain hour between midnight and dawn to form at convenient distances from the fort in four columns of attack and a reserve. . . . A certain number of scaling ladders, axes, and fascines were to be borne by particular columns. A commanding officer, with a second to replace him in case of accident, was named, and a point of attack designated for each column. The cavalry were to be stationed at suitable points around the fort to cut off fugitives . . . . These dispositions were [later] modified . . . . The immediate direction of the assault seems to have been intrusted to General Castrillon, a Spaniard by birth and a brilliant soldier. Santa Ana took his station, with a part of his staff and all the bands of music, at a battery about five hundred yards south of the Alamo and near the old bridge, from which post a signal was to be given by a bugle-note for the columns to move simultaneously at double-quick time against the fort. . . .

When the hour came, the south guns of the Alamo were answering

Reproduced courtesy of the Library of Congress

SANTA ANNA

Although undated, this photograph was obviously taken in later life.

the batteries which fronted them; but the music was silent till the blast of a bugle was followed by the rushing tramp of soldiers. The guns of the fort opened upon the moving masses, and Santa Ana's bands struck up the assassin note of *deguello*, or no quarter. But a few and not very effective discharges of cannon from the works could be made before the enemy were under them, and it was probably not till then that the worn and wearied garrison was fully mustered. Castrillon's column arrived first at the foot of the wall, but was not the first to enter. The guns of the north, where Travis commanded in person, probably raked the breach, and this or the fire of the riflemen brought the column to a disordered halt, and Colonel Duque, who commanded the battalion of Toluca, fell dangerously wounded; but, while this was occurring, the column from the west crossed the barrier on that side by escalade at a point north of the centre, and, as this checked resistance at the north, Castrillon shortly after passed the breach. It was probably while the enemy was thus pouring into the large area that Travis fell at his post, for his body, with a single shot in the forehead, was found beside the gun at the northwest angle. The outer walls and batteries, all except one gun . . . were now abandoned by the defenders. In the mean time Cos had again proved unlucky. His column was repulsed from the chapel, and his troops fell back in disorder behind the old stone stable and huts that stood south of the southwest angle. There they were soon rallied and led into the large area by General Amador . . . . He probably followed the escalade of the column from the west.

This all passed within a few minutes after the bugle sounded. The garrison, when driven from the thinly manned outer defences, whose early loss was inevitable, took refuge in the buildings before described, but mainly in the long barrack; and it was not till then, when they became more concentrated and covered within, that the main struggle began. They were more concentrated as to space, not as to unity of command; for there was no communicating between buildings, nor, in all cases, between rooms. There was little need of command, however, to men who had no choice left but to fall where they stood before the weight of numbers. There was now no retreating from point to point, and each group of defenders had to fight and die in the den where it was brought to bay. From the doors, windows, and loopholes of several rooms around the area the crack of the rifle and the hiss of the bullet came fierce and fast; as fast the enemy fell and recoiled in his first efforts to charge. The gun beside which Travis fell was now turned against the buildings, as were also some others, and shot after shot was sent crashing through the doors and barricades of the several rooms. Each ball was followed by a storm of musketry and a charge; and thus room after room was carried at the point of the bayonet, when all within them died fighting to the last. The struggle was made up of a number of separate and desperate combats, often hand to hand, between squads of the garrison and bodies of the enemy. The bloodiest spot about the fort was the long barrack and the ground in front of it, where the enemy fell in heaps.

... According to Mr. Ruiz, then the Alcalde of San Antonio, who, after the action, was required to point out the slain leaders to Santa Ana, the body of Crocket[2] was found in the west battery ...; and we may infer that he either commanded that point or was stationed there as a sharpshooter. The common fate overtook Bowie in his bed in one of the rooms of the low barrack, when he probably had but a few days of life left in him; yet he had enough remaining, it is said, to shoot down with his pistols more than one of his assailants ere he was butchered on his couch. ...

The chapel, which was the last point taken, was carried by a *coup de main* after the fire of the other buildings was silenced. ... The inmates of this last stronghold, like the rest, fought to the last, and continued to fire down from the upper works after the enemy occupied the floor. ... Towards the close of the struggle Lieutenant Dickenson,[2] with his child in his arms, or, as some accounts say, tied to his back, leaped from the east embrasure of the chapel, and both were shot in the act. Of those he left behind him, the bayonet soon gleaned what the bullet had left; and in the upper part of that edifice the last defender must have fallen. ...

The Alamo had fallen. ... Travis and his band fell under the Mexican Federal flag of 1824, instead of the Lone Star of Texas, although Independence, unknown to them, had been declared by the new Convention four days before at Washington, on the Brazos. They died for a Republic of whose existence they never knew. The action, according to Santa Ana's report, lasted thirty minutes. ... Castrillon, not Santa Ana, was the soul of the assault. The latter remained at his south battery, viewing the operations from the corner of a house which covered him, till he supposed the place was nearly mastered, when he moved up towards the Alamo, escorted by his aids and bands of music, but turned back on being greeted by a few shots from the upper part of the chapel. He, however, entered the area towards the close of the scene, and directed some of the last details of the butchery. ... About the time the area was entered, a few men, cut off from inward retreat, leaped from the barriers, and attempted flight, but were all sabred or speared by the cavalry except one, who succeeded in hiding himself under a small bridge of the irrigating ditch. There he was discovered and reported a few hours after by some laundresses engaged in washing near the spot. He was executed. Half an hour or more after the action was over a few men were found concealed in one of the rooms under some mattresses. The officer to whom the discovery was first reported entreated Santa Ana to spare their lives; but he was sternly rebuked, and the men ordered to be shot, which was done. ... A negro belonging to Travis, the wife of Lieutenant Dickenson, ... and a few

Mexican women with their children were the only inmates of the fort whose lives were spared.

* * *

The [best] estimate ... of [the number of] infantry which formed the assaulting force of the Alamo ... [is] 2,500 .... 500 killed and wounded. ...

* * *

... A few hours after the action the bodies of the slaughtered garrison were gathered by the victors, laid in three heaps, mingled with fuel, and burned, though their own dead were interred. On the 25th of February, 1837, the bones and ashes of the defenders were, by order of General Houston, collected, as well as could then be done, for burial by Colonel Seguin, then in command at San Antonio. The bones were placed in a large coffin, which, together with the gathered ashes, was interred with military honors. The place of burial was a peach orchard, then outside of the Alamo village and a few hundred yards from the fort. ... Its identity is irrecoverably lost.

As is well known, all attempts to locate the remains of the Alamo heroes have failed. Of several monuments to them, the earliest, made from stones of the fortress, was erected in 1841, the latest, the well-known Alamo Cenotaph in Alamo Plaza, in 1939.

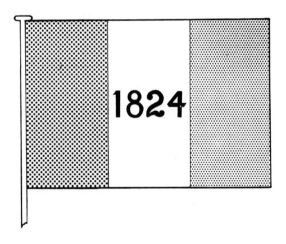

The Myth-Makers
and Military "Experts"

THE MYTHS, legends, and hoaxes that have sprung up around the Alamo, the siege, and the men who died there have, up to this point, been studiously avoided. There is, however, a class of stories not strictly factual that may have some basis in fact and thus be in some measure true. At best, it cannot now be determined with certainty where, in such stories, fact ends and fiction begins. The story of Lieutenant Dickerson's attempt to escape with his child is one that even Potter takes seriously. The Moses Rose escape story, on the other hand, is generally believed to be fictitious; but it *could* be true. Certainly we do not have the facts at hand to *disprove* it.

The only concern we can have here with any of these stories is that some of them concern Bowie, Crockett, and Travis, their conduct during the siege, how they died, and even their alleged "survival." They range from patently ridiculous fabrications to anecdotes that can be disproved by the testimony of eyewitnesses, by circumstances, and by our knowledge of the men involved. Some of them are repeated here, not because they require refutation, but because of their interest to students of the lives of the three subjects of this book.

The "survival" stories are perhaps the most common. One such yarn about Crockett originated with General Cos, who told it to a Dr. George Patrick in 1836, when Cos was a prisoner at Anahuac. It seems that Patrick expressed an interest in whether the General saw Crockett at the Alamo, whereupon Cos told him an absurd story of finding Crockett locked in one of the rooms of the barracks after the siege, spotless and well-dressed — presumably in buckskins and coonskin cap! Obviously he was trying to create the impression that Crockett had not participated in the fighting, even to the point of soiling his hands! According to Cos, he identified himself and told how, while on a visit, he had accidentally got caught in the Alamo after it was too late to escape. As in the majority of the survival stories concerning these three men, Crockett is portrayed wholly out of character, begging abjectly for his life, as he would never have done, only to be murdered by order of Santa Anna.[1] Josephus Conn Guild also perpetuated the persistent rumor that Crockett and five others survived the siege. He avowed that they

... surrendered to Castillion [sic], under promise of his protection, but being taken before Santa Anna, they were by his orders instantly put to death. Col. Crockett fell with a dozen swords sheathed in his breast.[2]

Is this not the type of story told countless times in the past about famous men after they died? Actually, no one would have been more likely to know the facts concerning Crockett's death than General Cos. Did he fabricate this malicious tale in an attempt to ruin Crockett's reputation? If so, he failed miserably.

Niles' National Register for April 25, 1840, carried a note that Crockett's son, John, then a congressman from Tennessee, had received "information inducing him to believe that the report in relation to his father being in one of the mines of Mexico, is correct."[3] The June 6 issue of the same year carried another note to the effect that *"The Texas Sentinel* pronounced the story ... to be a hoax."[4] But John Crockett was in sufficient doubt as to his father's death to write to the Secretary of State, whom he asked to institute an investigation of the matter through the minister to Mexico.[5]

The source of John Crockett's agitation was undoubtedly a letter dated February 6, 1840, from William C. White to the editor of a paper identified merely as "the Gazette." White had allegedly met a man who said he was Crockett, working in the Salinas mine near Guadalajara. Whether this prisoner was only seeking a means to escape, or had some other motive, no one knows; but he related a plausible story of his capture by the Mexicans and acted desperately (and convincingly) anxious to let his wife and children know of his fate. A clipping of this letter was enclosed with the letter referred to above of John Crockett to the Secretary of State. It seems likely that, had there been anything to this statement, the matter would not have been dropped, particularly as the request for an investigation was made by a congressman to the Secretary of State. It seems likely that this may have been merely a device of the prisoner to attract attention to his plight. The ruse would have been particularly logical if he were an American.

James Bowie's death was probably not a good subject for the myth-makers, since his accident occurred soon after he entered the Alamo and literally kept him confined to a cot for the rest of his life. Nevertheless, Madame Candelaria, who acted as his nurse and who apparently never told exactly the same story twice about the siege, stated on one occasion that Bowie "died of pneumonia the day before the battle of the Alamo." By "battle" it is assumed she meant the last day of the siege. But she persisted in her story that she received two wounds from Mexican soldiers while shielding him with her body, an act that would have been wholly illogical if he had been dead at the time.[6]

A. J. Sowell, in his *Rangers and Pioneers of Texas*, tells a story related to him by a Mexican fifer named Polin, who entered the Alamo after the siege, following Santa Anna as he sought to identify some of the dead Texans. In this astonishing story Polin stated that, just as the pile of bodies of the Texans was to be ignited, some soldiers brought in a cot upon which lay a sick man whom the captain of the detail identified as "no other than the infamous Bowie." The considerable conversation of the two deals with Bowie's alleged disloyalty in fighting against Mexico, and ends in violence. The gruesome details hardly bear repetition, but the Captain first (allegedly) had Bowie's tongue cut out, then had him pitched alive on the burning funeral pile. Only a fertile and warped imagination could have invented these and the remaining details, but Polin must have had such an imagination.[7] Madame Candelaria, Mrs. Dickerson, and Francisco Ruiz, alcalde of San Antonio, as well as others, testified that Bowie was found dead on his cot after the siege. There is almost no doubt that this was the case.

In spite of the evidence that Travis died early in the siege from a bullet in the forehead, the myth-makers also gave various versions of his death. Two Mexican messengers, Borgarra and Perez, stated that he shot himself rather than be taken prisoner by the Mexicans. Even Andrew Briscoe, Travis' close friend, whose account of the siege was published in the *New Orleans Post and Union* of March 28, 1836, so stated.[8] Again, the weight of evidence is against this allegation.

Another version of Travis' death was provided by one G. Norton Galloway in 1886, on the basis of a story allegedly told him by a Mexican soldier. It seems that *neither* Travis nor Crockett was killed during the siege, but, "utterly worn out by sleepless nights of watching and long-continued fighting," they fell asleep among the corpses, and were allegedly not detected! This account continues:

> When discovered, Colonel Travis gave a Mexican soldier some gold, and while conversing with him, General Cos, with whom Colonel Travis had dealt very generously when San Antonio was captured by the Americans, appeared. Cos warmly embraced Travis, and induced other Mexicans, among them General Castillion [sic], to join with him in asking Santa Anna to spare Travis' life. Then David Crockett also wearily arose to his feet from among the corpses. The brutal Santa Anna was terribly enraged at the disobedience of his orders, saying: "I want no prisoners," and turning to a file of soldiers ordered them to shoot the heroes. Colonel Travis was first shot in the back. He folded his arms stiffly across his breast and stood erect until a bullet pierced his neck, when he fell headlong among the dead. David Crockett fell at the first fire, his body being completely riddled with bullets. Even a cat that was soon after seen running through the fort was shot, the soldiers exclaiming: "It is not a cat, but an American."[9]

The spectacle of not one but *two* survivors feigning death under the scrutiny of Mexican soldiery, and succeeding in it for any length of time, is ridiculous enough; but no one aware of the former relationship between Travis and Cos would have expected them to embrace! The detail of the surviving commander in chief trying to bribe the Mexican soldier with gold is also absurd and out of character. As already stated, the evidence is clear that Travis, with a bullet in his forehead, fell across a gun carriage dead soon after the siege began, and he was so found by the inpouring Mexicans.

The burden of evidence and reason is against the above-related stories, which represent only part of the myth-making surrounding the Alamo, a subject of sufficient interest that a book has been written about it.[10]

❋   ❋   ❋

Was the Alamo a "glory trap"? There have been all degrees of opinion as to the folly or wisdom of what occurred there. Military "experts" and self-styled military critics have characterized the sacrifice of the defenders as unnecessary and indefensible folly, stating that it was poor military tactics and that it could have been easily avoided by several kinds of alternative action. Shades of opinion extend to the other extreme — i.e., the most extravagant hero-worship, which will permit no criticism of the heroes or anything they did. We are a little less than a century and a quarter from this famous event, long enough, one would think, that some mature judgments of it could be made; yet, curiously enough, even for many non-Texans, it remains difficult to consider the defensive side of it dispassionately. The story of the great self-immolation of the Alamo defenders is surcharged with emotion so powerful that we cannot avoid it. Nor do we want to. Like all great stories, it has too much to say to us that goes beyond fact and reason. May it always be so!

The motives of most of the men who died at the Alamo remain their secret. The other defenders are not so well known as Bowie, Travis, and Crockett because their lives are for the most part undocumented; but their heroism is without question. And are we so interested in *why* they stayed as long as there was any real hope that reinforcements would arrive? For what made these men great, if it was not that they remained *after* that hope had to be abandoned? Let us assume, then, that they were motivated by a high sense of duty and devotion to Texan freedom. Most of them were hard-headed realists who must have seen the practical aspects of the situation. If they did not make a decisive stand against the Mexicans *at that moment*, the Texan cause might be lost. Even though the Alamo had been all but stripped of supplies and weapons, it would have been disastrous to abandon it to the Mexicans, who were obviously much better off, militarily, than the Texans. Had this been allowed, it is doubtful that any Texan force that could have been assembled, even months later, could have retaken it.

The men in the Alamo were actually caught in a web of circumstances from which there *was* no honorable escape. If they were "trapped," it was by all that is noble and unselfish in the spirit of man. That is why they have long ago ceased to be only "Texas heroes," but are revered wherever their story is told, along with all others who have given of themselves to "the last full measure" in the cause of freedom.

The last was felled the fight to gain—
Well may the ruffians quake to tell
How Travis and his hundred fell
Amid a thousand foemen slain,
They died the Spartan's death
But not a hopeless strife —
Like brothers died; and their expiring breath
Was freedom's breath of life.

BIBLIOGRAPHICAL
AND OTHER NOTES

The completeness of the bibliographical citations in the following notes makes it unnecessary to include in this book separate bibliographies on James Bowie, David Crockett, and William Barret Travis, and on the siege of the Alamo. The reader may, however, find useful a few short bibliographies contained in published works. All of the books listed below are available in public libraries:

On Bowie:
Claude Leroy Douglas, *James Bowie; the Life of a Bravo* (Dallas: Banks Upshaw and Co., 1944).
Raymond W. Thorp, *Bowie Knife* (Albuquerque: University of New Mexico Press, 1948). This is not, of course, a biography, but it contains a brief bibliography of value to anyone interested in the history of the Bowie knife.

On David Crockett:
Constance Rourke, *Davy Crockett* (New York: Harcourt, Brace and Co., 1934).
James A. Shackford, *Davy Crockett, the Man and the Legend* (Chapel Hill: University of North Carolina Press, 1956).

On William Barret Travis:
At this writing there is no published bibliography on Travis that is anywhere near complete.

On the Alamo and the Siege:
John Myers Myers, *The Alamo* (New York: E. P. Dutton and Co., 1948).

JAMES BOWIE

Notes to Chapter 1 — Bowie's Forebears and Childhood
[1]See Walter Worthington Bowie, *The Bowies and Their Kindred* ... (Washington, D. C.: Press of Cromwell Bros., 1899), p. 258.
[2]See *William and Mary College Quarterly and Historical Magazine*, X, No. 4, April 1902, p. 278.

[3]See account by J. S. Moore in the *Galveston Daily News* for Sept. 8, 1875. Referred to by Amelia Williams in her "A Critical Study of the Siege of the Alamo and of the Personnel of Its Defenders," *Southwestern Historical Quarterly*, XXXVIII, No. 2, Oct. 1933, Chap. III, p. 90, footnote 2.

[4]Bowie, *op. cit.*, pp. 260-61.

[5]William S. Speer and John Henry Brown, *Encyclopedia of the New West* (Marshal, Texas: U. S. Biographical Publishing Co., 1881), p. 433.

[6]See *DeBow's Review*, XIII, July-Dec. 1852, "Early Life in the Southwest — the Bowies," p. 378; John Henry Brown, *Indian Wars and Pioneers of Texas* (Austin, Texas: L. E. Daniell, 189?), p. 135; and Bowie, *op. cit.*, p. 261.

[7]*DeBow's Review*, XIII, *op. cit.*, p. 378.

[8]See Raymond W. Thorp, *Bowie Knife* (Albuquerque, N. M.: University of New Mexico Press, 1948), p. 119.

[9]John Henry Brown, *op. cit.*, p. 135.

[10-12]*DeBow's Review*, XIII, *op. cit.*, pp. 378-79.

[13]John Henry Brown, *op. cit.*, p. 135.

[14]*DeBow's Review*, XIII, *op. cit.*, p. 379.

[15]Bowie, *op. cit.*, pp. 261-62.

[16-18]*DeBow's Review*, XIII, *op. cit.*, pp. 379-80.

[19]See Josephus Conn Guild, *Old Times in Tennessee* (Nashville: Tavel, Eastman and Howell, 1878), p. 107.

Notes to Chapter 2 — "Those Wild Bowie Boys"

[1]Josephus Conn Guild, *Old Times in Tennessee* (Nashville: Tavel, Eastman and Howell, 1878), p. 107.

[2]Thomas B. Thorpe, *The Mysteries of the Back-Woods* (Philadelphia: Carey and Hart, 1846), pp. 141-43.

[3]*Niles' National Register*, LVI, July 20, 1839, pp. 324-25.

[4]See Thorpe, *op. cit.*, p. 139.

[5]Summarized from Thorpe, *op. cit.*, p. 38.

[6]*Ibid.*, pp. 39-43. Quotation is from pp. 42-3.

[7]See William Darby, *The Emigrant's Guide to the Western & Southwestern States & Territories* . . . (New York: Kirk and Mercein, 1818), pp. 76-7.

[8]See William B. Dewees, *Letters from an Early Settler of Texas* . . . compiled by Cara Cardelle (pseud.) (Louisville, Kent.:

Morton and Griswold, 1852), pp. 137-38.

[9]*DeBow's Review*, XIII, July-Dec. 1852, "Early Life in the Southwest — the Bowies," p. 380.

[10]*Ibid.*, p. 380.

Notes to Chapter 3 — Fortunes for the Taking

[1]Based on material in *DeBow's Review*, XIII, July-Dec. 1852, "Early Life in the Southwest — the Bowies," pp. 380-81.

[2]See Henderson Yoakum, *History of Texas*...(New York: Redfield, 1855), I, pp. 180-84. Some of the material on the early history of Galveston Island is also summarized from Yoakum.

[3]*Ibid.*, pp. 183-84.

[4]Summarized from J. O. Dyer, "A Truer Story of the Bowie Knife," *Galveston Daily News*, March 21, 1930, p. 25, columns 6 and 7.

[5]Yoakum, *op. cit.*, I, p. 196.

[6]*DeBow's Review*, XIII, *op. cit.*, p. 381. For a detailed description of a commonly used method of smuggling slaves into the country, see *Niles' Weekly Register*, XV, Dec. 12, 1818, p. 269.

[7]See Claude Leroy Douglas, *James Bowie: the Life of a Bravo* (Dallas: Banks Upshaw and Co., 1944), p. 25.

[8]Sparks is quoted in Edward S. Ellis, *The Life of Colonel David Crockett* (Philadelphia: Porter and Coates, 1884), pp. 222-23.

[9]See same newspaper article referred to under note 4 above.

[10]Quoted by Raymond W. Thorp in his *Bowie Knife* (Albuquerque: University of New Mexico Press, 1948), p. 126, from William S. Speer and John Henry Brown, *Encyclopedia of the New West* (Marshal, Texas: U. S. Biographical Publishing Co., 1881), pp. 436-37.

[11]From a document copied from the records of Bexar County by Evelyn Brogan in her *James Bowie, a Hero of the Alamo* (San Antonio: T. Kunzman, 1922), pp. 35-7.

[12]*DeBow's Review*, XIII, *op. cit.*, p. 381.

[13]See Josiah Hazen Shinn, *Pioneers and Makers of Arkansas* (Little Rock, Ark.: Genealogical and Historical Publishing Co., 1908), as quoted by Raymond W. Thorp, *op. cit.*, p. 82.

[14]See Noah Smithwick, *The Evolution of a State*, compiled by Nanna S. Donaldson (Austin: Gammel Book Co., 1900), quoted by Thorp, *op. cit.*, p. 82.

[15]*DeBow's Review*, XIII, *op. cit.*, p. 381.

[16]See *Ibid.*, p. 381.

[17]See Francis W. Johnson, *History of Texas and Texans*, 2 vols. (Chicago and N. Y.: The American Historical Society, 1914), quoted in Thorp, *op. cit.*, p. 83.

[18]From Amos A. Parker, *Trip to the West and Texas . . . 1834-5 . . .* (Concord, N. H.: White and Fisher, 1835), p. 185.

[19]See Horace H. Shelton, "Texas Heroes — James Bowie . . . ," in *Under Texas Skies*, II, No. 6, Nov. 1951, pp. 25-6.

[20]For a thorough demolishment of Samuel G. Bastion's detractions of Bowie, see Raymond W. Thorp, *op. cit.*, pp. 79-81.

Notes to Chapter 4 — The Bowie Knives — a Collective Invention

[1]*DeBow's Review*, XIII, July-Dec. 1852, "Early Life in the Southwest — the Bowies," p. 381. The account is supposed to be based on an interview of John Bowie by some unknown writer. The "great duel" referred to is described in Chapter 5 of this biography of Bowie.

[2]See *Galveston Daily News*, XLVIII, No. 338, Mar. 31, 1890, p. 4, col. 6.

[3]See J. Frank Dobie, "Bowie and the Bowie Knife," *Southwest Review*, XVI, No. 3, April 1931, p. 356.

[4]See *Harper's Weekly*, "Concerning Fire-Arms," V, No. 240, Aug. 3, 1861, p. 495. Summarized by Robert F. Scott in "Who Invented the Bowie Knife?," *Western Folklore*, VIII, No. 3, July 1949, p. 196.

[5]The Jones article was first published in the Centennial Edition of the *Arkansas Gazette* for Nov. 20, 1919, as part of an unpublished manuscript of the then late J. N. Smithee, "The Bowie Knife and the Man Who Made It." Dan W. Jones's article, which takes up a probable four-fifths of the Smithee article, is titled "True History of the Bowie Knife, With a Biographical Sketch of Its Inventor, James Black."

[6]Andrew J. Sowell, *Rangers and Pioneers of Texas . . .* (San Antonio: Shepard Brothers and Co., 1884), pp. 126-27.

[7]Among these later authors are Amelia Williams, John Myers Myers, Walter Worthington Bowie, and Claude L. Douglas.

[8]The version of this letter quoted was found in *Niles' National Register*, LV, Sept. 29, 1838, p. 70.

[9]See letter from John S. Moore to W. W. Fontaine, April 25, 1890, *Fontaine Papers*, Archives of the University of Texas. J. M. S. du Fosset kept notes concerning the Bowies, while Lucy Leigh Bowie and Walter Worthington Bowie were well supplied with family archives.

[10]See *The American Flag* (Matamoros), II, No. 114, July 10, 1847, p. 1.

[11]Charles Hooton, *St. Louis Isle, or Texiana* . . . (London: Simmonds and Ward, 1847), p. 21.

[12]See Henry C. Mercer, "The Bowie and Other Knives," *Bucks County Historical Society Papers*, IV, 1917, p. 612.

[13]See Dobie, *op. cit.*, p. 362.

[14]*American Notes and Queries*, II, No. 21, Mar. 23, 1889, p. 251.

[15]See footnote 8 above, *Ibid.*, p. 70.

[16]Lucy Leigh Bowie, "Famous Bowie Knife, Its History and Origin," *Bucks County Historical Society Papers*, IV, 1917, p. 622.

[17]*Ibid.*, p. 620.

[18]See footnote 1 above, *Ibid.*, p. 381.

Notes to Chapter 5 — Bowie Knives and Duelling Pistols

[1]See John Lyde Wilson, *The Code of Honor; or Rules for the Government of Principals and Seconds in Duelling* (Charleston: T. J. Eccles, 1838), quoted by Thomas McAdory Owen in his *History of Alabama and Dictionary of Alabama Biography*, 4 vols. (Chicago: S. J. Clarke, 1921), I, p. 22, and elsewhere.

[2]See the *Telegraph and Texas Register* for January 5, 1839. The story of anti-duelling movements and legislation is an interesting one, worthy of a more thorough investigation than it has yet received.

[3]An act of February 20, 1839. I do not know whether this bill was passed by both houses of Congress and signed into law. The version of it that I saw is in *Niles' National Register*, LVI, issue of March 30, 1839, p. 69.

[4]See notes to Chapter 4 of the Bowie biography, number 8.

[5]Timothy Flint, *Recollections of the Last Ten Years* . . . (Boston: Cummings, Hilliard and Co., 1826), p. 181.

[6]This detail is related by Raymond W. Thorp in his *Bowie Knife* (Albuquerque: University of New Mexico Press, 1948), p. 12. It is not in the *Niles' Weekly Register* for Nov. 17, 1827, one

of his sources for the Sandbar affair, so he must have obtained it from the other, the *New Orleans Argus* for October 1, 1827.

[7]Walter Worthington Bowie, *The Bowies and Their Kindred* (Washington, D. C.: Cromwell Bros., 1899), pp. 273-74. It seems very unrealistic to anyone reading about this affair today to expect that so many members of both factions in this bitter feud could get close enough together to oversee a duel between representatives of the opposing sides without the conflict broadening. There had already been violence between the Maddoxes and Wellses. Col. Robert Crain and General Cuney were mortal enemies; Wright and Bowie, likewise; Alfred Blanchard and Thomas J. Wells, ditto. Indeed, the conduct on both sides, as portrayed in the various accounts, suggests that a general fight was anticipated, even hoped for. Moreover, champagne and brandy were hardly fluids calculated to extinguish the flames of hate!

[8]See Emerson Hough, *The Story of the Outlaw* (New York: The Outing Publishing Co., 1907), pp. 38-9, for a brief sketch of Sturdivant's career.

[9]See Raymond W. Thorp, *op. cit.*, p. 130, for this detail. My account is summarized mainly from one in the *Galveston Daily News*, XXXVIII, No. 300, March 6, 1889.

[10]Ben C. Truman, *The Field of Honor* . . . (New York: Fords, Howard, and Hulbert, 1884), p. 290.

[11-14]These brief quotes taken from *Ibid.*, pp. 291-93.

[15]*Ibid.*, pp. 294-95.

[16]This account is taken from the *Democratic Telegraph and Texas Register*, XV, No. 25, June 20, 1850, p. 3, columns 3 and 4.

[17]Quoted in part and summarized from *American Notes and Queries*, I, No. 5, June 2, 1888, pp. 49-50.

[18]Walter W. Bowie, *op. cit.*, p. 275.

[19]Quotation is from a version of this story that appeared in the *Galveston Daily News*, XXXVIII, No. 300, Mar. 6, 1889. Others are in William S. Speer and John Henry Brown, *Encyclopedia of the New West* (Marshal, Texas: U. S. Biographical Publishing Co., 1881), p. 438, and in *American Notes and Queries*, I, No. 5, June 2, 1888, p. 50.

[20]Mentioned in Horace H. Shelton, "Texas Heroes — James Bowie . . . ," *Under Texas Skies*, II, No. 6, November 1951, p. 28.

[21]From the *Jacksboro* (Texas) *Echo*, XI, No. 46, May 25, 1877,

p. 2, col. 7.

[22]Referred to in WPA processed series, *San Francisco Theatre Research Monographs*, edited by Lawrence Estevan, Vol. 11, XXII, "Edwin Forrest," p. 26. Issued at San Francisco in March 1940.

[23]Quotations are from the *Galveston Daily News*, XXXVIII, No. 300, Mar. 6, 1889. Other versions appeared in Truman, *op. cit.*, p. 116, and in the *San Francisco Chronicle*, XXXIII, No. 44, Febr. 28, 1881.

[24]See Speer and Brown, *op. cit.*, pp. 436-37.

[25]Summarized from Effie August Bowie, *Across the Years in Prince George's County* (Richmond, Va.: Garrett and Massie, 1947), pp. 700-01.

Notes to Chapter 6 — Love and Lipan Silver

[1]See Horace H. Shelton, "Texas Heroes — James Bowie...," *Under Texas Skies*, II, No. 6, Nov. 1951, p. 27. (Published by Texas Heritage Foundation, Austin, Texas.)

[2]James Bowie's baptismal record was translated from Spanish into English by Evelyn Brogan and included in her *James Bowie, a Hero of the Alamo* (San Antonio: T. Kunzman, 1922), p. 33.

[3]See Theresa M. Hunter, *Romantic Interludes from the Lives of the Texas Heroes* (San Antonio: The Naylor Company, 1936), pp. 19-25.

[4]John Henry Brown, *Indian Wars and Pioneers of Texas* (Austin: L. E. Daniell, 189?), as quoted by Thorp in *Bowie Knife* (Albuquerque: University of New Mexico Press, 1948), p. 125.

[5]See J. A. Quintero, "The San Saba Gold and Silver Mines," *The Texas Almanac for 1868* . . . (Galveston: W. Richardson & Co., 1867), pp. 83-5.

[6]Reprinted from the Nov. 1898 newspaper mentioned in the text by *Frontier Times*, XXVII, issue of October 1949, pp. 14-15.

[7]*Ibid.*, p. 15.

[8]Henderson Yoakum, *History of Texas* . . . (New York: Redfield, 1855), I, p. 290, footnote.

[9]John Henry Brown, *History of Texas from 1685 to 1892* . . . (St. Louis: L. E. Daniell, 1892), I, pp. 170-75. There are a few discrepancies between Rezin's and James's accounts. James mentions a Mateo Dias not included in his brother's list of partici-

pants in the battle; he also lists a "Daniel Buchanan," while his brother's version of the name is "David Buchanan." I have not seen the Spanish version of James's account, but referring to the Governor as "your lordship" and to an Indian chief as a "captain" suggests that it may not have been translated with much care. Still another account of the battle was made by Cephas K. Ham, one of the participants, although I have not seen it.

[10]See Hunter, *op. cit.*, p. 27.

[11]A typewritten copy of this letter, of which I have a photostatic copy, is filed with the Nacogdoches Archives, Archives Division, Texas State Library, Vol. 83, pp. 112-13.

Notes to Chapter 7 — Nacogdoches and After

[1]For a brief account of these battles, see James W. Parker, *The Rachel Plummer Narrative* ... (Palestine, Texas: publisher not shown, 1926), pp. 79-80.

[2]Henderson Yoakum, *History of Texas* ... (New York: Redfield, 1855), I, pp. 298-99.

[3]Charles Adams Gulick, Jr., and Katherine Elliott (editors), *The Papers of Mirabeau Buonaparte Lamar* (Austin: Von Boeckmann-Jones Co., ?1923), III, p. 270.

[4]*Ibid.*, pp. 271-72.

[5]John Henry Brown, *Indian Wars and Pioneers of Texas* (Austin: L. E. Daniell, 189?), p. 136.

[6]John J. Linn, *Reminiscences of Fifty Years in Texas* (New York: D. and J. Sadlier and Co., 1883), pp. 302-04.

[7]This will was not probated until March 7, 1839, and not filed for record until August 11, 1852. See *Dallas Morning News* for Jan. 7, 1895, p. 4, for a copy of the document. Half of his estate Bowie willed to his brother Rezin, the other half to his brother-in-law Alexander B. Sterrett, and his sister Martha, but he also provided for payment of certain debts and left provision to "support and educate my nephews ..., children of my brother, Stephen Bowie, deceased." Ursula he regarded as already provided for by the terms of the marriage contract.

Notes to Chapter 8 — The Battle of Gonzales to the Siege of Bexar

[1]As quoted by Andrew Jackson Houston in his *Texas Independence* (Houston: The Anson Jones Press, 1938), p. 75.

[2]William Kennedy, *Texas: Its Rise, Progress and Prospects* (London: 1840; New York: 1841), II, p. 111, as summarized by Yoakum, I, p. 366.

[3]Anna J. H. Pennypacker, *A New History of Texas for Schools* (Tyler, Texas: Pub. by the author, 1888), footnote, p. 61.

[4]From "General Austin's Order Book for the Campaign of 1835," in *Quarterly of the Texas State Historical Association*, XI, No. 1, July 1907, pp. 32-3.

[5]See Andrew J. Sowell, *Early Settlers and Indian Fighters of Southwest Texas* (Austin: B. C. Jones and Co., 1900), p. 5.

[6]*Ibid.*, p. 6. Fannin's concession to Bowie in allowing him to sign the battle report first was probably made only in the interests of harmony. Bowie was thoroughly imbued with the psychology and prejudices of the volunteer soldier. His distaste for playing "second fiddle" to any "regular army" officer was responsible for his later clash with Travis at the Alamo.

[7]As quoted from the original by Henry Stuart Foote in his *Texas and the Texans*...(Philadelphia: Thomas, Cowperthwait & Co., 1841), II, pp. 121-25. A more lively account was written by Creed Taylor, a Texan participant at Concepcion. See James De Shields, *Tall Men with Long Rifles* (San Antonio: The Naylor Co., 1935), pp. 36-42.

[8]See "General Austin's Order Book for the Campaign of 1835," referred to in my note 4 directly above, p. 32.

[9]See *Ibid.*, p. 34.

[10]Eugene C. Barker (ed.), *The Austin Papers*, part of the *Annual Report of the American Historical Association for the Year 1922* (Washington, D. C.: Government Printing Office, 1928), II, p. 759. The original of this letter is in the Samuel May Williams Papers, which are in the custody of the Rosenberg Library, Galveston, Texas.

[11]*Ibid.*, III (Austin: University of Texas, 1927), p. 229, "Minutes of the Council of War."

[12]Yoakum, *History of Texas*...(New York: Redfield, 1855), II, p. 17.

[13]*Ibid.*, p. 18.

[14]See Andrew J. Sowell, *op. cit.*, pp. 7-8.

[15]Quoted by Raymond W. Thorp on pp. 136-37 of his *Bowie Knife* (Albuquerque, New Mexico: University of New Mexico

Press, 1948), from John Henry Brown, *Indian Wars and Pioneers of Texas* (Austin: L. E. Daniell, 189?), p. 136.

Notes to Chapter 9 — The Still-Restless Guns —
Bowie Enters the Alamo

[1]Yoakum, II, p. 454, Appendix 1, Doc. No. 8.
[2]*Ibid.*, p. 52.
[3]*Ibid.*, p. 58.
[4]*Ibid.*, p. 460, Appendix 1, Doc. No. 16.
[5]Quoted from Joseph E. Field, *Three Years in Texas . . .* (Greenfield, Mass.: J. Jones, and Boston: A. Tompkins, 1836), p. 27.
[6]Quoted by Horace H. Shelton in his "Texas Heroes — James Bowie . . . ," *Under Texas Skies*, II, No. 6, Nov. 1951, pp 26-7.
[7-8]Originals in Texas Army Papers, Texas State Library.
[9]The two quotations in this paragraph are from Reuben M. Potter, "The Fall of the Alamo," *Old South Leaflets*, No. 130 (Boston: The Directors of the Old South Work, n.d.), pp. 5 and 6.
[10]Harriet Smither (ed.), *Papers of Mirabeau Buonaparte Lamar* (Austin: Von Boeckmann-Jones Co, ?1926), V, pp. 93-4.

DAVID CROCKETT

General Note:

The reader may wonder why the Crockett biography is not documented as are those of Bowie and Travis. The main reason is that it is based largely upon the so-called "autobiography," actually a compilation of several of Crockett's works known as *The Life of Davy Crockett by Himself,* which has gone through so many editions that page references to any one of them would be all but meaningless. Public familiarity with this work and with the main facts of Crockett's life — especially since the recent Crockett "boom" in this country — also make it supererogatory to fill in the gaps in this brief biography, which many a reader can do for himself. Whether the "autobiography" was written by Crockett in collaboration with someone or exclusively by him with only editorial corrections by some other hand is unimportant. What is important is that the authentic picture of the man shines forth from its pages unmistakable, unique, identifiable, as it never has from any biography of the man yet written.

Most of this condensation is in my own words, but those passages that are used verbatim are, of course, enclosed in quotation marks or printed in smaller type.

WILLIAM BARRET TRAVIS

Notes to Chapter 1 — Youth and Education

[1]See *William and Mary College Quarterly*, XVIII, 1910, pp. 141-44, for a delineation of some of the branches of the Travis family of Virginia from about 1637 to about 1872.

[2]See Thomas McAdory Owen, *History of Alabama* . . . (Chicago: S. J. Clarke Publishing Co., 1921), IV, p. 1681. The number of Travis children varies in the different accounts from seven to ten. Also, no modern historians give North Carolina as William's birth place, virtually ending a controversy of long standing over which of the Carolinas can claim him.

[3]See Cyrus Townsend Brady, *Conquest of the Southwest* . . . (New York: D. Appleton and Co., 1905), p. 101. Amelia Williams, in her well-known "Critical Study of the Siege of the Alamo . . . ," includes a brief sketch on Travis in which she discusses and pretty well refutes the "foundling" story. See *Southwestern Historical Quarterly*, XXXVII, No. 2, Oct. 1933, p. 80, footnote 2.

[4]See John Myers Myers, *The Alamo* (New York: E. P. Dutton and Co., 1948), p. 114.

Note to Chapter 2 — Did Young William Meet Lafayette?

[1]This material, except for its deduced connection with Travis, is summarized mostly from contemporary newspaper accounts and, to a relatively minor extent, from B. F. Riley's *Makers and Romance of Alabama History* (? place: ? publisher, 1915), pp. 564-78.

Notes to Chapter 3 — A Marriage Is Blessed and Blighted

[1]For this account see Theresa M. Hunter, *Romantic Interludes from the Lives of the Texas Heroes* (San Antonio: The Naylor Co., 1936), pp. 33-45.

[2]From a photostatic copy of the letter in the University of Texas Library, quoted by Amelia Williams in her "Critical Study . . . ,"

Chap. III, *Southwestern Historical Quarterly*, XXXVII, No. 2, October 1933, pp. 85-6, footnote.

[3]From a "Private Journal" of William Barret Travis, which he kept from August 30, 1833, through June 26, 1834. It is also referred to as his "Diary," which is the name I have chosen to use. See p. 23. Page references are to a typewritten copy of the original, which is in the James Harper Starr Collection at the Eugene C. Barker Texas History Center, Austin, Texas.

[4]*Ibid.*, p. 74.

[5]Ruby Mixon of Fort Worth, Texas, has written a thesis, "William Barret Travis, His Life and Letters," unpublished (to my knowledge) at this writing, and the only full-length biography of the man yet attempted. I have not seen this work, but it is possible that it throws some light on the relationship of Travis with members of the Cato family other than Rosanna both before and after he came to Texas.

[6]Diary, p. 2.

[7]*Ibid.*, p. 32.

[8]*Ibid.*, p. 59.

[9]*Ibid.*, p. 82.

[10]*Ibid.*, p. 90.

[11]*Ibid.*, pp. 101-02.

[12]See Amelia Williams, *op. cit.*, p. 87. In his diary, Travis mentions visiting a Cummins family a number of times and of performing legal services for both a James and a John Cummins. One mildly titillating entry, which may refer only to his relationship to the Cummins family as a whole, reads as follows:

— went to Cummins's — recepcion frio, pero conclusion muy caliente — [Reception cold, but conclusion very hot.]

This quotation is from p. 93 of the typewritten copy of the diary.

[13-14]Diary, p. 85.

[15-16]*Ibid.*, p. 89.

[17]*Ibid.*, pp. 101-02.

[18]*Ibid.*, p. 107.

[19]*Ibid.*, p. 114.

[20-21]*Ibid.*, p. 122,

Notes to Chapter 4 — "Buck" Travis at Anahuac

[1]N. D. Labadie, "Narrative of Anahuac, or Opening Campaign

of the Texas Revolution," *Texas Almanac for 1859* (Galveston: W. and O. Richardson, ?1858), p. 31.

[2]Henry S. Foote, *Texas and the Texans* ... (Philadelphia: Thomas, Cowperthwait & Co., 1841), II. All quotations in the paragraph are from p. 15.

[3]Capt. Creed Taylor narrative, quoted by James De Shields in *Tall Men with Long Rifles* ... (San Antonio: The Naylor Press, 1935), pp. 6-7. Practically all of this work consists of notes dictated by Captain Taylor and edited by De Shields, who does not state where the notes were obtained.

[4]See Charles Adams Gulick, Jr., and Katherine Elliott (editors), *The Papers of Mirabeau Buonaparte Lamar* (Austin: Von Boeckmann-Jones Co., ?1923), III, pp. 233-35.

[5]Labadie, *op. cit.*, p. 32. See also the Patrick Jack account footnoted directly above, in which Jack stated that Bradburn gave this actually anonymous letter as his reason for arresting Travis. That it was just an excuse for the action is fairly obvious.

[6]*Ibid.*, p. 36.

[7]One bright spot in the treatment of the prisoners is related in an account of Patrick Jack, already referred to. He stated that, while they were generally treated with "barbarous inhumanity," a Lt. Juan "Cortena" (Cortinez) supplied them with better food than the stale bread and boiled beans allowed them by Bradburn, presumably at his own expense. See Charles Adams Gulick, Jr., and Katherine Elliott (editors), *op. cit.*, III, p. 235.

Notes to Chapter 5 — Citizen and Lawyer

[1]See Robert H. Williams, Jr., "Travis — a Potential Sam Houston," *Southwestern Historical Quarterly*, XL, July 1936 — April 1937, pp. 154-60.

[2]*Diary*, p. 72.

[3]See Amelia Williams, "A Critical Study . . . ," Chap. III, "The Leaders at the Alamo," *Southwestern Historical Quarterly*, XXXVII, No. 2, Oct. 1933, p. 82, including footnote 11.

[4]*Diary*, pp. 121-22.

[5]*Ibid.*, pp. 85-6.

[6]*Ibid.*, p. 78.

[7]See Amelia Williams, *op. cit.*, p. 82.

[8]*Diary*, p. 120. Williamson, nicknamed "Three-Legged Willie"

because of a withered, doubled-up leg that forced him to wear a peg leg, was quite a local character in San Felipe from its early days. Contrasting with his serious interest in the Texas Revolution and his fine professional mind was a lighter side. He was a great storyteller and wit.

⁹*Ibid.*, p. 100.

¹⁰*Ibid.*, p. 35.

¹¹*Ibid.*, p. 53.

¹²"The Reminiscences of Mrs. Dilue Harris," *Quarterly of the Texas State Historical Association*, IV, July 1900 — April 1901, pp. 101-02.

¹³Diary, pp. 118-19.

Notes to Chapter 6 — The Cautious Diarist

¹Diary, p. 54.

²⁻⁵*Ibid.*, p. 55.

⁶*Ibid.*, p. 56.

⁷*Ibid.*, p. 107.

⁸*Ibid.*, pp. 11-12.

⁹*Ibid.*, p. 34.

¹⁰⁻¹¹*Ibid.*, p. 32.

¹²⁻¹⁴*Ibid.*, p. 120.

¹⁵*Ibid.*, p. 121.

¹⁶See Macum Phelan, *A History of Early Methodism in Texas, 1817-1866* (Nashville: Cokesbury Press, 1924), pp. 45-9, *passim.* That Travis had a heartfelt interest in religion is evidenced by his co-sponsorship of and attendance at religious meetings. His letter of Aug. 17, 1835, subscribing to the New York *Christian Advocate and Journal*, quoted by Mr. Phelan on pp. 48-9, is a direct appeal to the Methodist Church to send missionary preachers to Texas.

¹⁷Diary, p. 106.

¹⁸*Ibid.*, p. 3.

¹⁹*Ibid.*, p. 1.

²⁰*Ibid.*, p. 8.

²¹*Ibid.*, p. 83.

²²*Ibid.*, p. 97.

²³*Ibid.*, p. 116.

²⁴*Ibid.*, p. 82.

[25]*Ibid.*, pp. 89-90.

[26]*Ibid.*, p. 73.

[27]*Ibid.*, p. 83.

[28]*Ibid.*, entry for Sept. 6, 1833, p. 3.

[29]Travis could not, of course, have read Charles Kingsley's *Westward Ho!*, which was not published until 1855.

[30]Diary, p. 89. Travis' "affair" with this anonymous sweetheart and his attitude toward women are discussed in Chapter 3.

[31]*Ibid.*, entry for Dec. 15, 1833, p. 52.

[32]*Ibid.*, p. 119.

[33]*Ibid.*, p. 50.

Notes to Chapter 7 — More Trouble at Anahuac

[1]See Zachary T. Fulmore, *History and Geography of Texas, as Told in County Names* (Austin: Published by the author, 1915), p. 142.

[2]See Eugene C. Barker, "Difficulties of a Mexican Revenue Officer in Texas," *Quarterly of the Texas State Historical Association*, IV, July 1900 — April 1901, p. 194.

[3]Letter quoted by Adele B. Looscan in "The Old Fort at Anahuac," *Quarterly of the Texas State Historical Association*, II, issue for July 1898, p. 23, and in Barker, *op. cit.*, p. 197, footnote 3.

[4]See "The Reminiscences of Mrs. Dilue Harris," *Quarterly of the Texas State Historical Association*, IV, July 1900 — April 1901, p. 125.

[5]Letter quoted in Barker, *op. cit.*, p. 197. The original letter is in the Bexar Archives.

[6]As quoted by John Henry Brown in his *Life and Times of Henry Smith* . . . (Dallas: A. D. Aldridge & Co., 1887), pp. 59-61.

[7]See Charles Adams Gulick, Jr., and Katherine Elliott (editors), *The Papers of Mirabeau Buonaparte Lamar* (Austin: A. C. Baldwin and Sons, ?1921), I, p. 206, doc. No. 204.

Notes to Chapter 8 — Same Story — Different Ending

[1]James K. Greer (ed.), "The Journal of Ammon Underwood, 1834 — 1838," *Southwestern Historical Quarterly*, XXXII, No. 2, Oct. 1928, p. 136.

[2]"The Reminiscences of Mrs. Dilue Harris," *Quarterly of the Texas State Historical Association*, IV, July 1900 — April 1901, p. 125.

³Harriet Smither (ed.), *The Papers of Mirabeau Buonaparte Lamar* (Austin: Von Boeckmann-Jones Co., ?1927), VI, p. 178.

⁴Quoted in John Henry Brown, *Life and Times of Henry Smith* . . . (Dallas: A. D. Aldridge & Co., 1887), p. 59.

⁵From a letter of Travis to Bowie, dated July 30, 1835, quoted in Yoakum, *History of Texas* . . . (New York: Redfield, 1855), I, p. 343.

⁶Letter quoted by Eugene C. Barker in "Public Opinion in Texas Preceding the Revolution," *Annual Report of the American Historical Association for 1911*, I, p. 224, footnote 2. The original is in the Mexican Archives.

⁷Letter quoted in Brown, *op. cit.*, pp. 69-70.

⁸⁻⁹*Ibid.*, p. 69.

¹⁰This letter is published in Harriet Smither (ed.), *The Papers of Mirabeau Buonaparte Lamar* (Austin: Von Boeckmann-Jones Co., ?1926), V, p. 81, doc. No. 225.

¹¹Quoted by Eugene C. Barker in his "Difficulties of a Mexican Revenue Officer in Texas," *Quarterly of the Texas State Historical Association*, IV, July 1900 — April 1901, p. 202.

¹²Letter, Travis to Austin, Sept. 22, 1835, quoted by Eugene C. Barker in his "William Barrett Travis, the Hero of the Alamo," *Publications of the Southern History Association*, VI, No. 5, Sept. 1902, pp. 420-21. Also printed in the *Austin Papers*.

¹³This letter is quoted by Adele B. Looscan in her article, "The Old Fort at Anahuac," *Quarterly of the Texas State Historical Association*, II, May 1898 — June 1899, p. 26.

¹⁴See "The Reminiscences of Mrs. Dilue Harris," *Quarterly of the Texas State Historical Association*, IV, July 1900 — April 1901, p. 127.

¹⁵Letter, Travis to J. W. Moore, Aug. 31, 1835, printed in the *Houston Morning Star*, Mar. 14, 1840.

Notes to Chapter 9 — Scouting and Recruiting to Duty at Bexar

¹"Stephen Austin's Order Book for the Campaign of 1835," *Quarterly of the Texas State Historical Association*, July 1907, No. 1, p. 31.

²*Ibid.*, quotations from p. 37.

³*Ibid.*, p. 41.

⁴*Ibid.*, p. 47.

[5]From a photostat of the original, which is in the Army Papers, Texas Archives, Texas State Library.

[6]See Homer S. Thrall, *A Pictorial History of Texas* (St. Louis: Thompson and Co., 1879), as quoted by Dabney White in his *East Texas, Its History and Its Makers* (New York: Lewis Historical Publishing Co., 1940), III, p. 1260.

[7]Original letter is in the Texas State Library.

[8]See Travis' letter of Dec. 17, 1835, to James W. Robinson in Charles Adams Gulick, Jr., and Katherine Elliott (editors), *The Papers of Mirabeau Buonaparte Lamar* (Austin: A. C. Baldwin & Sons, ?1921), I, pp. 264-65.

[9]*Ibid.*, p. 264.

[10]See Robert H. Williams, "Travis — a Potential Sam Houston," *Southwestern Historical Quarterly*, XL, July 1936 — April 1937, pp. 154-60.

[11]From a photostat of the original letter of December 3, 1835, which is in the Army Papers, Texas Archives, Texas State Library. For further details on Travis' suggested cavalry force and its approval by Austin, Houston, and the General Council, see Eugene C. Barker, "The Texan Revolutionary Army," *Quarterly of the Texas State Historical Association*, IX, April 1906, pp. 234-35.

[12]These quotations are from a photostat of the original Travis letter of January 28, 1836, which is in the Army Papers, Texas Archives, Texas State Library.

Notes to Chapter 10 — The Settling Doom

[1]Reuben M. Potter, "The Fall of the Alamo," *Old South Leaflets*, No. 130 (Boston: The Directors of the Old South Work, n.d.), p. 5. According to a note in this undated reprint, the essay was first published in the *Magazine of American History* for January 1878.

[2-3]Originals of these letters are in the Texas State Library.

[4-6]Originals of these letters are in the Army Papers, Texas Archives, Texas State Libarary.

[7]Potter, *op. cit.*, pp. 5 and 6.

[8-9]Originals of these letters are in the Army Papers, Texas Archives, Texas State Library.

[10]Both the reproduction and the quotation are from the origi-

nal letter, which is in the Bancroft Collection of Documents in the Bancroft Library of the University of California, whose Director has kindly permitted its use as an illustration in this book.

¹¹See John Sutherland, *The Fall of the Alamo* (San Antonio: The Naylor Co., 1936), p. 8.

¹²This information is summarized from footnote 32, Chapter II of Amelia Williams' "A Critical Study of the Siege of the Alamo . . . ," *Southwestern Historical Quarterly*, XXXVII, No. 1, July 1933, pp. 10-11.

¹³See Sutherland, *op. cit.*, p. 14.

¹⁴*Ibid.*, summarized from pp. 17-19.

Notes to Chapter 11 — "Give Me Help, Oh My Country!"

¹As quoted by John Henry Brown, *Life and Times of Henry Smith* . . . (Dallas: A. D. Aldridge & Co., 1887), pp. 297-98. Brown seems to have tampered with both punctuation and spelling in his version. Mary R. Brown in her *Condensed History of Texas for Schools* . . . (Dallas: published by the author, 1895), shows Travis' typical use of dashes instead of periods, of "&" for "and," and a "P.S." that differs slightly. It reads "Send an expresses to San Felipe with the news — night & day — " The plural "expresses" makes more sense than "express." Travis could have intended "Send *as* expresses to San Felipe with the news — " He was understandably excited, so his handwriting was not the best.

²Yoakum, *History of Texas* (New York: Redfield, 1855), II, p. 78.

³See *Ibid.*, also II, p. 78.

⁴The original of this famous letter is in the Army Papers, Texas Archives, Texas State Library. I worked from a positive photostat of it in the Manuscripts Division of the Library of Congress.

⁵⁻⁶*Ibid.*, Notes on the cover of the famous letter. The original may be easier to decipher, but I have reproduced all I could make out from the photostatic copy.

⁷*Ibid.*, back of letter. Compare with Amelia Williams' version in her "Critical Study . . . ," *Southwestern Historical Quarterly*, XXXVII, No. 4, for April 1934, p. 306, where she corrects some spelling and adds the word "as." The "N b" could mean "Nota bene" (note well), although there is some doubt that a semi-literate man, as Smithers obviously was, would know this Latin

expression. If it does not mean that, its significance remains a mystery, at least to me.

[8]If Amelia Williams had the original letter to work from here, she may, as stated above, have been able to read some words that I could not. Still her reading of "heavy" for "long" preceding "cannonade" is puzzling. I could make out only five words in the last sentence, and the last name, while undoubtedly "Martin," looks more like "Malther."

[9]This rendering may also not be as complete as would be possible to make, working with the original letter.

[10]This letter was published in the *Arkansas Gazette* of April 19, 1836.

[11]Included in Henry S. Foote, *Texas and the Texans*... (Philadelphia: Thomas, Cowperthwait & Co., 1841), II, pp. 219-22.

[12]The article and letter are on page 1, column 6, of the issue of the *Texas Monument* cited.

[13]Amelia Williams, in her "Critical Study...," Chap. III, gives some details concerning the provisions of this will. The document is apparently in the handwriting of John Rice Jones, who administered Travis' estate. See *Southwestern Historical Quarterly*, XXXVII, No. 2, October 1933, p. 88.

Notes to
THE SIEGE

[1]This abridged version of the Potter account is taken from an undated reprint published in Boston by "The Directors of the Old South Work" as one of the *Old South Leaflets*, No. 130, and is titled "The Fall of the Alamo." The date of publication is not shown, but this is apparently not the earliest version of the work, which, according to a note on page 24, "was first printed in the *Magazine of American History*, January, 1878 . . . ." The material I have quoted is taken from pages 6-23.

[2]Most of Potter's peculiar spellings of names and other words and his sometimes equally odd punctuation are retained. His use of the personal pronoun, his editorializing, and some other matter not now of much interest have been omitted.

[3]Potter is incorrect in stating that this quotation, which is not completely accurate, is from Travis' letter of March 3 to the

Government. It is from another letter of the same date to "a friend," published in the *Houston Telegraph and Texas Register* for March 24, 1836, p. 144.

Notes to
THE MYTH-MAKERS AND MILITARY "EXPERTS"

[1]See J. Frank Dobie *et al.* (editors), *In the Shadow of History* (Austin: Texas Folklore Society, 1939), pp. 42-7.

[2]Josephus Conn Guild, *Old Times in Tennessee* (Nashville: Tavel, Eastman and Howell, 1878), p. 266.

[3]*Niles' National Register*, LVIII, Mar. — Sept. 1840, p. 128.

[4]*Ibid.*, p. 224.

[5]For the John Crockett letter, see Frederick C. Chabot (ed.), *Texas Letters* (San Antonio: Yanaguana Society Publications, 1940), V, pp. 73-4.

[6]This account appeared in the *San Antonio Daily Express* for February 11, 1899, p. 5.

[7]For this account, see Andrew J. Sowell, *Rangers and Pioneers of Texas* (San Antonio: Shepard Brothers and Co., 1884), pp. 146-49.

[8]This letter is quoted by Amelia Williams in her "Critical Study . . .," *Southwestern Historical Quarterly*, XXXVII, July 1933, pp. 41-2, footnote 88.

[9]G. Norton Galloway, "Sketch of San Antonio," *Magazine of American History*, XV, No. 6, June 1886, pp. 532-33.

[10]See especially Adina de Zavala, *History and Legends of the Alamo* . . . (San Antonio: published by the author, 1917).

The stanza concluding the book is taken from Reuben M. Potter's "Hymn to the Alamo," as published in *The American Flag, Cameron County and Matamoros Advertiser*, November 29, 1848, p. 1.

INDEX

(Since the names of Bowie, Crockett, and Travis appear on almost every page of their respective biographies, no detailed breakdown under their names is furnished in this index.)